NOTABLE AMERICAN HOUSES

The
AMERICAN HERITAGE
History of
NOTABLE AMERICAN HOUSES

Author and Editor in Charge
Marshall B. Davidson

Biographical Essays
Margot P. Brill

Published by
AMERICAN HERITAGE PUBLISHING CO., INC.
New York

Staff for this Book

EDITOR
Marshall B. Davidson

ART DIRECTOR
Philip Lief

ASSOCIATE EDITOR
Margot P. Brill

COPY EDITOR
Brenda Bennerup

PICTURE EDITORS
Mary Leverty
Maureen Dwyer

EDITORIAL ASSISTANT
Donna Whiteman

American Heritage Publishing Co., Inc.

PRESIDENT AND PUBLISHER
Paul Gottlieb

EDITOR-IN-CHIEF
Joseph J. Thorndike

SENIOR EDITOR, BOOK DIVISION
Alvin M. Josephy, Jr.

EDITORIAL ART DIRECTOR
Murray Belsky

GENERAL MANAGER, BOOK DIVISION
Andrew W. Bingham

Library of Congress Catalog Card Number: 75-149724
International Standard Book Numbers: 07-015467-8, regular; 07-015468-6, deluxe

Introduction

The pages that follow tell the story of life in America in terms of the houses Americans have planned, built, and lived in across the breadth of the land. It is a story that reaches back into the European past, as far back as ancient Greece and Rome, and at times looks to the distant Orient. It continues for three hundred years in these New World surroundings—and it remains unfinished. For our notions of what a good house should look like and how it might best serve our needs and purposes are always changing, never more radically than in recent years. Yet men have always lived in "modern" times, even if they may never have been so acutely aware of the fact as we are today. Whatever their age, all the houses included here were at the time they were built up-to-date solutions to the problems of shelter and style, of comfort and convenience. From the evidence they present we can reconstruct the growth of ideas, of cultural patterns, and of practical expedients that have led to the problems and possibilities that are our present inheritance.

In any event, herewith is a selection of the best and, for the most part, the most typical houses that have been built in this country from the first permanent structures of the early colonial settlements to the achievements of the present day. The selection includes houses of the great and of the not so great. However, in all cases they are significant expressions of American experience and tradition. Each speaks reliably of a particular place and time in history, and of certain social and individual circumstances. They all speak of the needs and the dreams and the tastes of the people who owned and lived in them. These have been the homes of men and women who have literally left their mark on the land. In a number of cases their interest and importance is magnified by association with the lives of men and women who have played some memorable part in the nation's past. In considering such places as Mount Vernon and Monticello, it is difficult to disassociate their qualities as houses from their appeal as the shrines of heroes. Yet it must be remembered that there have been few more dedicated and informed householders than George Washington and Thomas Jefferson, men who were attentive to every detail of the planning, construction, and design of their celebrated dwellings. In those examples as in the others chosen for illustration, the character of the house itself represents a meaningful standard of accomplishment in the evolution of the American home and of American domestic architecture.

History is not an end in itself; it should provide data by which we can evaluate the happiness of life under various circumstances. We sometimes tend to use the present as an absolute standard for judging the past, a tendency that reduces much that once was important in its own right to the level of seeming merely quaint. Nothing that is properly understood remains quaint. In dealing with houses, the better we understand those of the near and distant past, the closer we come to certain fundamental and enduring human values. The flow of time obviously cannot be reversed; the past can never be recaptured in anything like its completeness, although some romanticists would have it that way if they could. To idealize the past is as misleading as to glorify the present. But if we view the past as perceptively as may be and for its own sake, we may indeed find ways of better evaluating our present condition. We can thus, at least, hope to escape from what the late Bertrand Russell referred to as "the parochialism of time."

Almost three and a half centuries ago, in one of the earliest English books on architecture, Sir Henry Wotton observed that the three basic attributes of a good building were "Commoditie, Firmeness, and Delight"—his succinct way of saying that such a building must efficiently serve its intended purposes, that it must be soundly constructed, and that it must be attractively designed. Actually that is a timeless formula, one that the ancient Roman architect Vitruvius had outlined some fifteen hundred years earlier. It is fair to say that those are the attributes that give shape, substance, and character to the dwellings we are about to consider. Timeless as the formula may be, however, every age has interpreted it in a different manner. What served "commoditie" at one time in history has seemed woefully inadequate at another; what was a delight to the eyes of one generation was an affront to the eyes of the next; and even what constituted "firmeness" has been reconsidered with the advances of technology.

More than matters of style or fashion or of technological development were responsible for those changing interpretations. Concepts of living, of the good life, played an important role. The first permanent dwellings built along the Atlantic seaboard, from Massachusetts to Virginia, interesting and picturesque as they were, were innocent of any formal style. They were made to accommodate a way of life that followed centuries-old customs. Under the heavy weight of tradition, ignorant of the deliberately organized refinements in living being developed abroad, the earliest settlers continued an unvarying, rudimentary domestic routine in which such concepts as comfort, convenience, privacy, and specialization in household arrangements played little or no part. No doubt what those forebears of ours did not know about they did not miss. But it was a gradually increasing awareness of just those concepts that would dictate the evolution of the American home in the following several centuries—along with, to be sure, a progressive technology and a self-conscious regard for formal styles as tastes changed and would continue to change over the years to come.

In the course of time America has probably produced more different designs for living, in terms of both architectural style and domestic functions, of exterior form and interior detail, than any other single nation over the same span of years. The inspiration for those various designs has come from numerous alien sources, as already remarked. But important factors have influenced and modified such foreign strains in different ways in different regions of the country. The extremes of climate in some areas, the great diversity of the land itself, and the nature of its abundant resources have all led away from the original models toward distinctive native interpretations and creations. The relative scarcity of manpower in a rapidly expanding economy has generated a reliance on laborsaving shortcuts to accomplishment, which in turn encouraged other native variants of borrowed traditions and practices both in building and in homemaking.

In America, also, more quickly and generally than in other lands, the fashions and amenities favored by the well-to-do have been adapted to the circumstances and brought within the reach of a large public. The average American's quest for ever-increasing comfort and convenience has, indeed, often been the subject of both ridicule and serious comment. However, it has also led to emulation, since it is apparent that man's spiritual welfare can be nourished even in the presence of good plumbing, lighting, heating, and other practical domestic facilities and appointments. In other respects as well American houses have in late years provided models for international emulation. Where once, and for long, they were obviously derivative in their styles and patterns, they have become forthrightly native and original expressions which, at their best, are exemplary contributions to the world of domestic architecture.

Walt Whitman once wrote that to understand America one had to appreciate "the pull-down-and-build-over-again spirit"; and it is true that no other nation has so deliberately and repetitively destroyed the old to replace it with the new. There is affirmation in this. To discard the past has been an act of faith in an illimitable tomorrow. But this attitude has also involved a downright indifference to houses and monuments of irreplaceable value. What we have left of such structures, tangible witness to our American heritage, is rapidly diminishing. As the rest may go, so will go precious aspects of our environment, to which, it is hoped, this book bears witness.

The Editors

1

Our

Medieval

Legacy

*A*mong the many and mixed reasons that brought the first settlers to this country, the prospect of building and owning their own homes was never absent. Even for those whose spiritual need was an overriding motive in moving to the New World, such a prospect gave additional point to the pricks of conscience. Why then, asked the staunch Puritan John Winthrop before he left England to venture across the Atlantic, "should we stand striving here for places of habitation...& in the meane time suffer a whole Continent as fruitfull & convenient for the use of man to lie waste wthout any improvement?" Why, indeed. Over all the years since Winthrop voiced that rhetorical question, some such sentiment has played a strong part in bringing hopeful newcomers from abroad to these shores. Even in today's crowded and hurried world, with so much of the continent already built upon and paved over, there is still room enough in the land to plan or dream about the houses of tomorrow.

For the very first arrivals, three and a half centuries ago, some sort of shelter—almost any kind of shelter—was obviously a most immediate and pressing need. It was all very well for Captain John Smith in his *A Description of New England* to praise the climate along the northeast coast of America as healthy and invigorating, as any summer visitor might do. But the Pilgrims approached Plymouth Harbor in the biting cold of mid-December, 1620, under leaden skies and amid snow flurries and wind-driven rains. As it fell upon them, spray from the sea froze until their clothes were like iron casings. They were also occasionally exposed to a hail of arrows as they reconnoitered along the shore. And, as Governor William Bradford plaintively wrote, "they had now no freinds to wellcome them, nor inns to entertaine or refresh their weatherbeaten bodies, no houses or much less townes to repaire too, to seeke for succoure."

On Christmas Day they began building their first house, "for commone use to receive them and their goods"; but it was only about twenty feet square, and it caught fire a few weeks later. Over the course of the next nine months they put up seven dwellings, not much shelter for the one hundred and two men, women, and children who had been crammed aboard the *Mayflower* —not enough by far. During that first bitter season, not surprisingly, half the company died "wanting houses and other comforts...." Even two years later there were still only about twenty houses standing in the colony. In 1623,

Opposite: doorway and entry of the Ironmaster's House at Saugus, Mass., erected in the 1640s

Bradford recounted, a further group of settlers came to Plymouth looking for "greater matters then they found or could attaine unto, aboute building great houses and such pleasant situations for them as them selves had fancied; as if they would be great men and rich all of a sudaine. But they proved castls in the aire."

In the other early colonies as well, anything remotely resembling such castles in the air had to wait until the first, acute problems of settlement were overcome. At Jamestown the first landfall had been made in a milder climate and in a more clement season, in the spring of 1607. But when relief ships arrived eight months later, in midwinter, the first contingent was still "utterly destitute of howses, not one as yet built, so that they [the first settlers] lodged in cabbins and holes within the grounde...." Characteristically, for he was a born promoter, John Smith also advertised this area as a "delightsome land...heaven and earth never agreed better to frame a place for mans habitation...." But Jamestown was in malarial country, among its other disadvantages and perils, and here, too, at the beginning the mortality rate was tragically high. Eighty-five per cent of the population of the community died during the winter of 1609–10. A dozen or so years later one reporter declared that even then "ther Howses are generally the worst yet that ever I sawe, ye meanest Cottages in England beinge every waye equall (if not superior) with ye most of the beste."

Powhatan, the Indian sachem, was somewhat more impressed. When the settlement needed food in the winter of 1608, he offered to swap one hundred and fifty hogsheads of corn for a house similar to one that had been built for John Ratcliffe, briefly president of the colony and a man given to undue extravagance; apparently it was the largest dwelling in the community. John Smith actively worked on such a structure for Powhatan until the project was abandoned. (As an anticlimax to that episode, shortly thereafter Ratcliffe constructed a fort at Point Comfort, which did not serve him well, for he was thereupon slain by Powhatan.)

At Salem, New Amsterdam, and, toward the end of the seventeenth century, at Philadelphia, the firstcomers also put up in the most primitive shelters, be it caves, covered holes in the ground, or whatever, until they found time and means to build adequate, permanent dwellings. Thus it was in such rude, improvised structures, as Edward Johnson reported, that the earliest arrivals at Salem "made shift to rub out the Winters cold by the Fireside...turning down many a drop of the Bottell, and burning Tobacco with all the ease they could, discoursing betweene one while and another, of the great progresse they would make after the Summers-Sun had changed the Earths white furr'd Gowne into a greene Mantell." (Those remarks remind us, incidentally, that the *Mayflower* was supplied with ample provisions of "hot waters" and beer and that John Alden was the cooper charged with the maintenance of the barrels these were stored in.)

In good season "orderly, fair, and well-built houses" sprang up in each of the infant settlements along the Atlantic seaboard. Among them were larger and finer structures, both private and public, than any that have survived from that early period. No house remains standing in Virginia, for ex-

A portrait of Sir William Berkeley

ample, that is comparable to and contemporary with the "wilderness palace," called Green Spring, that was erected in Jamestown about the middle of the seventeenth century as a countryseat for Sir William Berkeley, governor of the colony—a mansion that his widow termed "the finest seat in America & the only tollerable place for a Governour." Even in dilapidated condition, before it was finally demolished, Green Spring was still an impressive pile when the architect Benjamin Henry Latrobe sketched it in 1798. Thus, too, the original building of the Old College at Harvard, constructed before the middle of the century, was the most ambitious structure of its time in New England. There were those who feared that this "Wooden Colledg...may afford as many Schismaticks to ye Church, & ye Corporation as many Rebells to the King, as formerly they have done, if not timely prevented." Moreover, the students were scandalously wearing their hair long "after the manner of Ruffians." (The minister at Rowley, Massachusetts, actually cut off his nephew from his inheritance because he insisted on wearing his hair long.) However, the college building itself was not soundly constructed and soon deteriorated, although the rebellious and hirsute tendencies of the student body has persisted—or returned—to trouble authorities of a later date.

Such structures and others of less pretension owed their essential character to the particular origins of their owners and builders, whether they came from Ipswich, Dedham, Essex, or Cambridge in old England, from old Amsterdam or elsewhere in the Low Countries, or wherever. For the colonists quite naturally tended to re-create as faithfully as circumstances permitted that part of the world they had forsaken; those aspects of it, at least, with which they were most familiar and which they most fondly remembered. They planned and built in accordance with deeply rooted habits and traditions. Aside from the wilderness setting, there was little to distinguish the first solid habitations they put up in the New World from those they had quit in the Old; and that setting itself was soon modified and domesticated as villages came into being and grew into little cities whose streets and profiles also resembled the long-settled communities of England, principally, and of Holland. In spite of an abundance of empty land, it was reported in 1663 that Bostonians were building their houses "close together on each side of the streets as in London." Barely a generation later a touring Englishman observed that "a Gentleman from *London* would almost think himself at home at *Boston*."

No doubt that comparison was somewhat exaggerated. However, it serves as a reminder that until the great fire of 1666, in the course of which most of the city was reduced to charred ruins, London was essentially medieval in character, as indeed were the smaller towns and rural villages from which so many of the early English colonists migrated. And so in consequence were the New World offshoots of those communities that were their models. Two centuries later, in America as in England, there would be a great reawakening of interest in the Middle Ages, an interest that expressed itself at a popular level in architecture as well as in such historical novels as Sir Walter Scott's *Ivanhoe* among innumerable others. That Gothic Revival style, as it was called, was a highly self-conscious effort to evoke a romantic image of

Top: the Old College, Harvard, 1642
Above: Green Spring, in 1798 sketch

the Middle Ages—a fashionable trend that, as will later be told, coincided with one of the most imaginative and progressive periods of American home building. The medievalism of the seventeenth century, on the other hand, was simply the survival of ancient practices and attitudes that had not significantly changed for centuries past. There is no better way to illustrate that point than to consider together the little brick church of St. Luke's at Smithfield, Virginia, and Sunnyside, the home of Washington Irving near Tarrytown, New York. The former, built in 1632, just twenty-five years after the founding of Jamestown, with its buttresses, pointed-arch windows, and steeply pitched roof, is a tiny, distant, but direct descendant of the great Gothic cathedrals of an earlier England. In spite of superficial resemblances, Irving's "little nookery," as he referred to Sunnyside, was a farmhouse remodeled in the mid-nineteenth century to create a picturesque reminder of a past that could never be recovered.

It is altogether unlikely that such words as *architecture* and *style* were even in the vocabulary of the early settlers, much less in common usage. For the most part their dwellings were innocent of any formal design; rather they were more or less direct expressions of a way of life that had not changed radically for some centuries. At one long remove from developments abroad, and anxious to preserve a familiar way of life, those colonists tended to perpetuate customs that, at least in fashionable circles, were being discarded for newer modes overseas. Thus, in some respects and for a time, the newly founded world was less new than the old one that had been left behind.

As the migration to America gathered momentum, the standard of comfort in English houses was steadily rising. Yet, even a bare generation before the founding of Jamestown, one reporter noted with amazement how many houses in England had been "modernized" with chimneys and glass windows during his own lifetime. Earlier householders had commonly been content with an open hearth in the center of a room, with an escape for the smoke through a mere hole in the roof (some such primitive arrangement was observed by a traveler in America as late as 1798). There were those who deplored the degeneracy of the new improvements for, as they claimed, the smoke that had filled a room in other times not only hardened the timbers of the structure but also "was repourted to keepe the good man and his familie from the quacke or pose, wherewith as then varie few were oft acquainted."

Window glass was a luxury of sorts until the seventeenth century and continued to be in the colonies before adequate glass factories were established. ("Bring oiled paper for your windows," one early colonist wrote to a friend in England who was planning to come to the New World.) Windows had indeed long been regarded as cherished personal property, apart from the rest of the home, and were often designed so that they could be removed and stored for safety or convenience. In the past, even the kings of England carried their Gothic casements from castle to castle along with their tapestries, beds, and other furnishings.

As just suggested, the changing fashions that were progressively affecting English home life in the sixteenth and seventeenth centuries evoked a lingering nostalgia for those "good old days" when customs were simpler and

Top: Gothic survival; St. Luke's
Above: Gothic revival; Sunnyside

the national fiber was of stouter stuff. It was almost a reflex of the conservative English character to hark back to an earlier time associated with abundant hospitality and unfettered, robust, and "natural" manners. As late as 1681 a leading character in a current drama proclaimed: "For my part I think 'twas never good days, but when great Tables were kept in large Halls; the Buttery-hatch always open; Black Jacks, and a good smell of Meat and *March* beer; with Dogs' turds and mary-bones as Ornaments in the Hall: These were signs of good Housekeeping."

He was, of course, referring to the great manorial halls of medieval and even Elizabethan England, those lofty rooms of all purposes, with open timber roofs that were, indeed, the core and substance of the house; those rooms where everyone—"knight, page, and household squire"—lived, ate, and slept, where the estate business was administered, and where, in inclement weather, the more tender livestock found shelter. The scene in a hall of that type described in the quotation above recalls the motion picture in which Charles Laughton as Henry VIII feasted on great joints of beef, tossing the bones over his shoulder onto the rushes covering the floor behind him for the dogs to finish. Such a great hall, built in 1341, with its open hearth at the center and its high, timbered roof, survives in its essential character at Penshurst Place in Kent—and others can be seen about the English countryside.

Remote as those large, ancient, and picturesque establishments may seem from colonial America, they were nevertheless recalled in the modest dwellings constructed in this country during the seventeenth century. For in these, too, the hall, so called, was the principal room of the structure, the area in which, typically, most domestic functions of the household centered. At times and in certain seasons, at least, it was in the hall that the whole family would congregate to share the warmth of its open fire, to cook over it, to dine, sleep, mend, or read as occasion demanded or permitted. An average family consisted of nine or ten persons. Since the hall also had to accommodate a complement of furniture and other household paraphernalia and to serve as a storage space of sorts, the circumstances must have tired body and spirit alike. There was little enough room when the hall was occupied, and simply no possibility of privacy. Those points were poignantly made by one pair of travelers who in 1679–80 put up for the night with a Quaker family near Trenton. "Although we were too tired to eat," they lamented, "we had to remain sitting upright the whole night, not being able to find room enough to lie upon the ground."

To carry an analogy between such small, cramped quarters and the great, lofty halls of medieval England much further would be misleading. In both cases, it is also true, the roughly hewn timber framework of the structure was left exposed to view, without apology and, usually, without embellishment. However, it was just another of the inconveniences of the early New England hall that the ceilings were often so low that a man of average height would have to duck to avoid knocking his head on the central beams. In his youth Benjamin Franklin, a man of modest stature, cracked his head on such a beam in Cotton Mather's house, whereupon he was proferred a maxim he always remembered: "when you come to a low place, stoop!"

The great hall of Penshurst Place

Not all the houses that were constructed during the first few generations of colonization were of wood. As will be told, stone and brick were also used, in New England as in other regions. In any case, men skilled in the use of all these materials—masons, carpenters, sawyers, and others—and equipped with tools for working them were early on the scene in the New World, and with them most of the popular building techniques of the Old World were quickly transplanted to the wilderness. For obvious reasons wood was from the beginning, and still is, America's principal building material. (To this day most American houses, by far, are wooden.) By the early seventeenth century timber was becoming scarce in England, and what remained was needed for shipbuilding. But the first settlers in this country, and later generations that moved the frontier inexorably westward, were confronted with an almost overwhelming abundance of timber, dense forests on a scale that Europe had not known for centuries past. Wood was not only plentiful, but it was easily worked by competent craftsmen. In this country there remains no more impressive example of such competence in handling large structural timbers than the interior framing of the "Old Ship" meetinghouse in Hingham, Massachusetts, built in 1681 and so called because its intricate arrangement of beams, rafters, and trusses recalls an inverted ship's hull. They span an area forty-five feet across, which is probably wider than most of the great halls of medieval England.

In many parts of the world—in India, Central and South America, East Africa, and other places—European colonists settled in regions where the native population had long since developed a relatively sophisticated culture with traditional building techniques adapted to the local climate and other conditions. It goes without saying that under those circumstances competent native craftsmen, familiar with available building materials and how best to use them, could be drafted, enslaved perhaps, into the service of the newcomers. The Indians of North America, however, had little to teach the colonists in the arts of building or the amenities of living. The mat- and bark-covered Indian shelters, "wyndoes they have none, but the light comes in at the doore," towns frequently on the move with the season, with the hunt, or before tribal enemies, and a culture that lacked iron and steel tools, all were no models for men with a bent to improve their lot and to witness the more wonderful works of God.

Not only did the colonists have to do their own building, but they had to learn from experience how best to cope with the peculiar conditions of their new environment. Winters in the New World were generally both longer and more severe, and the summers hotter, than settlers from the cool, temperate climate of England and western Europe were accustomed to. In New England, for instance, because of the greater severity of the climate, and because of the availability of better materials, the colonists soon abandoned thatch, so commonly used in England, in favor of wooden shingles for roofing. The fact that thatch posed a serious fire hazard was something else again. Early records of the Plymouth Plantation and the Massachusetts Bay colony abound in references to houses that went up in flames because of sparks lighting on thatch roofs. About noon on March 16, 1631, wrote Governor

Woodwork of Old Ship meetinghouse

DOROTHY ABBE

John Winthrop, for instance, "the chimney of Mr. Sharp's house in Boston took fire..., and taking the thatch burnt it down, and the wind being N.W., drove the fire to Mr. Colburn's house...and burnt that down also...."

Those first New Englanders also very soon learned the necessity of covering the exterior walls of their frame buildings with clapboards as protection against the weather and for greater warmth. Half-timbered houses, with plaster walls exposed to the elements within the structured framework, a traditional English style of building, were simply not practical in the New World. Clapboards were in fact among the earliest exports from the colonies. They were already being shipped out of Plymouth to England, where they were in demand, in 1622 or 1623. From the beginning the shortage of manpower in a land so rich in resources led Americans to develop laborsaving devices, and thus it was that water-powered sawmills quickly started to replace traditional hand-worked pitsaws; this before such contrivances were common in England, where they continued to be discouraged for fear of technological unemployment. In 1646 the General Court of the Massachusetts Bay Company awarded a patent, probably the first issued in this country, to one Joseph Jenkes for "manufactures of engins of mils to go by water, for speedy dispatch of much worke wth few hands." A very few years later, in 1650 and 1651, it was estimated one mill alone, in Exeter, Massachusetts, produced about "four score thousand...boards and some planks." Remembering that the population of Boston was doubling about every twenty-five years, and that the city, like others, kept burning down, thatch or no thatch, such stepped-up production was vital to keep pace with the needs of those communities.

The Yankees, to whom we are inclined to attribute such inventiveness and ingenuity, never were all English in origin to be sure. Over the first two centuries people from other lands joined the migration to New England, people whose names rank high in the "Yankee" hierarchy. The Crowninshields came from Germany, the Wendells from Holland, the Faneuils and the Reveres from France, and so on. Nevertheless, though it was an amalgam of sorts, the New England community had a firm English Puritan base.

New York, on the other hand, was from the start polyglot at every level. The infant city of New Amsterdam on the tip of Manhattan Island was founded before Boston—at a moment in history when old Amsterdam was crashing the barriers of world trade. It was a sailor's town and a trading place from the start, a place where life was quickened by the constant traffic of people from the world at large. Yet, in that little wilderness outpost, and all up and down the Hudson River valley, the Dutch settlers placed a clear and dominant imprint of their native traditions. Before the English took over the colony in 1664, New Amsterdam had developed into a tiny replica of a typical Dutch trading city—of Amsterdam, Leiden, or Hoorn. Its *gutte*, or "canal," running through the heart of the community, "whereby at high water boats goe into ye towne"; its curving streets and its neat gardens and orchards; its nestling houses of parti-colored brick and tile, stepped gable ends facing the street; its free spending, cosmopolitan population, all seemed strange and interesting to visitors from the other colonies.

Early dwelling with thatched roof

The Dutch also built in wood, but their urban structures were typically of brick or, less frequently, stone. In 1641–42 a four-story stone tavern, its steep roof covered with red pantiles and capped by a belfry, was built near the waterfront. The Dutch governor was delighted that he now had an ample inn "to accomodate the English who daily passed with their vessels from New England to Virginia." The Dutch apparently referred to these intrusive neighbors from New England as "Johnnies," and since the Dutch word for Johnny is *Janke*, they became known as Yankees. "Doe not forbeare to... crowd on," the governor of Connecticut was advised the year that tavern was completed, "crowding the Dutch out of the places where they have occupied, without hostility or any act of violence." And so the Yankees did. When a little fleet from England arrived for the formal take-over, there were numerous Englishmen already among the fifteen hundred inhabitants to watch New Amsterdam become New York "without a blow or a tear."

There, in Albany (Beverwyck), and along the majestic river valley connecting those two centers, the Dutch tradition lingered. Noah Webster heard a sermon delivered in Dutch at Albany as late as 1786. We still use such Dutch words as *cookey, stoop, boss, dope,* and others. But inexorably, over the years, the buildings the Dutch had raised, like those built by the Huguenots and Walloons who accompanied and followed them, gave way to others in the English tradition. The tidy interiors, with their scoured plank floors and tiled hearths and walls, their built-in beds, and other reminders of a way of building and of living transplanted from old Holland, all but vanished from the American scene.

Like the early settlers of New England, those who colonized the South were predominantly of English stock. No doubt they came with as many mixed motives as did their northern neighbors, albeit for the most part they did not share the Pilgrims' and Puritans' quarrel with the established church of England. That particular difference is very clearly to be seen in a comparison of two structures already mentioned: the little church of St. Luke's, so like the typical sixteenth- and seventeenth-century Anglican parish churches of England, and the barnlike, foursquare "Old Ship" meetinghouse at Hingham, an original New World architectural form suited to the Puritans' form of worship. The Virginians also, many of them, came from villages and rural areas that still lingered in the fading glow of the Middle Ages. And their first permanent homes also reflected the persistence of medieval building traditions and a rather rudimentary way of life, unchanging for long years past, that centered about a principal room, or hall, and its large fireplace. They, too, were familiar with frame construction, and they, too, displayed their native ingenuity by quickly resorting to water-powered sawmills. (There apparently was one operating in Virginia in 1625, before the earliest mention of such a device in New England.) In 1656 a description of Virginia referred to the "pleasant" buildings that could be seen there at that later date, "built of wood, yet contrived so delightfull, that your ordinary houses in England are not so handsome, for usually the rooms are large, daubed and whitelimed, glazed and flowered, and if not glazed windows, shutters which are made very pritty and convenient." To such relatively simple homesteads

The stone tavern at New Amsterdam

the early Virginia settlers, as those in nearby Maryland, gave affectionate and beguiling names—Resurrection Manor, Brick Billy, Kis Kis Kiack, Christ's Cross (shortened to Criss Cross), The Ending of Controversie, and so on.

However, there were other circumstances that made for differences between North and South in matters of building, of living, and of cultural patterns; differences that became increasingly evident with the passage of time. Although Virginians and their closer neighbors in the southern colonies did indeed come almost entirely from England, they came from virtually all parts of the mother country rather than, as the New Englanders so largely did, from one relatively limited area—and the houses they built in the New World express that varied regional inheritance in the different forms they took. There is nothing like a standard type of seventeenth-century southern house.

In the warmer climate of the South, to dissipate the heat of the cook's fire, among other reasons, chimneys were placed at the outer ends of houses, rather than centered within a cluster of rooms to conserve that heat as in New England. To take full advantage of the cross ventilation made possible by chimneys so placed, the centers of many Virginia houses were soon broken through with a hallway running from front to back. Like the Dutch, the Virginians showed a preference for brick construction, in spite of the abundance of timber that was available. The small size of bricks and their standardized production recommended them for masonry, and at least in some of the areas of England from which Virginians emigrated brick masonry was well understood. Thus, there were bricklayers among the settlers in Jamestown in 1607, and bricks were being produced there or nearby almost immediately.

In the end, the single most important factor in shaping a separate regional culture, social structure, and economy in Virginia and surrounding areas was the almost obsessive concentration on the cultivation of tobacco. Although tobacco was well known to Englishmen long before the colony was settled, growing that "divine herb" was not in the original plans of the settlers there. As soon as cultivating it proved both feasible and profitable, however, the Virginia colonists went about it with single-minded devotion. At one point tobacco grew in the very streets of Jamestown. About twenty-five hundred pounds were exported to England in 1616. Two years later the figure had already risen to fifty thousand pounds and production was rapidly increasing. By the very nature of things Virginia was almost exclusively a rural society, with no urban center of consequence to distract its populace from the peculiar rounds of plantation life. Before the seventeenth century ended, Virginia's history was being shaped by a relatively few planters whose holdings were large and whose slaves were many. Despite the abiding legends of Virginia cavaliers whose ancestry traced back to the Norman Conquest and before, the British gentry were only rarely represented among the early emigrants to Virginia. Those who rose to prominence and fortune owed their advantages more to their own efforts than to their pedigrees.

By the end of the seventeenth century almost a third of a million people had come to claim their futures under British rule in the New World. English colonies had been planted or acquired everywhere along the American coast, from the St. Croix River in the North to the Ashley in the South. (Early in

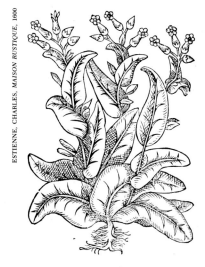

ESTIENNE, CHARLES. *MAISON RUSTIQUE*, 1600

The tobacco plant, Nicotiana

the next century Georgia and Nova Scotia, the thirteenth and fourteenth colonies, were added at either end to serve as buffers for the others against the French, Spanish, and Indians.) By then, two important influences were giving new shape to domestic life all along the eastern seaboard: for the most part the colonists had made the necessary adjustments to conditions in their new habitat, and they were entertaining with growing interest those new manners and fashions of living so rapidly spreading in England.

In the meantime, other communities of totally different character had sprouted up in the New World beyond the boundaries of English authority. The Spanish were the first Europeans to venture on the North American scene. Spain was then, in the mid-sixteenth century, at the height of its imperial power, and as its bands of determined warriors and explorers pushed north into Florida and New Mexico and beyond, it seemed likely enough that they might possess the entire continent before the English laid serious claim to any part of it. When the Spanish ambassador at London learned from a spy of the first Virginia colony, he reported the news to his king, adding, "I hope that you will give orders to have these insolent people quickly annihilated."

Even after Spain's power in Europe seriously declined, New Spain grew on, reaching up still farther into what is now part of the United States. St. Augustine was settled in Florida as early as 1565, the first permanent white settlement in the northern continent. Then, about the time Jamestown was settled, the Spanish settlement of La Villa Real de la Santa Fé de San Francisco de Asis—Santa Fé, in short—was grafted on an Indian pueblo as a frontier outpost. Had the wealth of precious metals the Spaniards hoped to discover actually been there, the hamlet would have become an important center of Spanish rule for a vast inland area. There, in any case, still stands the Palace of the Governors of New Mexico, the oldest dwelling built by white men still standing in this country.

The adobe and timber Palace of the Governors, the main structure of those Royal Houses (Casas Reales) built around 1610 in Santa Fe, N.M., to fortify the newly founded frontier outpost

SANDAK

Old New England

The Yankee Tradition

Scattered about the New England countryside are several dozen houses that were raised in the seventeenth century and that have withstood most of the hazards — fire, neglect, hurricanes, and wreckers' tools — to which such structures have been exposed for three centuries or more. The number is diminishing, and few that have survived have escaped some alteration of their original fabric.

Wrought-iron knocker-latch

PAULUS LEESER

Most have been added to at some time; windows and chimneys have been replaced; clapboards have been painted diverse colors; and, often, the houses themselves have lost the immediate surroundings that once contributed to the character of their sites. Others have been lovingly restored to their earlier state. Some that had completely disappeared have been meticulously reconstructed. One way or another, enough evidence remains to provide a fair understanding of the physical appearance, inside and out, of those early dwellings and of how they functioned.

Even before the end of the eighteenth century such venerable structures were already a subject of curiosity. In 1796 the Reverend William Bentley of Salem noted in his diary the recent death of an elderly neighbor whose family had lived in the same house for several generations past. The windows of the house, wrote Bentley with curious interest, were "of the small glass with lead in diamonds & open upon hinges. The Doors open with wooden latches...the chest of drawers with knobs, & short swelled legs. The large fire places, & the iron for the lamp.... The Beds very low, & the curtains hung upon the walls." Here, apparently, the seventeenth century had lingered on, untouched by passing time. Although Bentley does not mention it, the house had probably never been painted. As late as Bentley's own day, painting the exteriors of houses was still not common practice, especially in rural districts. Even in the cosmopolitan town of Salem early in the nineteenth century, the efforts of one successful businessman to improve his home were met with caustic remarks from his associates. "Sam is feeling his oats," they sneered. "He's begun to paint his house." The paint earliest applied to New England houses, red ocher commonly mixed with fish oil, was called "Indian red," not from any association with local aborigines but because the "real kind" of red earth that was used came from the East Indies; it had long been known in Europe.

Whatever their limitations, and by today's standards there were many, such houses were built by time-tested, widely understood methods, raised by communal effort, and completed with what seems to us an instinctive good sense of proportion and fitness, an unstudied and decided appreciation of form — an understanding of simple beauty that was a by-product of knowing and sound craftsmanship.

On the eighth of June, 1683, such a house was raised as a parsonage for the Reverend Joseph Capen by the community at Topsfield, Massachusetts, on a twelve-acre lot of land allotted to him by the town. And there, perched on a knoll overlooking neighboring meadows, the Parson Capen House, carefully restored, still stands as a faithful reminder of the Puritan past.

OVERLEAF: *the Parson Capen House, built at Topsfield, Mass., in 1683*
SAMUEL CHAMBERLAIN

19

The Ironmaster's House at Saugus, Mass., is a landmark of the first company town in America.

In *The House of the Seven Gables* Nathaniel Hawthorne prophesied that to escape the dead hand of the past, each generation would build anew its houses and public buildings. For somewhat different reasons we are approaching that goal today through hasty construction and planned obsolescence. However, in contradiction of any such purpose, the typical seventeenth-century New England house was laboriously built to last through generations of daily use, as was the Turner House in Salem, Massachusetts, so redolent of the past, that has since been renamed from the title of Hawthorne's novel. Additions to the original two-room structure over the years transformed it into a picturesque agglomeration of elements. By the mid-1800s it had been altered so often that Hawthorne himself was confused; at one point the house actually had eight gables. Another many-gabled house, that of the ironmaster at Saugus, Massachusetts, has been restored to its original state. Its first tenants were hired to manage the ironworks founded by John Winthrop, Jr., in the 1640s, an enterprise that shortly thereafter went bankrupt. Most typical of the changes made to gain space was the lean-to added in the back of the house, like that of the Whitman House in Farmington, Connecticut. In outline it resembles a medieval saltbox, whence the name given to this type of dwelling.

Above: the basic element of the House of the Seven Gables was a two-room structure, which was added to from time to time over the years to come.

Left: raised in 1664, the Whitman House in Farmington, Conn., is a New England "saltbox." The lean-to at the back was added sometime after 1700.

23

A diamond-pane casement window on the Ironmaster's House at Saugus, Mass.

Nearly every feature of the typical seventeenth-century New England house was derived directly from old English precedents. The examples illustrated on the foregoing pages, with their overhanging second stories and their decorative pendant knobs, their casement windows and their clapboard walls, would not have seemed out of place in south-eastern England. Just what the reason was for the framed overhang, or jetty as it was called, is not clear. It probably was a contrivance intended to strengthen the frame of the house, and in doing so it added interest to the profile of the structure. Windows, either hinged casements or fixed units (fresh night air was considered noxious in sleeping rooms), were small and few to limit costs and to conserve heat. Blown glass, almost entirely imported in the seventeenth century, was typically cut into diamond-shaped panes from round disks that were spun, in a semimolten state, at the end of the glassmaker's tool until they flattened out sufficiently and congealed. That swirling motion can still be detected in the irregular so-called music lines it left on the lustrous surface of such old glass. Metallic impurities in the glass mix resulted in attractive discolorations—purples, greens, ambers—with prolonged exposure to light. After 1700 double-hung sash windows became almost universally popular equipment. Yet, as Bentley observed, casements, with their panes set in diagonal lead bars, long remained in use. During the Revolution the lead from some of them was melted into bullets. The solid front doors were made of two layers of boards, or battens—arranged vertically on the outside, horizontally on the inside—studded with a pattern of large-headed nails.

Opposite: overhang and pendant of the Parson Capen House at Topsfield, Mass.

Right: batten, nail-studded door of the Ironmaster's House in Saugus, Mass.

A steep staircase in Parson Capen's entry leads to the bedchambers on the second floor.

All but the rudest seventeenth-century New England houses included a parlor, or "best" room, which, as the name implies, contained the finer furnishings and was reserved for such special occasions as entertaining important guests. Often it also served as the parents' bedroom. Seating facilities in this room were sometimes lined up in a row against the wall, and as a 1691 inventory implies, were apt to exceed the number of occupants: the parlor of John Bowles of Roxbury, Massachusetts, contained "13 Leather chairs," "6 Turkey work chaires," and "4 Stools wth: needle work covers." At an early date in some houses the cooking operations were removed from the hall to a separate kitchen, often placed in a lean-to at the back of the house. In this annex the kitchen itself commonly opened onto a buttery at the cool end, a small bedroom at the opposite end. The latter made a convenient room for tending the ill. Until late in the century, even in the better houses no effort was made to conceal or disguise the posts and beams of the building's framework.

CAL. SACKS

BED ROOM	KITCHEN	BUTTERY
HALL		PARLOR
	PORCH	

A lean-to usually included space for a buttery and bedroom as well as a kitchen.

Structural timbers, the skeleton of the house, were left exposed in early rooms.

A   Massachusetts   press   cupboard

Colonists did well to heed the proverb "early to bed, early to rise" and make the most of the daylight hours out-doors. Illumination from candles and lamps provided little light at night. Even by day the few small, rudely glazed windows did little to mitigate the gloom within doors. At best indoor space was cramped, although, in the absence of closets, chests and cupboards alleviated the clutter by serv-ing for the storage of everything from tools to the family Bible and clothing. The press cupboard shown above with its overhang and pendants reflects the current architectural forms. Turkey "carpitts" on table tops (they were not yet used on floors) added color to a somber setting. People with the means hung their beds with curtains that could be closed to provide warmth and a modicum of privacy and to exclude any breath of fresh air.

The Abraham Browne House, Watertown, Mass.

A diamond-pane casement window with lead bars from the Whipple House, constructed in 1639 at Ipswich, Mass.

ELIOT ELISOFON, COURTESY *LIFE* MAGAZINE

Above: a fieldstone hearth and brick baking oven in back, about 1660
Opposite: the brick chimney of the Ironmaster's House at Saugus, Mass.

For the colonists the New England winter was so cold it "froze the blood"; adequate heating was a matter of utmost importance. From the first, massive central chimneys about which all the rooms were clustered formed the very core of the homes; their boldly outlined stacks, rising above the roof tops, were like capstones of such structures. Entire families passed the coldest days—often weeks—of the year huddled beside the cavernous hall fireplace, where a fire burned continuously. Built to accommodate enormous logs and the vessels used for cooking quantities of meat, these units left much to be desired in the way of convenience, safety, and effectiveness. Housewives risked catching fire to reach bake ovens at the rear. A pot of boiling liquid crashed to the hearth of one Captain Denny's house, scalding four tots "in so terrible a manner that one died." Currents of air that fed the large flames were sucked through every crack and cranny of the structure. It was not a unique occasion when the ink froze as Samuel Sewall was writing before a fire. The consumption of firewood was prodigal. As forests receded, the problem of an adequate supply became an urgent concern of all the northern towns.

LEFT: ELIOT ELISOFON. RIGHT: LIBRARY OF CONGRESS

Above: three flues joining a central chimney
Right: chimney of the Eleazer Arnold House

The Whipple House garden today contains over sixty varieties of gaily colored flowers and herbs that were known in the 1600s.

John Winthrop, Jr., amateur physician and horticulturist

Gardens were nearly as indispensable to the Puritans as the roofs over their heads. Since there were few doctors in the early New England Eden, settlers relied chiefly on the ordinary housewife and her knowledge of herbs to cope with such exigencies as easing the pains of childbirth, treating wounds, curing snakebites, and laying out the dead. Her bailiwick usually included a fenced-in area just beyond the front door, where she cultivated plants "for meate and medicine," as well as for dyes, insecticides, cleansers, cosmetics, and deodorants. One man well versed in "Physicke," John Winthrop, Jr., transplanted his English garden to America in seed form. Ipswich, the town he founded in 1634, soon burgeoned into a "store of orchards and gardens," where families like the Whipples distilled "syrup of clove gilly flowers," angelica, mint, strawberry, and rose water. Sometimes colonists learned about healing properties of native herbs from the Indians, but more often they gleaned the "vertues" of plants and recipes for pills and potions from herbals brought over from England. These works listed parsley, sage, rosemary, and thyme—used strictly for seasoning today—as remedies for "torments of the gut," palsy, "stench of the mouth," and madness, respectively. Chervil and dill were said to provoke lust, while St. Johnswort was a standby against witches. Samuel Sewall, who liked to stroll in his garden, perhaps read that yarrow "stayeth the shedding of hair," and gathered it one day. Another time he observed the body of a long-departed friend, well preserved in a coffin filled with tansy, a highly reputed worm preventative.

Maifon Ruſtique,
OR
THE COVNTRIE
FARME.

Compiled in the French tongue by
Charles Steuens and *Iohn Liebault* Doctors of
Phyficke.

And tranflated into Englifh by RICHARD SVRFLET Practitioner in
Phyficke.

Alfo a fhort collection of the hunting of the Hart,
wilde Bore, Hare, Foxe, Gray, Conie ; *of*
Birds and Faulconrie.
*The Contents whereof are to be feene in
the Page following.*

Printed at London by Edm.Bollifant,
for *Bonham Norton.*
1 6 0 0

The title page of an herbal once owned by John Winthrop, Jr.

33

The Practice of Building

There was no such thing as a professionally trained architect in America throughout the seventeenth century or for scores of years to come. Until after the Revolution artisans with more or less highly developed skills, rather than designers schooled in the arts and sciences, were responsible for domestic and public building.

In the colonies the word *architect* did not come into common usage until the early decades of the eighteenth century. The word, incidentally, stemming from the Greek *arkhitektōn* meaning master builder, apparently had been introduced into the English language by John Shute in his *First and Chief Groundes of Architecture*, which first appeared in 1563. However, even there its usage was limited to the vocabularies of those with special pretensions. By 1620, when the Pilgrims set sail for America, *architect* had yet to become a household word. At that time moneyed aristocrats were among the few able to afford the luxury of architect-planned mansions, and there was only a handful of people whose training, activities, and reputations warranted the title of architect. Emigrants to the New World, like their middle- and lower-class countrymen who stayed at home, neglected matters of style and fashion in favor of more elementary, practical, and traditional construction.

Housebuilding, or more accurately "hutbuilding," was the oldest craft practiced in England's New World possessions. The first immigrants possessed only a rudimentary knowledge of construction and worked under difficult pioneer conditions. According to Captain John Smith, Jamestown's earliest inhabitants arrived in May, 1607, but by September "As yet...had no houses to cover us, our Tents were rotten, and our Cabbins worse than nought." And even the following January the colonists were

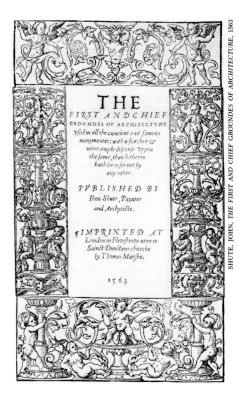

SHUTE, JOHN, THE FIRST AND CHIEF GROUNDES OF ARCHITECTURE, 1563

A title page from the first edition of the book that Anglicized the word architect

"utterly destitute of howses, not one as yet built." Similarly in New England William Wood observed that settlers had come over "rawly and uncomfortably provided, wanting all utensils and provisions which belonged to the well being of Planters." He strongly recommended that in the future would-be builders bring with them "All manner of Iron-wares... nailes for houses," axes, augers, saws, froes, wedges, and glass.

Of the one hundred and two passengers on board the *Mayflower* only one has been positively connected with the crafts. The cooper, John Alden, may have been the sole Pilgrim competent enough with tools to erect Plymouth's first wooden dwellings. Although William Bassett, a master mason from Sandwich, arrived between 1621 and 1623 and Governor William Bradford made passing references to carpenters in 1624 and

1626, skilled labor at Plymouth remained scarce for years. At the Massachusetts Bay colony in 1633 workmen were commanding such exorbitant fees that the Court fixed the rates for wages: the services of carpenters and masons were valued at two shillings a day, while those of common laborers were assessed at a mere eighteen pence. By 1634 William Wood still had ample reason to write that among the men most "fit for these plantations" would be "an ingenious Carpenter, a cunning Joyner, a handie Cooper, and a good brickmaker, a Tyler, and a Smith."

The housewrights (*wright* was another name for a carpenter) accompanying John Endecott to Salem in 1628 represented the first group of newcomers adequately prepared to conduct large-scale building operations in New England. This happened considerably earlier in the South, where skilled brickmakers numbered among Virginia's first settlers. By 1650, however, the influx of immigrants had alleviated New England's labor shortage, and men in the building trades were supplanting flimsy, temporary shelters with "fayre houses." These artisans came equipped with neither plans, cross sections, scale models, nor pattern books. Without consciously striving to achieve one style or another, they faithfully reproduced from memory the framed and boarded homes in which they had lived in the villages and farms of East Anglia, a stronghold of medieval tradition. Conservative by nature, these craftsmen had little desire to innovate, but used structural techniques and forms dating back to the Middle Ages, which had been painstakingly passed down from one generation to the next under the prevailing master-apprenticeship system. Required to meet the exacting standards of his craft guild in the Old World, the building tradesman took pride in the training that had taught him how to do a job thoroughly. Whatever refinements colonial buildings may have lacked, these were not due to incompetent workmanship. The Puritans were not indifferent to beauty, but they did eschew extravagance. In addition craft boundaries in the mother country had been precisely defined, but in America there was neither the necessity for, nor any possibility of displaying, highly specialized skills. The self-sufficient New England community demanded a greater degree of versatility from its citizens. A builder might not be a jack-of-all-trades, but he was expected, at the very least, to master more than one. As the early nineteenth-century diarist William Bentley reflected about his home town of Salem in Massachusetts, "the arts were better understood in the first generation . . . than in any succeeding. The first settlers were from old countries & were men of enterprise. In a new Country they had only the necessities of life to provide for. . . . An ingenious Carpenter made rakes, a good mason laid cellar rocks & bricks in clay. A good painter became a glazier of glass windows set in lead. They taught what they practiced not what they knew."

Colonists generally were familiar with methods of production in virtually all the crafts and with the materials used; they were not likely to be fooled by shoddy workmanship or products. At the same time, a prospective homeowner supplied his builder with only the most summary specifications, expecting the workman to use his own discretion in structural questions as well as in details. Typical of the extraordinary latitude given builders was the contract, drawn in 1638, in which Deputy Governor Samuel Symonds of Ipswich ordered a two-story, four-

room house: "Concerneinge the frame . . . I am indifferent whether it be 30 foote or 35 foote longe; 16 or 18 foote broade. . . . You may let the chimnyes be all the breadth of the howse, if you thinke goode. . . . It makes noe great matter though there be noe particion vpon the first flore; if there be, make one biger then the other. . . . I leave [such problems] to you & the carpenters."

Toward the end of the seventeenth century, fashions introduced by royal governors and other later arrivals, improved communications between the colonies, and increased trade with the mother country generated in the wealthier classes a desire to own up-to-date clothing, furniture, and homes. Thus, builders began importing illustrated handbooks (which assumed the importance of builders' Bibles in the eighteenth century) in order to become conversant with the latest London styles and find suitable models to copy. Although no building manual has been traced with certainty in America before 1700, it is possible that copies of Joseph Moxon's *Mechanick Exercises* circulated across the Atlantic at an early date. First issued in serial form in 1678, the journal contained drawings closely resembling the early houses of New England. Another book that may have found its way to this country was Stephen Primatt's *The City and Country Purchaser and Builder.* The book included an H-type floor plan, one that was relatively new in England and unknown in the colonies at the time of its publication in 1667. This design could have served as the source for Philadelphia's Slate House, erected about 1698 by James Porteus for the merchant Samuel Carpenter. The completed residence was undoubtedly one of the city's finest, for it housed the hard-to-please proprietor William Penn during his second visit to America.

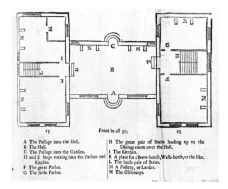

Above: "A Platform for a Mansion-House" illustrated in Stephen Primatt's City and Country Purchaser and Builder *of 1667*

Below: the Slate House in Philadelphia

Bottom: an elevation of a town house from Joseph Moxon's Mechanick Exercises

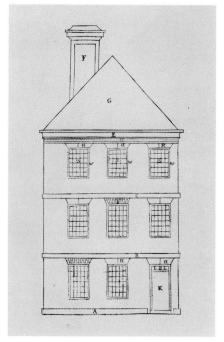

Smoothing a beam with an adze

Although architectural styles succeeded one another over the years, the basic constructional methods of the frame house remained unchanged for more than two centuries. Strong and durable oak gave the colonists their principal framing material. Trees were generally cut at the building site, where large timbers were hewn with a broadaxe, smoothed with an adze, and framed. However, early examples of "prefabrication" were not entirely uncommon: in 1630 John Winthrop "ordered his house to be cut and framed in Charlestown," but moved to Boston shortly thereafter, "whither also the frame of the Governor's house . . . was also carried" in separate sections. In the early days of settlement two-man pitsawing operations produced smaller planks and boards, but within a few decades this slow and inefficient process was made obsolete by water-powered sawmills. A new house required weeks—even months—of preparation for digging a cellar, erecting a chimney stack, and laying a wooden sill above the foundation.

A mortise-and-tenon joint

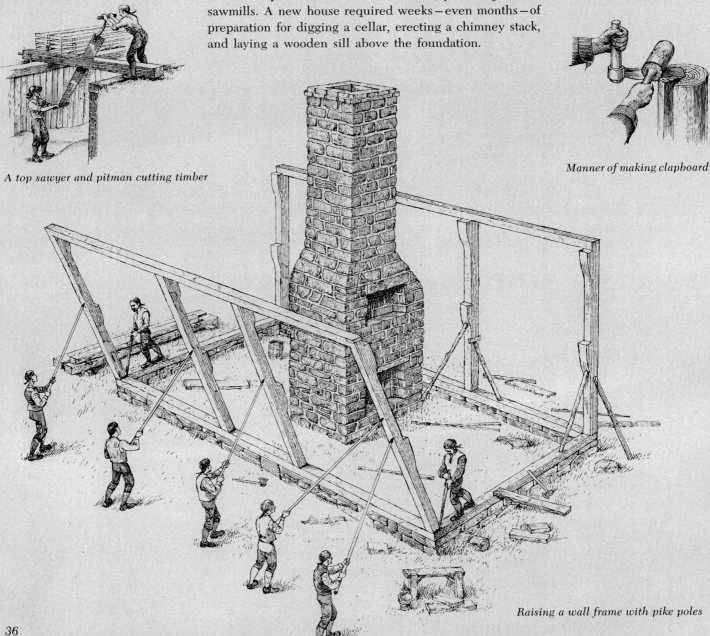

A top sawyer and pitman cutting timber

Manner of making clapboard

Raising a wall frame with pike poles

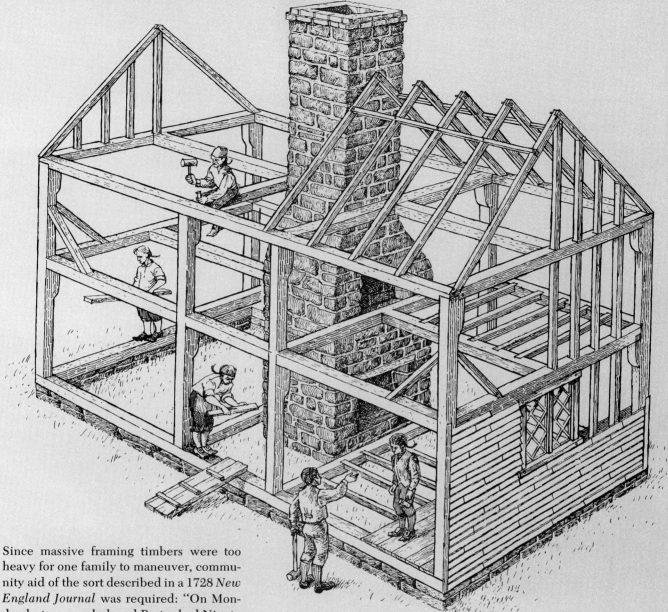

Skeletal structure of a frame house

Since massive framing timbers were too heavy for one family to maneuver, community aid of the sort described in a 1728 *New England Journal* was required: "On Monday last . . . our beloved Pastor had Ninety Men at Work for him, who cut & hew'd all the Timber needful for the Building his House; which we hope will be a motive to other Towns." At a typical house-raising, wall frames were assembled on the ground and secured with mortise and tenon (an extension of one piece of wood fitted into the socket of another). Then men using metal-tipped pike poles pushed each "broadside" to an upright position. Finally, side beams were locked into the front and rear walls by agile persons precariously perched on corner posts. House-raisings usually ended with food, rum, and some inevitable hell-raising. The custom continued long after 1774, when a new homeowner smugly reported that "no notice [was] given of raising untill the Night before for feare of a heard of grog brusers, not a man but invited."

The completed residence

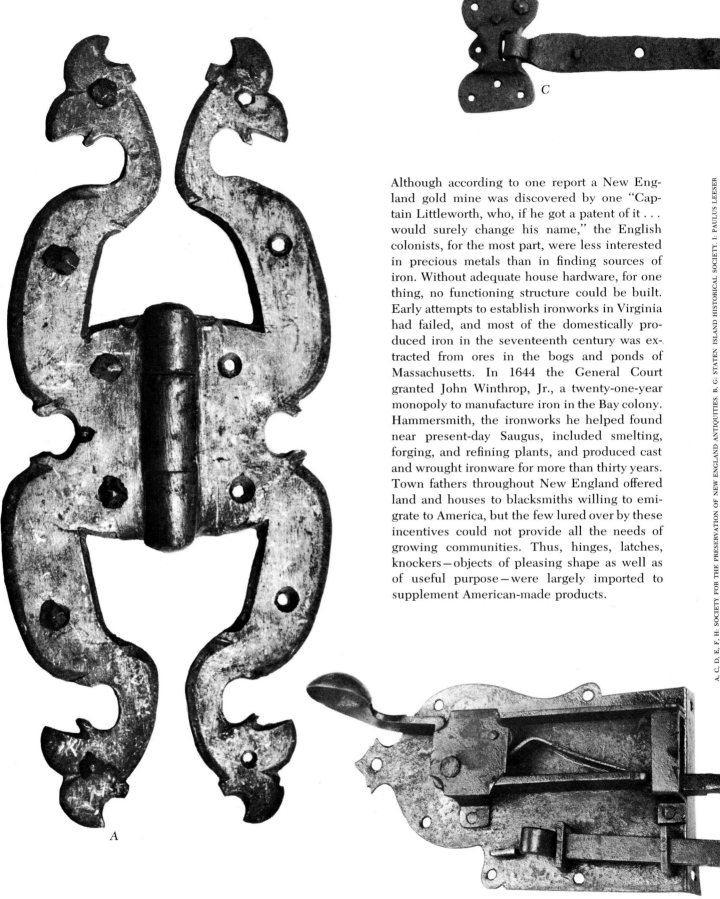

Although according to one report a New England gold mine was discovered by one "Captain Littleworth, who, if he got a patent of it . . . would surely change his name," the English colonists, for the most part, were less interested in precious metals than in finding sources of iron. Without adequate house hardware, for one thing, no functioning structure could be built. Early attempts to establish ironworks in Virginia had failed, and most of the domestically produced iron in the seventeenth century was extracted from ores in the bogs and ponds of Massachusetts. In 1644 the General Court granted John Winthrop, Jr., a twenty-one-year monopoly to manufacture iron in the Bay colony. Hammersmith, the ironworks he helped found near present-day Saugus, included smelting, forging, and refining plants, and produced cast and wrought ironware for more than thirty years. Town fathers throughout New England offered land and houses to blacksmiths willing to emigrate to America, but the few lured over by these incentives could not provide all the needs of growing communities. Thus, hinges, latches, knockers—objects of pleasing shape as well as of useful purpose—were largely imported to supplement American-made products.

A

B

C

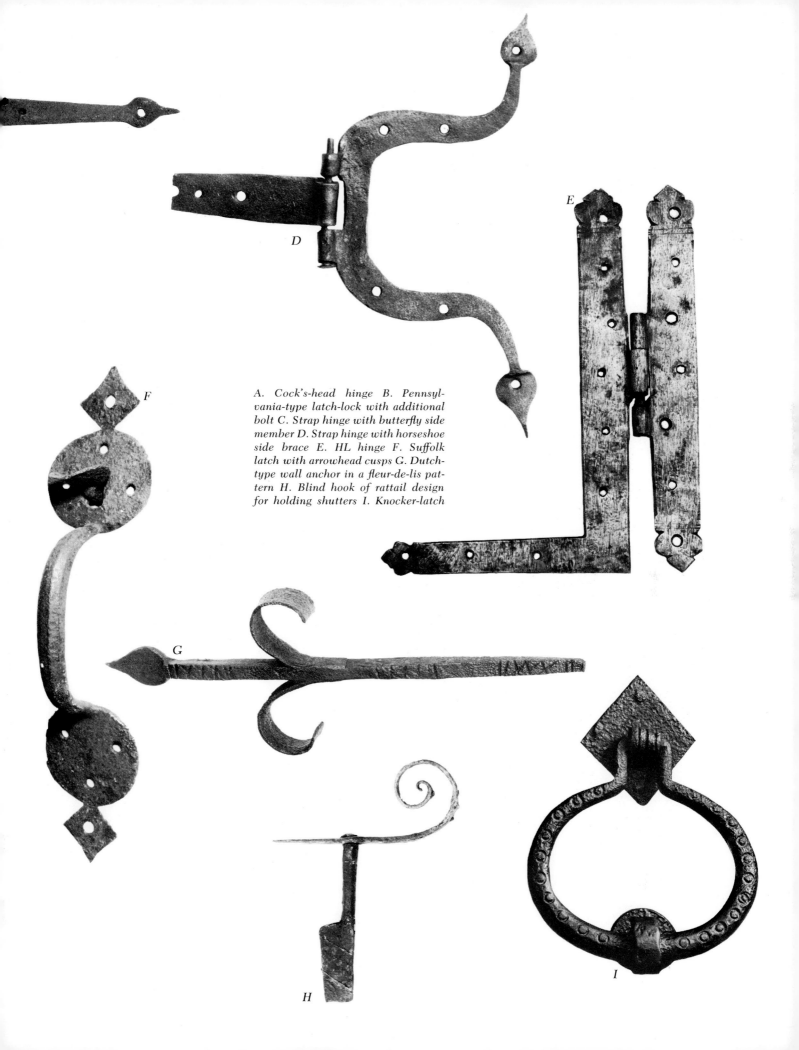

A. Cock's-head hinge B. Pennsylvania-type latch-lock with additional bolt C. Strap hinge with butterfly side member D. Strap hinge with horseshoe side brace E. HL hinge F. Suffolk latch with arrowhead cusps G. Dutch-type wall anchor in a fleur-de-lis pattern H. Blind hook of rattail design for holding shutters I. Knocker-latch

Despite the abundance of granite, sandstone, marble, and other minerals in rocky New England, the Puritans seldom built homes entirely of stone. Most took the Biblical words "founded upon a rock" quite literally and laid stone basements under houses, which from the ground up were usually of wood. Since stone had been scarce in their native southeast England, these settlers were generally unfamiliar with masonry construction. In addition, stone houses were believed to foster dampness. As late as 1784, when Thomas Jefferson tried to dispel the "unhappy prejudice," they were considered unhealthy. And wood required less labor to handle than huge boulders. The stone fences that still outline much of the New England countryside are monuments to the neighborly teamwork involved in hauling heavy stone heaps off newly cleared lands. Finally a lack of lime for mortar in most areas, except Rhode Island, inhibited the colonists from building with stone. Those who tried inferior substitutes were likely to share John Winthrop's fate; in 1631 he "erected a building of stone at Mistick," but "there came so violent a storm of rain . . . (it not being finished, and laid with clay for want of lime) two sides of it were washed down to the ground." Of the three stone houses known to have existed during the seventeenth century, only the residence of the Reverend Henry Whitfield in Guilford, Connecticut, survives. A pillar of the Puritan church, Whitfield came to America with his followers in 1639, founded Guilford, and within a year erected a dwelling of ledge stone, quarried a quarter of a mile away and bound with yellow clay and oyster-shell mortar.

Besides being a home, the Whitfield House served as fort, meetinghouse, town hall, and inn.

The Hudson River Valley
Heritage from the Dutch

In the late summer of 1609 Henry Hudson, an Englishman in the employ of the Dutch East India Company, sailed into New York Bay and ventured up the majestic river that now bears his name as far as the present site of Albany. He was searching for a way to the Orient, and at that point he turned back, frustrated. However, his otherwise fruitless exploration opened the path for Dutch traders, who came to bargain with the tawny natives for beaver, otter, muskrat, and other furs. By the 1620's several permanent trading posts had been established about the bay and along the river, including New Amsterdam, planted on what was to become the wealthiest small area on earth at the tip of Manhattan Island.

Almost everywhere the Dutch paused in their world commerce, they left tidy reminders of their prosperous homeland, and their settlements along the Hudson were no exceptions. The Dutch trading companies were actually more interested in collecting silks, tea, and spices from the Orient than in bargaining for animal pelts in the American wilderness. However, their little New World colonies took firm root as the fur trade flourished, and in the homes of those remote outposts life went on much as it did in old Holland, so far as that could be managed. For Pilgrims who had spent some years in Holland before moving to America this all seemed familiar enough, but for other colonists who came to trade in New Netherlands it was a world strangely different from any they were accustomed to.

Dutch customs and manners lingered along the Hudson Valley long after the English took

Early wrought-iron tie beam

NATHANIEL LIEBERMAN

over the area in 1664. To this day Dutch place names — Kinderhook, Cobleskill, Spuyten Duyvil, Brooklyn (Breuckelen) — are scattered all over the map of eastern New York State. Telephone books still list family names of such early settlers as the Van Rensselaers, Schermerhorns, De Peysters, and others. Washington Irving has woven everlasting magic into his stories of Diedrich Knickerbocker, Rip Van Winkle, and other genial folk whose adventures in this land of Dutch traditions he so fondly imagined. His fanciful legends have indeed become generally confused with historical fact. But the houses built by the early Dutch emigrants have largely vanished. In present-day New York City there is not even a trace of Peter Stuyvesant's New Amsterdam. A few miles upriver, however, in North Tarrytown, stands the stone manor house and the gristmill raised by Frederick Philipse in the early 1680s. Philipse had come from Holland about 1650 and for a time served as Stuyvesant's carpenter. Before he died in 1702 he had amassed an estate of ninety thousand acres, known as Philipsburg Manor, over which he ruled like a feudal lord. His ships carried profitable cargoes of all descriptions about most of the Western world. In spite of such great wealth, Philipse's original manor house had only four rooms. About 1720 his son and heir, Adolph Philipse, doubled the size of the house simply by duplicating the original structure, and thus it appears today, carefully restored and well tended. The frame gristmill that originally adjoined the house has been faithfully reconstructed.

OVERLEAF: *the Philipsburg Manor House and gristmill, North Tarrytown, N.Y.*
MARSHALL DAVIDSON

The Little Street, *by Jan Vermeer, pictures typical 17th-century Dutch brick houses.*

The Dutch governor's house, Albany, N. Y.,

as it appeared in the early 19th century

About the time the view shown below was drawn, a visitor observed that the settlement on Manhattan Island was but "the commencement of a town to be built here, and to be called New Amsterdam." Some years later, after the British occupation, a lady from New England described the town that had in fact been built. "The Buildings Brick Generaly, very stately and high," she reported, "though not altogether like ours in Boston. The Bricks in some of the Houses are of divers Coullers and laid in Checkers, being glazed look very agreeable." Nothing was immediately or significantly altered by the change from Dutch administration. From contemporary documents, feature after feature of the early city can be likened to those depicted in seventeenth-century Dutch paintings by Jan Vermeer, Pieter de Hooch, and others. Even in the mid-eighteenth century most of the houses were still "after the Dutch modell with their gavell [gable] ends fronting the street... the greatest number of brick, and a great many covered with pan tile and glazed tile." Albany was much the same. In that city, reported one traveler, there were about four thousand inhabitants, "mostly Dutch or of Dutch extract. . . . Their whole thoughts being turned upon profit and gain which necessarily makes them live retired and frugall." However, when James Fenimore Cooper visited New York in 1828 the scene was fast changing. "A few old Dutch dwellings yet remain," he reported, "and can easily be distinguished by their little bricks, their gables to the street, and those steps on their battlement walls. . . ."

A view of New Amsterdam, about 1650. The large building was a fort enclosing the "pretty large stone church," with its belfry rising above the roof tops.

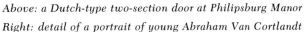

Above: a Dutch-type two-section door at Philipsburg Manor
Right: detail of a portrait of young Abraham Van Cortlandt

Like the exteriors, the interiors of New Netherland homes closely resembled those shown in Dutch paintings of the seventeenth century. On his visit to Albany in 1744, Dr. Alexander Hamilton of Maryland remarked that the Dutch families there "keep their houses very neat and clean, both without and within. Their chambers and rooms are large and handsome. They have their beds in alcoves so that you may go thro all the rooms of a great house and see never a bed. . . . Their kitchens are likewise very clean, and there they hang earthen or delft plates and dishes all round the walls in manner of pictures, having a hole drilled thro the edge of the plate or dish and a loop of ribbon put into it to hang it by. . . . They live in their houses in Albany as if it were in prisons, all their doors and windows being perpetually shut...indeed the excessive cold winters here obliges them in that season to keep all snug and close, and they have not summer sufficient to revive heat in their veins so as to make them uneasy or put it in their heads to air themselves." In some Dutch-type houses the stairs to the attic or upper story were nothing more than a ladder, to be let down when needed, or at best a stationary flight of ladder stairs. Also as in Dutch houses—as shown in paintings by the Dutch "little masters"—doors were typically divided in two horizontally. That feature was known in medieval England, and there called a *heck*, or "fence," door.

Ladder stair and alcove bed in the house of the ferry-keeper at the Van Cortlandt Manor, N. Y.

The Morning Toilet, *painted by Pieter de Hooch, showing an alcove bed and two-section door*

A selection of 17th-century Dutch tiles of various designs and colors, similar to those imported for use in the fireplaces and [...] and occasionally on the interior walls of early N[...] Netherlands houses.

A hooded, jambless, and tile-backed fireplace at the Van Cortlandt Manor, near Croton-on-Hudson, N.Y.

In 1704 when Madam Sarah Kemble Knight made an adventurous horseback trip from Boston to New York, she had a woman's eye for the tidy interiors she visited in the latter city. "The inside of them are neat to admiration," she wrote, "the wooden work, for only the walls are plasterd, and the Sumers and Gist [summer beams and girts] are plained and kept very white scowr'd as so is all the partitions if made of Bords. The fire places have no Jambs (as ours have) But the Backs run flush with the walls, and the Hearth is of Tyles and is as farr out into the Room at the Ends as before the fire, wch is Generally Five foot in the Low'r rooms, and the piece over where the mantle tree should be is made as ours with Joyners work, and as I supose is fasten'd to iron rodds inside." In one house she observed that the chimney corners and the hearths "were laid with the finest tile that I ever see, and the stair cases laid all with white tile which is ever clean, and so are the walls of the Kitchen wch had a Brick floor." Such hooded, jambless fireplaces backed with imported tiles were, as Madam Knight observed, virtually a standard feature of New Netherland houses. The hoods were usually hung with a cloth apron to discourage smoke from spilling into the room. Delft tiles came in endlessly varied patterns and colors, and they became popular in other colonies. In 1738 one Boston merchant advertised "Dutch Tyle, viz, Scripture (round and square), Landskips of divers sorts, Sea Monsters, Horsemen, Soldiers, . . . &c."

A detail of a painting by Pieter de Hooch showing a typical Dutch fireplace, similar to the one at the Van Cortlandt Manor

From the start, men of many different lands mingled with the Dutch along the shores of the Hudson. Albert Andriesse Bradt came from Norway and was dubbed *de Noorman.* Alexander Lindsay Glen came to Schenectady from Scotland. Jonas Bronck came in 1639 from Denmark and gave his name to the present borough of the Bronx. Thomas Chambers, an Englishman, was the first to purchase land at Wiltwyck, which was to be renamed Kingston. There were Schoonmakers from Hamburg, Kierstedes from Prussia, and Hoffmans from Sweden. And there were Walloons and French Huguenots in some numbers—and Jews from Brazil. In 1644 the Jesuit missionary Father Isaac Jogues heard eighteen different languages spoken in Manhattan alone. In rural areas between New Amsterdam and Albany, or Beverwyck, people of such diverse strains built their simple houses of local materials and in a manner altogether different from the brick dwellings of urban centers. Although they are commonly referred to as "Dutch colonial" houses, they owe nothing in particular to Dutch traditions, or to those of any other single country. Rather they represent straightforward expedients to meet the needs of shelter and protection, more or less international in their primitive character. Such is the stone house at New Paltz, New York, started by Abraham Hasbrouck, a Huguenot, in 1694, with attached structures built in the following years as further need required.

MARSHALL DAVIDSON

Stone house built at New Paltz, N. Y., by Abraham Hasbrouck in 1694 and 1712

Farther South

Tidewater Trends

As James I and London merchants envisaged it, Virginia was to be an urban colony, consisting of a series of trading centers. Jamestown, the capital of this tidewater domain, would become a miniature London with ships thronging its harbors and with such thriving industries as ironworks, glassworks, carpenters' shops, potteries, and wine presses. His Majesty's commercial emporium, however, proved to be a pipe dream. Instead, Virginia became a land of tobacco plantations, and Jamestown assumed the proportions of a rural hamlet where no more than a few dozen of the row houses, prescribed by its founders, stood at any one time. By the 1680s Jamestown was already in a state of decline, containing only "som 16 or 18 houses... and in them about a dozen familles...getting their liveings by keeping ordnaries, at extreordnary rates."

Almost from the start Virginians realized that wealth lay not in trade but in the South's genial climate and rich soil. They soon established farms and small plantations along the colony's many navigable waterways — the Potomac, York, James, and Rappahannock rivers, to name a few — which caused a pamphleteer to write in 1661 that "the families...are dispersedly and scatteringly seated upon the sides of Rivers; some of which running very far into the Country." An industrious yeomanry, made up largely of immigrants who had come over as indentured servants, constituted the backbone of the rural population and supplied England with most of her tobacco until the early 1700s when the rise of slave labor made tilling one's own land unprofitable.

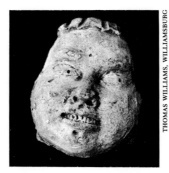

Plaster mask from Jamestown

The homes of these planters were simple structures of brick or frame covered with weatherboards. Unfortunately, no seventeenth-century wooden house survives; many, built of unseasoned timber, decayed in the damp climate; others, replaced by more pretentious dwellings, were converted into slave quarters and allowed to fall into ruin. At private wharves, usually a few feet from these riverside houses, ocean-bound ships would collect their tobacco cargoes and sail directly to England. Returning ships kept planters in remote places literally in the mainstream of English culture by bringing the latest clothing, books, and manufactured goods from London. The lonely life could also be alleviated by taking the family boat and visiting the home of a distant neighbor, often for days at a time. Entertaining strangers was another form of social contact. As Robert Beverley noted: "the Poor planters, who have but one Bed will very often sit up...all Night to make room for a weary Traveller."

Similar rural societies grew up farther south. Rice, rather than tobacco, brought prosperity to the area around Charleston, South Carolina, where early plantation houses reflected the English, Dutch, Huguenot, Scotch-Irish, and West Indian origins of their owners. Although altered over the years, Medway with its crow-stepped gables is still unmistakably Dutch in style. Built in 1686 by Jan Van Arrsens, Medway with its equally important front and back doors — facing land and river approaches respectively — anticipated an arrangement that characterized riverside architecture in the eighteenth century.

OVERLEAF: *Medway, the oldest extant house in South Carolina, was built of brick and covered with stucco.*
LOUIS SCHWARTZ, CHARLESTON

Indentured servants no sooner earned their freedom, a former bondsman wrote, "but they are ready to set up for themselves, and...live passingly well." One such person was Adam Thoroughgood, who came to Virginia in 1621, gained his liberty, and by 1629 had been elected to the House of Burgesses. As a reward for bringing one hundred and five settlers to the colony, Thoroughgood was granted in 1635 ten square miles of land on which he erected a home. Typical of early residences in the Virginia tobacco country, this

The Adam Thoroughgood House near Norfolk, Va.

Above: Bacon's Castle, depicted as a near ruin, in a nineteenth-century woodcut. It has since been restored.

Opposite: the gable end of Bacon's Castle with its triple clustered chimneys set diagonally upon a huge base

small but solidly built brick house bespeaks its owner's success. In about 1655 another immigrant, Arthur Allen, displayed his affluence in a more pretentious manor, of cruciform plan, which featured elaborately curved gables, a design of Flemish origin that had been fashionable in England during the reign of James I. When Nathaniel Bacon and his followers tried to overthrow Virginia's corrupt Governor Berkeley in 1676, they garrisoned themselves in this house— hence the name it has assumed, Bacon's Castle.

When in 1633 the second Lord Baltimore enjoined Catholics to treat Protestants "wth as much mildness and favor as Justice will permitt," he instituted an open-door policy that welcomed people of all faiths to Maryland. Such latitude in matters of religion extended to the early houses of the colony, which were similar in plan to those of Virginia, but exhibited a greater range of styles and individuality. Marylanders' zest for living was displayed in the sprightly patterns of glazed brickwork that adorned more than half their homes. A notable example is Make Peace with its "black-diapering" design running the length of an end wall. They also met the trials of colonial life with a sense of humor, as the names of their plantations—Hard Bargain, Penny Come Quick, Want Water, Dear Bought, and Peddy Coats Wish—bear witness. Perhaps the owner of Resurrection Manor hoped in time to reside in a more heavenly home. Maryland's distinctive medieval dwellings persisted well into the eighteenth century and were built concurrently with residences in the Georgian style. Although erected on its picturesque site in the early 1700s, West St. Mary's Manor with its clapboard sides and brick ends and prominent double chimneys clearly evokes its predecessors.

Above: Resurrection Manor, erected about 1660 on 4,000 acres of land

Opposite: brick detail from Make Peace, Maryland's most southerly house

West St. Mary's Manor, built beside a river on a land grant made in 1634

2

Georgian Classics

*B*efore the close of the seventeenth century twelve English colonies were firmly established along the Atlantic seaboard of America. Even such relatively late undertakings as South Carolina and Pennsylvania, founded some scores of years after Jamestown, Plymouth, and New Amsterdam had been settled, were already thriving communities. Each of the twelve had its unique history and situation, and for the most part each had assumed the separate character it would long retain, even as a state of the independent nation in much later years. That point was obvious enough to contemporary witnesses. "Fire and Water are not more heterogeneous than the different colonies in North America," concluded one eighteenth-century traveler after an extensive tour of the coastal regions. As Benjamin Franklin further explained, each of them had "peculiar expressions, familiar to its own people, but strange and unintelligible to others."

Some expressions were clear enough to anyone, as when the Virginian William Byrd complained to a friend about the "Banditti" from Massachusetts who anchored their vessels in the river near his estate to traffic with his slaves, "from whom," he caustically remarked, "they were sure to have a good Pennyworths." Or as when the New York merchant Gerardus Beekman described Connecticut as "that dam'd country." But apart from such signs of petty irritation, whatever the causes, there were wide differences in climate and physical surroundings, as well as in political and economic circumstances, which did in fact condition life in distinctive ways, and which led to significant variations in cultural and social patterns up and down the coast.

On the other hand there were factors that led toward more uniformity in those patterns. In some important respects the separate colonies were closer to the mother country than they were to one another; for all of them London set a common standard in matters of dress, literature, art, and architecture. As transatlantic communications increased, with more trade and travel, that standard became more immediate and pervasive in its influence. England enjoyed great prestige throughout the Western world in the eighteenth century. Europe was in fact swept by a wave of Anglomania; the French, Italians, Germans, and even Russians found in English institutions, English literature, and English customs and fashions worthy models to emulate. (As one small token of that enthusiastic admiration, Catherine the Great commissioned Josiah Wedgwood, the famous English potter, to provide her with an

Opposite: doorway and entrance hall of the Ashley House in Old Deerfield, Mass., about 1730

imperial table service decorated with views of great English countryseats.)

But nowhere was English precedent more highly respected than in eighteenth-century America. As the century progressed, a growing number of colonists were going "home" to Britain (*Our Old Home,* as Nathaniel Hawthorne called it) to read law at the Inns of Court, to take orders in the Anglican Church, to study medicine or art, and to savor the amenities of life as those were observed overseas. "It is the fashion to Send home all their Children for education," one reporter noted of South Carolinians, "and if it was not owing to the nature of their Estates in this Province, which they keep all in their own hands, and require the immediate overlooking of the Proprietor, I am of opinion the most opulent planters would prefer a home life [in Britain]." Even such ardent patriots as John Adams and Benjamin Franklin, men with sure instincts for what was valid and special in American colonial experience, looked to England for models and precedents in various departments of their lives. While he was in the field leading his fellow Americans in their struggle for political independence from Great Britain, George Washington still advised his workmen at home to depend on English pattern books in completing the improvements of Mount Vernon.

If not sudden, the rise of English prestige was a fairly rapid development that had its origins in the seventeenth century. Especially in the second half of that century England witnessed some remarkable changes, changes that soon made a strong impression on life in America. With the restoration of the Stuart monarchy under Charles II, following the overthrow of Oliver Cromwell's Puritan protectorate in 1660, and then again with the Glorious Revolution that brought the Dutchman William of Orange to the English throne in 1688, the old, insular traditions of the country were seriously undermined. Both those monarchs brought in their trains fresh ideas from the Continent—ideas that awakened England to the new world of Renaissance thought and art, with revolutionary consequences.

More than a century earlier Henry VIII and Cardinal Wolsey had brought craftsmen from Italy, where the Renaissance had reached its apogee, to practice their advanced skills in the alien atmosphere of the northern island. Around 1550 the Duke of Northumberland had dispatched John Shute to Italy to study the monuments of ancient Rome and the marvels of contemporary Italian architecture. The sketches he made there were shown to the king, and in time, as already mentioned, Shute published the first English book explaining the mysteries of the classical styles. However, these were but rare, early symptoms of an interest in such matters that a century or so later would become almost epidemic—an interest that, as it spread, converted England, and then America, from medievalism to modern manners of thinking and of living. For to this day, the intellectual and social life of the Western world is subtly molded by concepts that were adopted and practices that were fashioned by Italians of the Renaissance. When we eat with a fork we are observing a convention introduced to America, by way of England, from Renaissance Italy. Today's accountant, totting up corporate assets and liabilities, follows a bookkeeping system codified by a Franciscan monk in the fifteenth century. Our discussions of what subjects American school

A view of the great fire of London

children should study are distant echoes of an experiment in education begun in Mantua in the year 1423; and so on.

In their most overt, material form the new patterns in living were, of course, manifest in the houses and other structures that were raised during those changing times. The great fire of 1666 virtually wiped out medieval London; more than thirteen thousand buildings went up in flames, and the way was opened to a massive modernization of the city's architecture. One contemporary witness, rejoicing in the new appearance of the city as it was rebuilt, observed that "the dwelling houses raised since the fire are generally very fair, and built much more convenient and uniform than heretofore. Before the fire they were most timber houses, built with little regard to uniformity; but since the fire building of bricks has been the general way, and that with so much art and skill in architecture that I have often wondered to see in well-compact houses so many conveniences." To some degree, no doubt, that large-scale rebuilding in the new style accelerated its acceptance and its popularity in America. In 1686 an English visitor noted that most of the new houses then going up in Boston were made "conformable to our new buildings in London since the fire." The booming new city of Philadelphia also very early boasted an impressive number of brick dwellings "generally three stories high after the mode in London."

In such houses, built around the turn of the century, Renaissance influence found its earliest significant expression in America. Most of the fine houses raised during those years have disappeared or have been altered beyond recognition. However, with their emphasis on symmetry and formal order, their use of classical motifs, and their interior arrangements, they introduced those elements of style and comfort that prevailed throughout the eighteenth century. About 1712, for example, William Clarke, a wealthy merchant and member of the Governor's Council, built a house in the new mode on the corner of Garden Court and Prince Street, near the old North Square in Boston. The structure has long since been demolished, but it was a landmark of its day; its innovations included most of those features that distinguished the fashionable house of the new century from its predecessors.

Clarke's mansion was a three-story and attic brick building that contained twenty-six rooms. On the exterior the windows—sliding sash now, instead of casements—were arranged rhythmically on the facade, whose central feature was a more or less elaborate doorway framed with classical moldings and other carved details. In the seventeenth century, doorways, windows, fireplaces, and the like were simple, unadorned openings cut in the fabric of a house; here all these elements were treated formally as individual features of design. The attic dormers, for example, are capped with alternating triangular and arched pediments; the main doorway has its broken-arch pediment. In the interior of the older buildings, also, the structural elements of houses had been left exposed and largely undecorated; the functions of posts and beams, fireplaces and door openings, were frankly expressed. In the parlors of the Clarke House painted wood panels covered the plastered walls; elaborately carved fluted columns and richly gilded pilasters and cornices disguised or merely simulated truly functional features. The mantelpieces

The William Clarke House in Boston

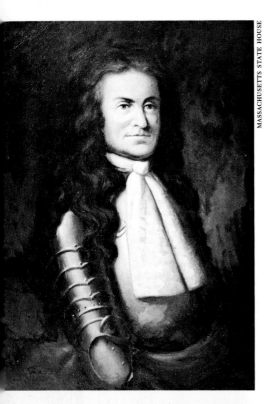

Top: royal governor, Edmund Andros
Above: portrait, Sir Christopher Wren

were ornately fashioned of Italian marble, and even the floors were formally designed with decorative inlays of exotic woods.

All this concerned more than mere formality of planning and designing; it involved new concepts of living in which comfort, convenience, and privacy played a growing role. The multiplication of rooms led to increased specialization in household arrangements—to separate rooms for cooking, dining, entertaining, sleeping, and so forth. Relieved of kitchen duties, fireplaces in the living quarters were smaller and more efficient. To keep a larger number of rooms as warm as might be, chimneys were built at either end of the house, allowing for a wide hall—the term "hall" now comes to mean a passageway—to run from the front to the back door. The hall of the Clarke House had a staircase, it was said, that was "so broad and easy of ascent" that one young occupant rode his pony "up and down with ease and safety."

Such accommodations were, of course, a measure of opulence as well as of sophistication. Clarke was qualified on both counts to raise and maintain his handsome establishment. His affairs prospered and his association with the royal governor may well have provided him with some special awareness of social and cultural developments in the courtly circles of London, where advanced styles were generated and promoted. In general the presence of royal governors in the colonies tended to heighten interest in the latest fashions from abroad; fashions in clothing and deportment as well as in architecture and household furnishings. Even Samuel Sewall, who tended to regard with disapproval the frivolous lives and wicked extravagance of the leaders of fashion in Boston, looked with some awe, if not respect, on Governor Edmund Andros in his scarlet coat and lace. On the memorable occasion when Sewall was introduced to His Excellency, he behaved with appropriate—which was complete—deference.

Nothing more impressively suggests the importance and dignity that surrounded the governor's office than the elaborate palace built at Williamsburg about the same time as Clarke's mansion, as a residence for the governor of Virginia (not to mention the other public buildings that served this colonial capital during the eighteenth century). In his first message to the Virginia Assembly, delivered in October, 1705, the new governor Edward Nott told them that he was "by the Royal Command to Recommend Earnestly to you Gentlemen . . . the Building a house fit for The Reception of Your Governor," although where the money was coming from was not immediately apparent. As it turned out, the structure would be financed by new duties on slaves and liquors imported into the colony.

As the official headquarters made for and approved by the queen's representative in Virginia, the palace must have made a memorable impression on the planters of the surrounding countryside—for its spacious and elaborate accommodations, if not for its architectural style, which was in fact not advanced by contemporary English standards. As Thomas Jefferson observed in his *Notes on the State of Virginia*, the palace was "not handsome without: but it is spacious and commodious within, is prettily situated, and, with the grounds annexed to it, it is capable of being made an elegant seat." Jefferson himself had occupied the building for a time when he was governor of the state. Shortly thereafter, in the winter of 1781, when it was being used as a hospital for American soldiers following the Yorktown campaign, the palace burned to the ground. (It has now been rebuilt in its original form.)

Both the capitol and the College of William and Mary had been built a few years before the palace and both were also large and impressive structures. As a passing note, in all these public edifices "modern" sash windows made their early appearance in America. Just when and where that device was invented is not clear, but it was obviously perfected in England around the 1680s. In his play *The Scowrers*, written in 1690, Thomas Shadwell tells the story of the roisterer Sir William Rant who, when he was "in beer," had an uncontrollable impulse to smash sash windows, an amiable eccentricity that made his glazier rich by repairing the damage that was done—a dramatic fiction that gives some idea of the ubiquity of the new fashion. That style soon crossed the Channel, for in 1698 a French nobleman proudly showed a visiting Englishman his "great sash window," which had been copied from a small model sent over from England. As the eighteenth century progressed such windows became the prevailing fashion throughout the colonies. In 1722 Benjamin Franklin printed a satirical piece in his Boston newspaper criticizing the extravagance of New England housewives in "new Glazing their Houses with new fashion'd square Glass." But the diamond-pane casement had by then seen its day. Actually, the college building at Williamsburg, which was completed about 1700, seems originally to have had casements, but these were quickly replaced by sash.

The college burned in 1705 but was soon rebuilt. It was probably the largest structure to have been built in the colonies. When Hugh Jones visited Williamsburg in 1722, he reported: "The Building is beautiful and commodious, being first modelled by Sir Christopher Wren, adapted to the Nature of the Country by the Gentlemen there [in Virginia]." Wren was one of England's most influential architects. His plan for rebuilding London after the great fire never was consummated, but it served as a prototype of the one developed more than a century later for Washington, D.C. He is best remembered for the fifty-two London churches which he designed and which, with their tall, graceful spires rising above low-pitched roofs, set a general pattern for the churches and meetinghouses that would become such an attractive feature of the American landscape in the following century and a half.

Wren was the earliest of a long succession of English architects, builders, and designers whose influence was strongly felt in eighteenth-century America. In a mounting volume of publications, which quickly found their way into bookstores and private and public libraries in the colonies, these men considered everything from the framing of timbers to the just proportions of the classical orders. It is safe to say that every house and public building of any pretension built in America during the eighteenth century owed some debt to one or another of those publications. Every educated man professed an interest in architecture and for them such references were indispensable. (When he was still a young man, Benjamin Franklin advertised in his own newspaper requesting the return of one such volume which he had lent long since to a negligent acquaintance.) Occasionally, a colonial building was all

THOMAS L. WILLIAMS

The governor's palace, Williamsburg

Top: *St. Paul's Chapel, New York City*
Above: *St. Martin's-in-the-Fields, London, the model for St. Paul's*

but indistinguishable from its English counterpart; St. Paul's Chapel in New York (miraculously still standing in that repeatedly burnt-out and rebuilt city), built in 1766, is almost a duplicate of St. Martin's-in-the-Fields in London that had been pictured in a very popular portfolio volume by one James Gibbs some years earlier. Gibbs' book was also indirectly responsible for designs that were incorporated in such outstanding structures as Independence Hall, Mount Vernon, and later, the White House, among others.

One reason why the governor's palace did not have a greater influence on the subsequent important buildings in Virginia was because of the increasing availability of manuals with more up-to-date designs. More than four score of such books were known in America before the Revolution. (William Byrd II, who constructed Westover on the James River, perhaps the most distinguished house in the colonies, had ten of the better-known titles in his library for his guidance.) The most elaborate of them presented English versions or adaptations of works by the great Italian Renaissance architectural designer Andrea Palladio, and of his English disciple Inigo Jones. (Jones' Banqueting House at Whitehall, London, built about 1620, was the first "correct" interpretation of Palladian architecture in England and as such a revolutionary development in its day.) In the British Isles the enthusiasm for those revived Renaissance and classical forms became virtually a cult, whose most prominent proponent was the third Earl of Burlington. Burlington was an amateur, not a professional, but he was lavish with his patronage and had working with him and for him several of the most gifted architects of the day. It was in recognition of his admirable and generous contribution that Alexander Pope addressed the earl:

> You show us, *Rome* was glorious, not profuse,
> And pompous Buildings once were things of use.

And he added perceptively:

> Just as they are, yet shall your noble Rules
> Fill half the Land with *Imitating Fools;*
> Who random Drawings from your Sheets shall take,
> And of one Beauty many Blunders make. . . .

It did at times seem that the land would be filled with constructions in the new style, whether imitations of Burlington's models or variations on the works of other designers. One satirist referred to the "buildings influenza" that was raging throughout England, an affliction that led many into debt in their feverish efforts to keep abreast of the style. In Ireland, it is said, the economic effects of the craze were so disastrous that the worst of curses was to wish that "the spirit of building" might come upon a man.

The colonies had their own building boom in the years subsequent to the establishment of Williamsburg, years of peace following the conclusion of Queen Anne's War, a boom underwritten by constantly increasing affluence. A good number of the finest surviving colonial dwellings, as well as a far greater number that have long since disappeared, were raised in the years roughly between 1720 and 1750. In these city mansions and countryseats the heritage of Renaissance patterns was expressed with a growing under-standing of academic refinements and, at the same time, with a freedom born of self-assurance. The extravagantly huge country houses of England, those monumental piles in the strict Palladian manner, were not imitated in America. Even in England they were as often ridiculed as praised. To accommodate imitations of Italian villas in the relatively chilly atmosphere of the British Isles meant the sacrifice of comfort to a desire for stateliness, and it involved fashionable conceits that offended common sense. Pope, who had nothing but encomiums for Lord Burlington's models, found Blenheim, the great palace given to the Duke of Marlborough in gratitude for his wartime services, an unlivable monstrosity. He put his complaint to rhyme:

> "Thanks, sir," cried I, "'tis very fine,
> But where d'ye sleep, or where d'ye dine?
> I find, by all you have been telling,
> That 'tis a house, but not a dwelling."

Compared to such an establishment, even the most ambitious American undertakings were modest and, it could be said, better adapted to their immediate surroundings. From Portsmouth, New Hampshire, in the north to Charleston in South Carolina, the new houses that were everywhere rising all paid heed to the prevailing fashion. But although they used a common language, so to speak, they spoke with regional accents. To quote Benjamin Franklin again and in a different context, each region had its "peculiar expressions" in architecture as in other forms of expression.

Colonists were not only visiting England in growing numbers as the eighteenth century advanced; they were increasingly traveling on business, for social reasons, or out of curiosity from colony to colony, and returning home with visions and notions born of their experience. The astonishment with which Madam Sarah Knight of Boston viewed the scene in New York early in the century has already been described (page 49). In the account of his travels through the colonies in 1744, the genial and witty Dr. Alexander Hamilton from Maryland made frequent observations about the strange customs, in buildings as in other matters, that he encountered in various regions. Just before the Revolution Josiah Quincy, Jr., of Boston found that in "grandeur, splendour of buildings, decorations," among other things of interest, Charleston, South Carolina, surpassed all he had seen or hoped to see in America. John Singleton Copley, the best of colonial artists, visited New York while his Boston house was being remodeled. He was his own architect and sent home frequent instructions for the guidance of his builders. At one point he wrote Henry Pelham, who was looking after such affairs in the painter's absence: "Should I not add Wings I shall add a peazer when I return, which is much practiced here, and is very beautiful and convenient." His comment confused Pelham so, Copley explained further: "You say you dont know what I mean by a Peaza. I will tell you than. it is exactly such a thing as the cover over the pump in your Yard, suppose no enclosure for Poultry their, and 3 or 4 Posts aded. to support the front of the Roof, a good floor at bottum, and from post to post a Chinese enclosure of about three feet

A self-portrait of the artist Copley

high. these posts are Scantlings of 6 by 4 inches Diameter, the Broad side to the front, with only a little moulding round the top in a plain neat manner. some have Collums but very few, and the top is generally Plasterd; but I think if the top was sealed with neat plained Boards I should like it as well. these Peazas are so cool in Sumer and in Winter break off the storms so much that I think I should not be able to like an house without. . . . I have drawn them in the Plan."

The freedom with which various builders in separate areas construed the "rules" of architecture, and which resulted in what seems to us such pleasing diversity, appalled Thomas Jefferson. In the range of his interests and talents Jefferson was a latter-day Renaissance man, a man whose studious approach to the principles of architecture and building allowed no compromise. The William and Mary College building he considered a "rude, mis-shapen" pile that might have been taken for a brickkiln except that it had a roof. "The genius of architecture," he wrote in his *Notes on Virginia,* "seems to have shed its maledictions over this land. Buildings are often erected, by individuals, of considerable expence. To give these symmetry and taste would not increase their cost. It would only change the arrangements of the materials, the form and combination of the members. This would often cost less than the burthen of barbarous ornaments with which these buildings are sometimes charged. But the first principles of the art are unknown, and there exists scarcely a model among us sufficiently chaste to give an idea of them...a spark may fall on some young subjects of natural taste, kindle up their genius, and produce a reformation in this elegant and useful art."

Few of his contemporaries would have agreed with such harsh criticism nor, as stated, can we from our present vantage. Jefferson's vision was in good measure fixed on considerations of style that were in advance of his time. Fashions in such matters constantly change. Generally speaking, the cultured amateurs and experienced builders of the eighteenth century solved many of the problems of house design and planning in such a satisfying manner that their patterns still have currency among traditionalists of today, and their remaining houses can still be comfortably lived in (with updated mechanical features). Beyond that, the typical house of this period handsomely expresses the best and most important aspects of colonial experience.

A profile sketch by John Singleton Copley of the house he was remodeling in 1771 on Mount Pleasant, his estate in Boston, with its "peazer" at either end. While he was away the artist wrote frequent letters to his home concerning the specific alterations he wished to have made.

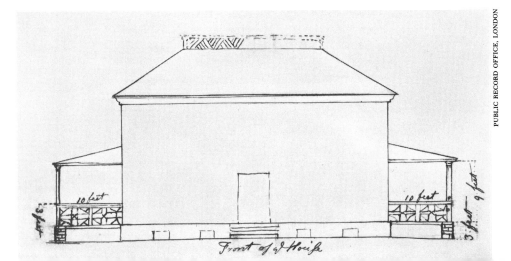

A Mode in Common

Georgian Similarities

Wherever capital was concentrated, Georgian architecture flourished. Early in the eighteenth century, wealth garnered by New England merchants, amassed by Pennsylvania privateers, and reaped by southern planters had contributed to the formation of an affluent society. Along the eastern seaboard a new class of "first families," of the sort described by the English architectural author

Iron gateway at Westover

William Kent as "emulous for distinction by an ostentatious display of their consequence and wealth," began investing as much energy in spending their money as they had in making it. Befitting their lofty status, they erected mansions in the fashionable Georgian mode, a style that in America actually appeared in the late Stuart period, and prevailed until the Revolution.

The houses shown on the forthcoming pages suggest that despite obvious regional differences Georgian architecture gradually evolved into something not unlike a universal style. A southern gentleman, accustomed to his spacious countryseat, might not find the compact home of a Yankee trader to his liking. However, even in the early phase of the style, before 1750, such far-removed structures as Captain Archibald Macpheadris' house in Portsmouth and William Byrd's Westover, with their standard plans and emphasis on formal order, reflect their locales or owners' personalities to a lesser degree than the pretensions of a well-to-do upper class.

Improved intercolonial communications helped disseminate the Georgian style. Ships plied the coastal routes and tidewater regions, supplying southern planters, who grew such

non-edible staples as tobacco or indigo, with northern foodstuffs. Although roads were generally poor, a highway and tavern guide was published as early as 1732 under the title of *The Vade Mecum for America: or a Companion for Traders and Travelers.* A basic cultural vocabulary was dispersed by artists like John Singleton Copley and Robert Feke, who painted prominent citizens in various colonies. And another bond was the one created by marriage; for instance, Abigail Adams of Massachusetts had Smith kinsmen in South Carolina.

After 1750 unvarying standards of elegance and sophistication existed from colony to colony. Finer homes everywhere were built according to the same general academic formulas. A New Yorker commented understandingly on Boston's "Very Spacious Buildings which together with their Gardens . . . Cover a Great deal Ground." A Quaker rhetorically asked of his lapsed brethren, "Has not our conformity to the World . . . in order to please ourselves and gain wealth. . . . naturally led us [to] the sumptuousness of our dwellings." Charlestonians were probably unsurpassed in their pursuit of pleasure. One of the richest, John Drayton, eloquently defended his peers. "At an early period," he rhapsodized, "gentlemen of fortune [formed] these happy retreats from noise and bustle; . . . elegant buildings arose, which overlooked grounds, where art and nature were happily combined. . . . And nature drawn from her recesses, presented landscapes, diversified and beautiful, where winds had not long before shook the trees of the forest, or savages had roamed."

Stratford, constructed between 1725 and 1730 on a sixteen-thousand-acre tract along the Potomac, became the ancestral home of the Lees.

Archibald Macpheadris' home, completed in the 1720s, was Portsmouth's first brick dwelling.

Early Georgian mansions, with their bold masses and classical detail, seem to embody the ambition and pride of the men who founded important mercantile and political dynasties. Thomas Lee, who rose from an aspiring merchant to governor of Virginia, surmounted his countryseat, Stratford, with chimneys enclosing roof-decks, from which he could watch his ships course the Potomac. This house was later the birthplace of the Confederate hero Robert E. Lee. At Portsmouth, New Hampshire, Scottish-born Archibald Macpheadris prospered in the fur trade and married the lieutenant governor's daughter, for whom he erected a suitably magnificent residence in the 1720s. Later, in 1762, the mansion received the first lightning rod in the colony, installed under the personal direction of Benjamin Franklin. Philadelphia, the "green country town" envisioned by William Penn, was soon plagued by such urban congestion that wealthy Quakers built rural retreats in the suburbs. Stenton so pleased its owner, James Logan, that the former secretary and chief justice of the colony refused to re-enter public service. He asked Penn's widow only that he "be allowed to live [with my wife] on our Plantation near Germantown under no other obligation . . . than . . . to advise . . . in your affairs for which she hath a great Zeal, yet more for her husband's peace." When not involved in politics, William Byrd lorded over his princely estate at Westover, a house as pretentious as Logan's was modest. After a visit there, the botanist John Bartram could not conceal a twinge of Quaker conscience or a trace of envy when he wrote: "Col. Byrd is very prodigalle . . . new Gates, gravel Walks hedges and cedars finely twined, and a little green house with . . . orange trees . . . in short he hath the finest seat in Virginia."

Stenton, erected near Philadelphia in 1728, housed James Logan's library—the third largest library in the colonies—on its second floor.

OVERLEAF: *Built in the 1730s on the James River, Westover has been described as the most beautiful Georgian residence in America.*
DEMENTI STUDIO, RICHMOND

Mount Pleasant, erected in the 1760s in Philadelphia's Fairmount Park, had flanking dependencies that were rare outside the South.

Built in 1765, Roger Morris' Manhattan mansion overlooks the Harlem River.

Among the great houses that arose after 1750, Mount Pleasant in Philadelphia was perhaps the most pretentious. It featured practically every device of late Georgian design, including Palladian windows, pediments, pilasters, and a grooved stuccoed surface simulating stone masonry. Built for a former privateer, John Macpherson, who won enough loot at sea to set up housekeeping in manorial splendor, Mount Pleasant did not take full advantage of its scenic site overlooking the Schuylkill River; its end walls lacked windows. Benedict Arnold purchased the estate in 1779, intending to settle there someday with the comely and wealthy Peggy Shippen, but the course of events altered his plans. Rich New Yorkers were beginning to complain that "living in our capital is become so very expensive, and what is worse that it is become so fashionable."

The facade of the Jeremiah Lee House is painted wood simulating masonry.

Money, however, was no object to Roger Morris, whose residence, with its colossal portico, was with one exception unique. Contrary to popular belief, such colonnaded porticoes did not become common in America until the 1800s. During the Revolution George Washington used this house (which is named the Jumel Mansion after a later owner) as his headquarters. New England extravagance was manifested in elegant town houses like the one owned by the prosperous Jeremiah Lee of Marblehead. Charleston planters were also handsomely housed. Dating from the late 1730s, John Drayton's countryseat on the banks of the Ashley River was architecturally advanced for its time. The structure, with its Palladian facade, so impressed the English parson Charles Woodmason, that he eulogized it in a panegyric: "What! Tho a second Carthage here we raise,/ A late attempt, the work of modern days,/ Here Drayton's seat and Middleton's is found,/ Delightful villas! be they long renown'd."

Superposed Doric and Ionic orders supporting the porch and balcony on the facade of Drayton Hall derive directly from Palladio's pages.

Although colonial gentlemen of the mid-Georgian period planned their mansions with a cold Palladian logic, their fertile imaginations ran riot when it came to embellishing their gardens. In England the seeds of a romantic rebellion against classicism had taken root in the area of landscape design, as evidenced by the vogue for "naturalistic gardens" containing architectural surprises in the form of Gothic ruins, Chinese pagodas, hermitages, classic temples, and mosques. These summerhouses, in addition to their ornamental value, provided rustic retreats for undisturbed trysts and the contemplation of nature. Designs for exotic buildings became available to people of cultivated tastes in America through such pattern books as Batty Langley's *Gothick Architecture, Improved by Rules & Proportions* and William Halfpenny's *New Designs for Chinese Temples, Triumphal Arches, Gardens, Seats, & Palings.* An octagonal plan proved to be the most popular in the colonies, and was the one chosen by George Washington for his bell-roofed garden houses at Mount Vernon. At Montpelier, James Madison erected a circular belvedere with freestanding columns, similar to a pavilion uncovered in the ancient Roman town of Herculaneum. Since the otherwise orthodox Palladian, Thomas Jefferson, considered summerhouses to be "play" architecture, not to be taken seriously, he felt at liberty, in 1771 and the year immediately following, to design a fantastical array of structures for the gardens at Monticello, including Chinese pavilions, a medieval tower with battlements, and a triumphal column that, had it been built, would have surpassed the one in Trajan's forum. However, the Revolution and subsequent events prevented these caprices from materializing.

A painted Chinese pagoda with a lattice railing, at Mount Pleasant in Philadelphia

Regional Preferences

From North to South

By the 1750s the thirteen colonies were pursuing such independent courses, politically, economically, and socially, that it seemed unlikely that they could ever work together for a common cause. "Everybody cries a union is absolutely necessary," wrote Benjamin Franklin in 1758, "but when it comes to the manner and form of the union their weak noodles are perfectly distracted." Although architectural differences from colony to colony were less pronounced because of the basic homogeneity of the Georgian style, each region imparted its own accent to the common language of classical forms, as the houses on the following pages illustrate.

In Virginia's tobacco kingdom, where towns were practically non-existent, plantations had to be largely self-sufficient communities with their own carpenters, brickmakers, blacksmiths, bakers, brewers, and slaves. On baronial estates ("King" Carter, for example, owned three hundred thousand acres) an untitled nobility built impressive mansions of stone and brick that, with their flanking dependencies, came closer than other colonial structures to approximating the Palladian manor houses of rural England. As one author put it, Virginians "live more like country gentlemen of fortune than any other settlers in America...[they] live in a state of emulation with one another in buildings (many of their houses would make no slight figure in the English counties), furniture, wines, dress, diversions, and this to such a degree, that it is rather amazing that they should be able to go on with their plantations at all."

A carved pineapple finial

New England, likewise, had a distinct Georgian vernacular. A deep-rooted Puritanism had lingered in this area, and Yankees cultivated a taste for elegance with something less than southern zeal. Even shortly before the Revolution, one Captain William Owen saw fit to remark, "The character of the Inhabitants of this Province [Massachusetts] is much improved, in comparison to what it was...but puritanism and a spirit of persecution is not yet totally extinguished." In the coastal and inland towns of New England the Georgian houses of wealthy merchants were constructed on a smaller scale than Virginia's regal residences. Dwellings continued to be built of wood, which was still in abundant supply in New Hampshire and Maine, and which was often grooved to simulate stone masonry. Many of the house carpenters and carvers were trained in the region's shipbuilding industries.

Charleston, a "melting pot" in its subtropical climate as well as in the diversity of its population, produced still another Georgian dialect. Unlike Virginians, Charlestonians took an active role in commerce, and their city developed into a thriving port. Seasonally, the rice aristocracy would flee the malarial marshes of their lowland plantations and retreat to town houses. To counter the penetrating dampness the first floors of their mansions were raised several feet above ground level. The sultry weather also encouraged the construction of spacious rooms, opening onto porches and piazzas that faced gardens, after the homes in the West Indies, whence came many of the city's residents.

The last of a group of stylistically similar houses raised in Virginia between 1725 and 1750, Carter's Grove, with its classical lines and harmonious relationship to its setting, represents the culmination of early Georgian plantation architecture. Begun in 1750 for Carter Burwell, grandson of the rich "King" Carter, from whom the estate inherited its name, and probably its financing, the mansion was constructed of red bricks fired on the premises, mortar, the lime for which was obtained from oyster shells delivered to Burwell's James River landing, and poplar, pine, and walnut cut at the site. The design of Carter's Grove has been attributed to Richard Taliaferro, a noted amateur architect from nearby Williamsburg. Plantation accounts list one David Minitree as the contractor-builder, whose superintendence of the job was so satisfactory that he received an extra twenty-five pounds "By a present." Richard Bayliss, a master-joiner, was brought over from England to execute the interiors which contain some of the outstanding examples of woodwork in the country. The superbly carved paneling, originally painted so as to hide the joints and variations in the wood used, has now been restored to a natural finish. Details of the entrance salon, many of which derive from William Salmon's *Palladio Londinensis*, all exhibit expert workmanship. Beyond the grand elliptical arch, the same consideration has been lavished on the stairway; the landings between floors, inlaid with a geometric pattern, are unique in America. The stair still bears scars incurred in 1781 when Colonel Tarleton of the British Light Horse Brigade was occupying the house. During what appears to have been a night of raucous horseplay, Tarleton or one of his officers charged up the stairs on his mount, hacking the handrail with his saber.

Above: on the mansion's important river front, the central hall widens into a spacious entrance salon.

Opposite: shaded by tulip poplars, Carter's Grove looks across terraced fields to the James River.

Bayliss' art is demonstrated in the Ionic pilasters, cornice, and arch of the second-floor hallway.

In his comparatively modest office, Carter Burwell kept detailed accounts that are still extant.

At Carter's Grove and similar Georgian establishments, areas associated with the running of the domestic economy were set apart from the great house. Even at the beginning of the eighteenth century, the historian Robert Beverley had observed of his fellow Virginians that "All their Drudgeries of Cookery, Washing, Daries, &c. are perform'd in Offices detacht from the Dwelling-Houses, which by this means are kept more cool and Sweet." Separate service buildings, generally smaller, simpler versions of the mansion itself, also housed schoolrooms, additional sleeping quarters, and actual offices where plantation business was transacted. The flanking office and kitchen wings at Carter's Grove, originally detached from the central structure, were connected to it via passages only in the twentieth century. Both dependencies antedate the main residence; the office, erected in the early 1700s, had served as the home of Nathaniel Burwell, Carter's father. From its completion in 1753, until 1790 when Carter Burwell II left it to build Carter Hall, Carter's Grove set a pattern for gracious living and entertainments as elegant as any offered by England's squirearchy. At one time or another most of Virginia's leading families partook of the Burwells' hospitality.

The family portraits, wing chairs, and carpet enhance the paneled grandeur of the east parlor.

Devoted almost exclusively to social purposes, the mansion's lower floor was fitted with the finest furniture, mirrors, hangings, carpets, plate, crystal, and china from London. The east drawing room, one of a pair of matching paneled parlors, with its formal Palladian ornament and fireplace framed by an architrave of white marble veined in gray, is said to have been the scene of a fatal duel. The drawing room to the west, containing an exquisitely carved Siena marble mantel, is popularly known as the "Refusal Room." Tradition has it that George Washington proposed to Mary Carter here and was turned down. And, in the same room, an even more ardent young swain, Thomas Jefferson, stammered out an awkward confession of love to Belinda (his term of endearment for Rebecca Burwell). Jefferson, then a naive nineteen-year-old student at the College of William and Mary, had vowed, "If I am to meet with disappointment, the sooner I know it, the more of life I shall have to wear it off.... If Belinda will not accept of my service, it shall never be offered to another." Although Miss Burwell's reply was negative, because she preferred the attentions of the dashing Jaquelin Ambler, whom she later married, time eventually cured the rejected suitor of his unrequited love.

Unlike earlier abodes, the Ashley House has sash windows, balanced chimneys, and a pedimented doorway.

The shell-topped cupboards and sunflower ornament atop pilasters in the Ashley parlor reveal Connecticut Valley tradition at its best.

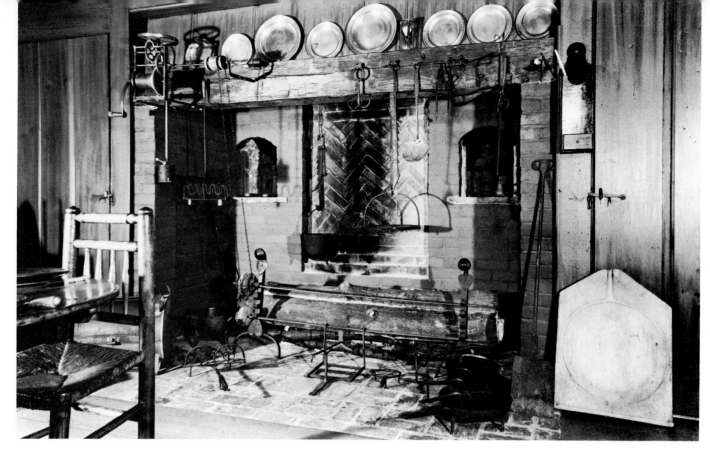

An enormous brick-lined fireplace in Parson Ashley's kitchen was equipped to feed a family of nine, as well as occasional Tory guests.

A secretary in the Chippendale style, made in New England

Deep in the hinterland of the Connecticut River valley, housewrights and carpenters submitted elements of Georgian design to their own imaginative processes and produced an ingenuous and engaging regional architecture. Built around 1730, the frame house purchased a few years later by the Reverend Jonathan Ashley of Deerfield, Massachusetts, embodies the salient features of the style. On first impression, the manse with its unpainted clapboard exterior, narrow windows, and lean-to addition containing a cavernous kitchen fireplace, recalls seventeenth-century structures, and appears to be better suited to a community still plagued with Indian raids than would a properly Palladian house. However, upon closer observation the dwelling's richly carved doorway, central-hall plan—one of the first of its kind in Deerfield—and fine interior woodwork indicate the arrival of a new order. For nearly fifty years, the divine officiated at christenings, weddings, and funerals in the sophisticated elegance of his paneled parlor. A man of controversial opinions, whose outspoken Tory sympathies in the years prior to the Revolution led to his being locked out of his church on many a Sabbath, the preacher's good taste was nevertheless unassailable. Although the handsome Chippendale secretary in the parlor did not belong to Ashley, the superbly fashioned piece, with its seasoned mahogany surfaces and architectonic proportions, typifies the sort of cabinetwork the parson owned and used.

The imposing brick mansion constructed for the wealthy merchant Miles Brewton was the most splendid of the town houses erected by fashionable Charlestonians in the period preceding the Revolution. Basically a late Georgian design, the residence, with its high basement and two-tiered classic portico, also took advantage of the sea breezes that swept the peninsula city. Ezra Waite, a self-described "Civil Architect, House-builder in general" from London, executed the elaborate woodwork inside and out. When a jealous rival implied that he had had nothing to do with the house, Waite vindicated himself in the *South Carolina Gazette*, stating that he "finished the Architecture, conducted the...said work in the four principal rooms; and also calculated, adjusted, and draw'd...the Ionick entablature, and carved the same in the front and round the eaves." Miles Brewton enjoyed his new town house for a brief six years before he and his family perished at sea in 1775. The dwelling then passed on to the deceased's sister, Mrs. Jacob Motte, who during the Revolution played unwilling hostess to the British officer Sir Henry Clinton, sequestering her daughters in the attic for the length of his stay. In the nineteenth century, the Union generals Meade and Hatch occupied the mansion, and thus probably spared it from the damage inflicted on its less-favored neighbors.

Opposite: occupants of the Brewton House could benefit from indoor-outdoor living in the shady spaces of the classic portico.

Completed in 1769, the Miles Brewton residence, with its ornate wrought-iron gates, recalls homes in southern European cities.

CAL SACKS

The magnificent rooms of the Miles Brewton House, with their paneling and carving of surpassing delicacy, attest to the skilled craftsmanship of Ezra Waite. A number of the decorative details of the woodwork may have been derived from designs in Abraham Swan's *British Architect*. The house has remained the property of Brewton's descendants, and such rooms as the first-floor drawing room (bottom, opposite) are furnished with objects acquired by members of the family over the years. On the far wall hangs a portrait, painted by the colonial artist Jeremiah Theus, of the mother-in-law of Mrs. Jacob Motte, who lived in the house during the Revolutionary War. Suspended from the stuccoed ceiling is a bronze and Waterford glass chandelier, brought from a family plantation in 1791. The room also contains many original pieces like the armchairs in the Chippendale style, made for Miles Brewton by Thomas Elfe, a prominent furniture maker of Charleston.

Left: Miles Brewton bought the English candlesticks on the dining room table.

Opposite: doorway flanked by Corinthian pilasters, topped by a broken pediment

On the tables of the first-floor drawing room are pieces of the China Trade porcelain collected by Miles Brewton for his new house.

The Art of Building

During the Middle Ages no special distinction was drawn between the architect of a structure and the manual workers, the masons and stonecutters, carpenters and joiners, whom he directed. He might as properly be termed a foreman or an overseer. With the Renaissance, however, the "inventor" of a building clearly disassociated himself from the construction workers. That new distinction was proudly emphasized by the great fifteenth-century Florentine architect (and man of many other talents) Leon Battista Alberti, who did not concern himself with the actual building of the works he designed. "For it is not a Carpenter or Joiner that I thus rank with the greatest Masters in other Sciences," wrote Alberti, "the manual Operator being no more than an Instrument to the Architect. Him I call an Architect, who, by sure, and wonder Art and Method, is able both with Thought and Invention, to devise, and with Execution, to compleat all those Works."

Not only had the architect become a gentleman but, conversely, gentlemen, like the Viscontis, Sforzas, and Medicis, had become connoisseurs of architecture. And as the influence of the Renaissance drifted northward to England, there too the status of the architect was improved and there too the gentry considered a knowledge of architecture a necessary part of their cultural equipment. In the late seventeenth century it was *Sir* Christopher Wren (he was knighted in 1675) who designed, among other buildings, those many parish churches in London already referred to; and it was the Earl of Burlington, a wealthy dilettante, who fraternized with architects and assumed for himself an equal standing in their profession.

In eighteenth-century America there were no architects of the stature or station of Wren, nor patrons as wealthy as Burlington. It has been said that in fact there were *no* architects, properly so called, in the colonies. However, only the most rigid and exclusive definition of the term could justify such a conclusion. Yet it is true that little or nothing is known of the designers and builders of most colonial dwellings, including some of the finest of them. As one example, across the York River from Williamsburg in Virginia stand the pathetic and picturesque ruins of Rosewell Hall, once among the most elegant and pretentious of all colonial mansions, the seat of the Mann Page family. One of its owners, a governor of Virginia, was an intimate friend of Thomas Jefferson. The two men built a tank on the roof for measuring rainfall and, it is said, Jefferson whimsically stocked it

The ruins of Rosewell, Va., built 1726

with fish so that they could enjoy sport on top of the house. Be that as it may, Rosewell was a magnificent monument. Although it was a unique structure, it was generally related to other fine buildings in Virginia that may have been designed by the same person, but who that person may have been cannot yet be determined. He was certainly not celebrated for his talents in any contemporary documents that have so far been discovered.

On the other hand, in a fair number of instances, the lives and accomplishments of such men can be traced through the records of the past clearly enough to provide a vivid picture of their personalities and their methods of working, as will be shown. In between those extremes more or less shadowy figures, some who were called or who called themselves architects, others merely overseers, or contractors, emerge from obscurity in connection with buildings here or there, then vanish from the scene.

In the colonies, as abroad, men of culture were normally expected to understand the principles of architecture, an accomplishment they not only used in their own interest but occasionally put to the service of their neighbors and communities. Thomas Jefferson is, of course, an outstanding example, although the number of houses he is said to have designed for friends and acquaintances is no doubt swollen by legend.

In 1749, when Jefferson was still but a child, another native-born Virginia gentleman, one Richard Taliaferro (pronounced and sometimes written "Toliver"), was referred to by the acting governor of the colony as "our most skillful architect." (He was also a burgess, justice of the peace, sheriff, and assemblyman.) If, as it is claimed, he designed such handsome and exceptional mansions as Westover (pages 70–71) and Carter's Grove (pages 76–79), his reputation was well earned. And if, as seems certain, he taught Jefferson himself the elements of architecture, on that score alone he had an indirect but important and lasting influence on the development of American architecture. Where he got his own training can only be guessed. Probably, like others of his time, he learned from actual experience on the job under the supervision of a more practiced tutor, and from the study of the numerous English manuals and pattern books that played such a large part in the design of American buildings of the period.

A number of well-to-do patrons brought skilled builders and architects from Britain to plan and construct their houses. As early as 1682 William Penn imported a young Scot, James Porteus, to build both a town house and a countryseat that would be suitable for the proprietor's residences, which Porteus did before proceeding to plan and construct a number of other distinguished houses in and about Philadelphia. In 1724, with a group of other leading Philadelphia housewrights, some prominent citizens among them, he founded the Carpenters' Company of the City and County of Philadelphia, modeled on an English precedent. The company provided schooling for builders and budding architects, who worked in a number of different colonies. In 1763 Benjamin Franklin turned to one of the members of the company to supervise construction of his new house in Philadelphia during his long absence in England.

Thus also, another young builder, William Buckland, was brought to Virginia as an indentured servant by George Mason and his brother to complete Gunston Hall, the Mason

Portrait of architect William Buckland

countryseat. In return for his services, the terms of his indenture assured him a free passage overseas, "twenty pounds a year, and meat, drink, washing, [and] lodging." After completing his indenture, he, too, went on to work in his own right for other patrons. In all probability Buckland worked on buildings designed by John Ariss, but he ended his career as an independent architect in a true sense of the word. In 1774 he finished a house in Annapolis that he had designed and planned, and also built, for Matthias Hammond, scion of an old Maryland family, owner of fifty-four tobacco plantations, and a young dandy who was never seen in public without his lace cuffs and a rapier. This extremely handsome residence marks the climax of Buckland's architectural career, and an anticlimax in the life of Hammond, who had commissioned the building as a wedding present for his prospective bride. Unhappily for him, before the wedding that was planned, the young lady ran off with another man, and Hammond retired to the country without occupying his dream house.

The most flexible, the most masterly, and perhaps the most prolific of colonial architects was Peter Harrison of Newport, Rhode Island. Like other contemporary practitioners Harrison had no formal training in architecture. Around 1738 he sailed to America as a crewman on his elder brother's ship, and soon thereafter became captain of his own ship. Several years later his vessel was captured by a French privateer and, with its crew, taken to Louisbourg. After his release and return to Newport he drew an accurate plan of the fortification of that "Canadian Gibraltar" that served the colonial troops ("Pepperrell's Yokels," they were called, because they were recruited from farmers, fishermen, and others undisciplined in military matters) when in 1745 after a siege of forty-nine days they finally stormed into Louisbourg and took it from the French. Governor Shirley, whose "mad scheme" it was to undertake that assault, was so pleased with Harrison's part in it that he commissioned the young man to design his new mansion, Shirley Place, in Roxbury, Massachusetts.

Meanwhile, Harrison, of Quaker parentage, had adopted the Anglican faith and fallen in love with Elizabeth Pelham, a well-born and willing young lady, with whom he eloped in the face of her family's objections and to avoid gossip concerning Elizabeth's advancing pregnancy. From then on, following the couple's return to Newport, although he was involved in diverse affairs, Harrison undertook one architectural commission after another. In 1747 he began building the Redwood Library, a charming small structure in the style of a classical temple. (Passing through Newport twelve years later the Reverend Andrew Burnaby from England noted with restrained enthusiasm that this little structure was "by no means inelegant.") Two years after that he designed King's Chapel in Boston, which never has been completely finished after almost two and a quarter centuries. Later came a house for John Vassall in Cambridge, Massachusetts, a structure that, apart from its architectural merit, is renowned as the later residence of Henry Wadsworth Longfellow; and he then built Christ Church, also in Cambridge. Fortunately, all three buildings still stand.

Eighteenth-century Newport was reputed to be "the receptacle of all religions." In 1759, for the Jews of Newport, Harrison designed Touro Synagogue, the second to be built in the colonies. It was, reported the *Newport Mercury* at the time of the opening ceremonies four years later, "an Edifice the most perfect of the Temple Kind in America." Even Burnaby, who saw it a-building, conceded that it would be "extremely elegant within when compleated," although he thought its handsome appearance would be spoiled by a

school "which the Jews insisted on having annexed to it for the education of their children." Happily, this delightful structure also still stands, smartly restored to its original condition.

So Harrison's career continued. At one time or another he was involved with everything from forts and lighthouses to public markets and private dwellings. He was a Tory, and toward the end of his life he was appointed collector of customs at New Haven. He died there at the age of fifty-nine in 1775. Tragically a mob of patriots thereupon burned his papers and library, including his drawings and some thirty important books on architecture. Following that, the name and accomplishments of this "ingenious Englishman," as Burnaby called him, slipped into obscurity, to return to notice only in recent years. He has since been named "the first American architect," which he was not, and called the most "masterly architect in the colonies," which he very probably was.

A sketch of the Redwood Library in Newport, R. I., designed by Peter Harrison in 1747

Going by the Book
Designs and Practices

The phrase "Georgian style," so often used in this chapter, is a very general term. It applies to a wide variety of structures, public and private, all of which in their plans and designs follow, more or less strictly, certain formal rules of architecture—rules that had their remote origins in ancient Rome and that filtered down through the ages to provide guidelines for the builders of colonial America. In the first century B.C. the Roman architect Vitruvius issued a ten-volume treatise, *De architectura*, which he dedicated to the emperor Augustus and which happened to be the only writing on architecture to survive from antiquity. Although Vitruvius' works had only a minor impact on his own times, they assumed a tremendous importance during the Italian Renaissance, and became virtually a bible for all progressive architects of that period. They first appeared in printed form in the late fifteenth century, and from then on were reprinted over and over again, and were translated into nearly all European languages.

Of all the Renaissance architects who turned to Vitruvius (and to the surviving remains of Roman architecture) for inspiration, by far the most influential was Andrea Palladio, who in the sixteenth century published his own treatise describing, explaining, and illustrating his "modern" interpretations of classical styles, and who referred to Vitruvius as "my sole master and guide." That publication fired the imagination of builders and architects throughout the Western world; it may in fact have been the most influential book on architecture ever written.

A design for the Ionic order

PALLADIO, ANDREA, I QUATTRO LIBRI . . . , 1581

"Were a modern architect to build a palace in Lapland, or the West Indies," complained the English artist William Hogarth in the eighteenth century, "Palladio would be his guide, nor would he dare to stir a step without his book." Palladianism did indeed spread like a rash from northern Italy, Palladio's main center of enterprise, to Poland, Norway, Hungary, Russia, and above all to England and to her American colonies. Even today Palladianism serves as a hallmark of elegance, imposing its forms and motifs on everything from the doors of kitchen refrigerators to water tanks on tall buildings.

A pocket version of Palladio's Book I, published in England in 1663, raced through twelve editions by 1733, which gives some indication of the prevailing interest in the subject. When a complete English edition of Palladio was published in 1715 under the patronage of Lord Burlington, the great apostle of Palladianism, new and detailed sources of guidance were opened to English readers and practitioners. Other versions of "dear Impeccable Palladio's rule," as Lord Bristol referred to the matter, quickly followed, and were in turn followed by still other books illustrating important English countryseats that had been erected in the Palladian manner. From thence it was but a short and logical step to the publication of designs frankly presenting individual, creative variations on the current themes. It was the realization of the designs in books more or less firmly rooted in Palladian principles, that constituted what we call Georgian architecture.

The southern facade of the central building of Mount Airy, obviously designed after the Gibbs engraving reproduced above. Built for John Tayloe to replace an earlier house, Mount Airy is one of the few major houses of Virginia executed in stone.

During the several decades preceding the Revolutionary War, in a number of the colonies impressively formal houses were built that were more or less strictly in the Palladian manner. In 1758 when Colonel John Tayloe started construction of Mount Airy in Virginia, for the building's southern facade he chose to follow closely an illustration published thirty years earlier in *A Book of Architecture* by James Gibbs, a Palladian disciple, as "A Design made for a Gentleman in Dorsetshire." Gibbs had warned his readers not to permit his designs to be changed "by the Forwardness of unskillful Workmen, or the Caprice of ignorant, assuming Pretenders," and in this aspect of Mount Airy his strictures were observed with rare fidelity. For the opposite facade Tayloe followed, less directly, a plate from another English pattern book, *Vitruvius Scoticus* by William Adam, father of the Robert Adam who revolutionized English architectural design in the next generation.

"A Design made for a Gentleman in Dorsetshire," from an engraving in James Gibbs' Book of Architecture, *published at London in 1728; the model closely followed for the southern facade of Mount Airy in Richmond County, Va.*

The northern facade of Mount Airy. In profile the structure, with its central building, projecting pedimented pavilion, and dependencies, recalls the Italian countryseats of Palladio.

Although Palladio's influence was most authoritative in England and ultimately, through further degrees of adaptation, in America, other sources of design were also followed in the colonies. The so-called Palladian window, with three openings, the central one arched and wider than the flanking ones, is a hallmark of Palladianism, and an architectural motif that was repeatedly used in America. Actually, the design was first illustrated in a published work by Sebastian Serlio, a somewhat earlier Renaissance architect. The broken-scroll pediment, so popular in Georgian architecture both here and in England, is a baroque form not to be found in Palladio at all. One exterior stone doorway at Westover that shows such a treatment is an almost exact copy of a plate published in a book nevertheless titled *Palladio Londinensis: or The London Art of Building*, by the Englishman William Salmon. Throughout the colonies, particularly in New England, local craftsmen translated such designs in native woods, often naively carved and painted to simulate stonework, with bold vigor and with complete freedom from academic restraints.

LEFT: SALMON, WILLIAM, *PALLADIO LONDINENSIS*, LONDON, 1734. RIGHT: WILLIAM H. PIERSON, JR., WILLIAMSTOWN. FAR RIGHT: METROPOLITAN MUSEUM OF ART ROGERS FUND 1946

A doorway design from Salmon's Palladio Londinensis

NATHANIEL LIEBERMAN

Above: Palladian window, from the facade of Mount Pleasant, Fairmount Park, Philadelphia
Opposite: Palladio's design for Vicenza Basilica, Italy; the motif for "Palladian windows"

South doorway at Westover, Charles City County, Va.

Carved wooden doorway of a building from Westfield, Mass.

Design for a so-called Venetian window from Batty Langley's
The City and Country Builder's and Workman's Treasury of Designs, *published at London in 1739 and well known in America*

A design for a chimney piece from Abraham Swan's British Architect, *published in 1745, and, beneath, a carved oak chimney piece
copied from that design for the Jeremiah Lee House, built in 1768 at
Marblehead, Mass. Plates from Swan's book were also used as
models at Mount Vernon and many other outstanding American
houses. An edition of the book was published at Philadelphia in 1775.*

A window at Mount Vernon closely corresponding to Langley's design. Even while in the field leading the colonial troops, Washington carefully followed building developments at home.

Design for a stucco ceiling from Langley's book and, beneath, a ceiling actually executed from that design at Kenmore, the house erected in Fredericksburg, Va., around 1752 by Colonel Fielding Lewis for his bride Betty Washington. This and other stuccowork at Kenmore was probably added to the interior in the mid-1770s, shortly before similar decorations were executed at Mount Vernon.

A design for a decorative window from James Gibbs' A Book of Architecture, first published in 1728, and, beneath, an exterior window in the pediment of the Matthias Hammond House, completed at Annapolis, Md., in 1774 under the direction of the successful immigrant architect William Buckland. The window as it was actually executed is quite obviously an adaptation of the design published by Gibbs.

The House Underfoot

Fashions in Floors

The Frenchmen who came to this country during the course of the Revolutionary War and the years immediately following were not altogether prepared for the surprises that awaited them here. Some were impressed by signs of luxury in a society that they had chosen to believe was both more primitive and more innocent than they found it to be. "It already appears," wrote one of them, somewhat irritably, "they have carpets, elegant carpets; it is a favourite taste with the Americans; they receive it from the interested avarice of their old masters the English." Another such visitor conceded that "good carpeting tends to concentrate the heat, which is an advantage in a country where...rooms are drafty." But both critics agreed that the American custom of keeping carpets laid even in the summer was needless vanity. As one of them concluded, "they sacrifice reason and utility to show."

However reliable those observations might be, other evidence suggests that throughout the colonial period, at least, floor coverings were by no means so common. In the seventeenth century they were indeed virtually unknown in America and were rarely used in England. Floors were left bare or covered with white sand that was swept with a broom into such agreeable patterns as "quaint circles and fancy wreaths." Even as late as 1781 still another of the French observers noted that while wealthy Americans had their floors covered with handsome carpets or painted cloths, "others sprinkle them with fine sand."

There were plenty of other homeowners, in America as in England, who simply did not

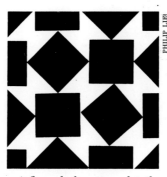

A floor cloth pattern detail

PHILIP LIEB

bother with floor coverings of any kind. Toward the middle of the eighteenth century one traveler noted that the Dutch inhabitants of Albany were "almost superstitiously clean in regard to the floor"; as another contemporary observed, by constant rubbing and scrubbing the rough planks in time became as smooth as if they had been planed. New Englanders apparently observed similar practices at the same time, since an advertisement of 1746 in the *Boston News-Letter* offered its readers "scouring Sand for Floors...."

However, as houses took on greater formality both inside and out, something more sophisticated was called for underfoot than primitively sanded floors or starkly bare floor boards, no matter how neatly scrubbed. Near Eastern rugs, long used as furniture covers, gradually found their way down onto the floors, but they were uncommonly expensive. As a cheaper alternative that was altogether effective in its own right, designs were painted, either directly on the floors or on canvas floor coverings, in imitation of the rugs and carpets or of the tile, marble, and parquet floors to be found in the great homes of England and, less frequently, in the fine houses of America. As the eighteenth century advanced, British carpet manufacturers produced increasing quantities of carpet—Wilton, Axminster, Brussels, Kidderminster, Scotch, and other types —at prices that fell within the budget of enough American householders to warrant a large export trade to this country; large enough to lend some credence to those observations made by the French visitors when they arrived on the scene.

Parlor of the Van Cortlandt Manor House with a marbleized, checkered painted floor overlaid with a carpet of Near Eastern origin

The architectural pattern books that were so widely used in colonial America for guidance in the construction and design of houses were supplemented by other manuals that provided instructions in diverse forms of interior decoration. Even in the seventeenth century there were English publications that advised professionals and amateurs alike in the simulation of marble, tortoise shell, and other rare materials with paints and varnishes applied to wood and canvas surfaces. In 1739 John Carwitham of London published a handbook, from which the illustrations shown on the opposite page are taken, representing "Various kinds of FLOOR DECORATIONS . . . both in Plano and Perspective Being useful Designs for Ornamenting the Floors of Halls Rooms, Summer Houses, &c. whither in Pavements of Stone, or Marble, or wth. Painted Floor Cloths...." Such patterns were apparently already fashionable in the colonies. When he died in 1728 William Burnet, who was governor of both Massachusetts and New York, left to his heirs "Two old checkered canvas' to lay under a table." Such commodities were locally produced as well as imported. In 1760, for example, a subscriber to the *Maryland Gazette* called for the return of his "convict serving man" who could imitate marble and paint floor cloths "as neat as any imported from Britain," and who had run away. Later in the century Abigail Adams wrote her niece from Paris that her writing room there lacked a carpet "to give it all an air of elegance"; in lieu of this there was a red-tile floor "in the shape of Mrs. Quincy's floorcloth tiles" back in Massachusetts.

Illustrations of "Floor-Decorations of Various Kinds" from the manual published by John Carwitham

The use of carpets as coverings for furniture lasted from the earliest days of settlement until after the Revolutionary War. At a court hearing held in Ipswich, Massachusetts, in 1676, one witness testified that more than forty years earlier his father had brought with him from England "a Turkey worked carpet...which he commonly used to lay upon his parlour table." References to such usage continued all through the next century. Several fashionable painters of the mid-eighteenth century showed family groups posed about tables covered with Oriental carpets of one sort or another, proof enough that the custom was still very much *à la mode*. As late as 1798 the first American edition of the *Encyclopedia* still defined a carpet as "a sort of covering of stuff" which was "commonly spread over tables"—or, it added, "laid upon the floor." By then carpets had in fact largely gone underfoot, so to speak, and were becoming a relatively common household accessory. The French troops marching south through the countryside to join Washington at Yorktown were astonished to find that the attractive rural homes they passed en route had carpets "even upon the stairs." Expert weavers in England, it was officially claimed, were producing carpeting "in the manner of Turkey carpets but much superior in beauty and goodness," and these, in turn, were being copied on canvas by colonial artisans for use on stairs as well as to cover the floors of principal rooms.

Right: "Turkey" rug like the one in the family portrait below

Above: the Royall family, painted by Robert Feke in 1741, posed about a rug-covered table
Opposite: 18th-century painted canvas floor covering from the Safford House at Salem, Mass.

Portrait of John Phillips, painted by Joseph Steward in 1793. Each of the two rooms has a wall-to-wall cloth of floral design.

Ever mindful of the comforts and the appearance of his home in Philadelphia, while he was in England Benjamin Franklin repeatedly sent back assortments of household furnishings, instructing his patient wife Deborah in their appropriate installation and use according to the latest London fashions. "In the great Case, besides the little Box," he wrote her in 1758 regarding one such shipment, "is contain'd some Carpeting for the best Room Floor. There is enough for one large or two small ones, it is to be sow'd together, the Edges being first fell'd down, and Care taken to make the Figures meet exactly: there is Bordering for the same. This was my fancy." In the years before the Revolution shops in virtually all the colonies were increasingly advertising English carpets of various types—carpets which were sometimes used for upholstery fabric for furniture as well as for floor coverings. In 1769 James Beekman ordered from England "as much fine wilton Carpeting as will cover 7 chier Bottoms...." In their efforts to compete with such English imports colonial artisans and entrepreneurs commonly reminded the local public that their products were as good as any to be had from abroad, a contention that would be hard to deny since so little actual evidence survives. The two different painted, wall-to-wall floor coverings shown in the portrait, opposite, of John Phillips provide a fair indication of designs that were available to the New England gentry in the years following the Revolution.

Trade card of Joseph Barnes, London, 18th century, who both made and repainted floor cloths.

As a quicker and less expensive substitute for freehand painting, stenciling was gradually refined as a craft in England in the second half of the eighteenth century. The same Joseph Barnes whose London trade card was illustrated on page 103, and who sold "all sorts of Floor Cloths," included both block printing and stenciling among the tricks of his trade. The basic equipment he used for stenciling carpets is illustrated below—a color tub, trowel, cutting knife, a scraper to prepare canvas surfaces, brushes, and other paraphernalia. In the portrait of John Phillips on page 102 the painted floor coverings are complemented by stenciled designs around the cornice, window trim, and baseboard of the rear room. In years to come such a "mechanical process" became an enormously popular form of decoration in this country for floors, carpets, walls, and furniture. As an economical shortcut to production that saved both time and energy, the method was ideally suited to the rapidly increasing demands of the American public.

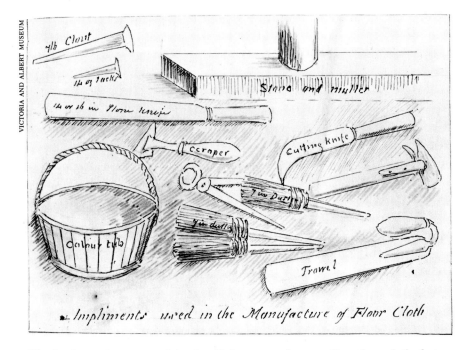

The basic equipment used in the 18th century for stenciling floor cloth designs

Downstairs and Up

The Rise of Style

Georgian interiors remained comparatively free from the academic disciplines that increasingly influenced exterior design during the eighteenth century. Despite the perennial controversy that raged in England between Palladian partisans on the one hand, who decried the "horrible shapes" of Far Eastern art, and equally jaundiced Orientalists on the other, who satirized the classicist's penchant for having not "a broomstick in [his house] which he has not had...carved according to some one of the five orders," interior architecture was generally unaffected by polemics. Although rooms at residences of the well-to-do were usually constructed according to classical formulas, with formal elaboration given to fireplace, window, and door openings, their embellishments derived from a variety of unclassical sources. Within the confines of a single parlor, for example, might cohabit peacefully a baroque broken pediment of the sort popularized by Christopher Wren, Chinese wallpaper, and rococo stuccowork in high relief on the ceiling, like that fashionable in France during the reign of Louis XV.

At large and luxurious establishments, the interior woodwork was painted in rich and varied hues that frequently matched the upholstery, wall hangings, and draperies that came into common use after 1750, which explains the numerous contemporary references made to green, blue, or yellow rooms. Owners who chose not to have wall-to-wall paneling often reserved such ornament for the fireplace wall. Paneling, carved chimneypieces, flooring, and stair balus-

Stairs at Carter's Grove, Va.

trades were, as a rule, made on the job, while marble mantelpieces, brass hardware, chandeliers, silk damasks and brocades, and wallpapers were largely imported from England. In the late 1730s the wealthy Boston bookseller and merchant Thomas Hancock became one of the most conspicuous consumers of his era when he ordered his London agent to send him some forty dozen panes of glass, twenty dozen blue and white Delft tiles, three marble hearths, walnut-framed looking glasses, and other adornments for his splendid new mansion on Beacon Hill. He also commissioned for his walls "painted papers" which were just coming into style. He specified that a "shaded Hanging" be made "as Cheap as Possible, & if they can make it more Beautifull by adding more Birds flying here & there, with some Landskip at the Bottom, [I] should Like it well.... In other of these hangings are great variety of different Sorts of Birds, Peacocks, Macoys, Squirril, Monkys, Fruit and Flowers, etc.—I think they are handsomer and better than Painted hangings done in Oyle." After mid-century, when paneling was gradually restricted to the dado, the trend toward decorative wall hangings grew. By 1768 colonial manufacturers were producing wallpapers and touting them in advertisements like one that offered a "most beautiful assortment of 1500 Pieces Paper, in 600 different patterns, from one to twenty-six colours." However, the finest rolls continued to come from England, or were imported from China via England. Beginning in 1784, American shippers conducted direct trade with China.

The parlor of the Hart House, built before 1675 in Ipswich, Mass., with one sheathed wall and exposed timbers

Paneled wall of Metcalf Bowler's countryseat, with fluted pilasters and tile-faced fireplace within molded frame

The walls of typical seventeenth-century houses were simply plastered over to secure and conceal the filling between the studs, without embellishment of any sort. Occasionally one or more walls were covered with a sheathing of wide boards, a practice which apparently was open to criticism for being unduly extravagant. When Thomas Dudley thus improved his walls in 1632 he was called before John Winthrop to justify such an expenditure. "His answer now was," reported the governor, "that it was for the warmth of his house, and the charge was little, being but clapboards nailed to the wall in the form of wainscot." Gradually more elaborate and formal treatment became popular. The walls of early Georgian houses were commonly entirely covered with panels which, like the fireplaces, windows, and doorways, were defined by classical moldings. As in other houses of the period, the rows of panels in a room in the countryseat of Metcalf Bowler, a Rhode Island merchant prince, are separated by fluted pilasters, also recalling classical designs. In later Georgian houses walls assumed more elaborate designs incorporating a rich display of academic ornament drawn from contemporary English pattern books, as in the splendid second-floor parlor of Philadelphia's last colonial mayor, Samuel Powel.

Fireplace wall of the upstairs parlor in Samuel Powel's Philadelphia home, with its elaborately carved and pedimented overmantel

Flock wallpaper of cut-up wool, adhered to stenciled canvas

After 1725, painted and papered wall surfaces vied for popularity with paneling. At one Newport residence, a unique series of paintings was applied to the plaster parlor walls about 1740. Decorated in the Chinese manner currently in vogue, the panel faces included unusual scenes of the Buddhist Hell and Chinese courts of punishment, as well as the ordinary Oriental fare of flowers and birds. The surrounding areas and moldings were originally painted to simulate marble. Acquired by the wealthy Metcalf Bowler in 1759, the structure (later known as the Vernon House) was remodeled into a stylish Georgian mansion with full paneling in the parlor that concealed the *chinoiseries* until they were

Charles Willson Peale's illusionistic portrait of his two sons

Detail from chinoiserie *paintings at the Vernon House, Newport*

uncovered in 1937. In a room of the Webb House at Wethersfield, Connecticut, the walls are covered with flockwork, made of pulverized wool applied to canvas to resemble cut velvet. George Washington spent five nights at this house during a 1781 conference with Rochambeau. A geometric wallpaper pattern of the 1790s is illustrated in Charles Willson Peale's portrait of his sons. Originally framed by a real doorway, with an actual step meeting the painted staircase, this picture, it was said, deceived Washington. According to Rembrandt Peale, "as he passed it, [he] bowed politely to the painted figures, which he afterwards acknowledged he thought were living persons."

Elements of the painted wall decorations at the Vernon House

OVERLEAF: *Chinese wallpaper, 1770, with painted designs*
HENRY FRANCIS DU PONT WINTERTHUR MUSEUM

Early 18th-century staircase with turned balusters

Above: a staircase with wedge-shaped steps and flat balusters, about 1726

Opposite: a staircase with latticework in the Chinese Chippendale manner

To accommodate domestic traffic from one floor to another the builder and architect have faced both practical problems of space and convenience and opportunities for imaginative design. In some early American houses a ladder set into a hole in the ceiling of the main floor provided an elementary means of serving the ups and downs of family life. Typically, seventeenth-century stairs consisted of short, steep, turning flights with wedge-shaped steps butted against the central chimney, contrived to occupy as little space as possible. As time passed, ornamental balusters were introduced—either flat sawn, as in the Pitt's Head Tavern in Newport, Rhode Island, or spiral turned, as in the Samuel Wentworth House from Portsmouth, New Hampshire, both shown here. With the gradual increase in the size of houses and with new emphasis on formal patterns, the staircase assumed special importance as an individual and prominent feature of interior design. At Bohemia, built about 1745, in Cecil County, Maryland, an elaborate arrangement of trellises in the so-called Chinese Chippendale style, with each of the panels in a different design, dominates the entrance hall of the house. The carving of the step-ends, or brackets, repeats the trellis motif.

The famous house built by Thomas Hancock on Beacon Hill in Boston, 1740, apparently initiated the tour de force of a double spiral in the main newel of its staircase, the inner one turning in the opposite direction from the outer. That highly decorative treatment was to be imitated in many later New England houses. Hancock's mansion, one of the finest built in the colonies, was demolished in 1863, at which time elements of the interior woodwork, including the newel post (shown here) among many other "antique curiosities," were auctioned off to the highest bidders. A similar main newel anchors the commodious and graceful staircase of The Lindens, built in 1754 in Danvers, Massachusetts, by Robert ("King") Hooper and removed in recent years to Washington, D. C. The handsome design of the staircase is enhanced by sensitively turned balusters that are arranged three to a tread. By the time Hooper planned his mansion the main staircase had developed into a commanding element of the interior architecture of fashionable houses, typically rising from a spacious entrance hall that ran the depth of the building and that opened through separate paneled doorways into the main rooms of the ground floor. In 1774 The Lindens, so named for the trees that stood about it on its original site, served as the temporary headquarters of Thomas Gage, governor of the Province of Massachusetts, at the invitation of Hooper, who was a confirmed Loyalist—an act of generous hospitality that annoyed his patriotic countrymen, especially at this time of acute tension between the colonies and the mother country. Redcoats were not popular visitors to these shores, but at The Lindens during Gage's residence, it was recalled, "The nights were given to revelry and dancing by the younger guests . . . when the officers of the regiment took part and made the scene picturesque with their bright scarlet uniforms."

Opposite: the entrance hall and staircase at The Lindens, built at Danvers, Mass., with French, 19th-century block-printed wallpaper

Right: newel post salvaged from the staircase in Thomas Hancock's house, built on Beacon Hill, Boston, in 1740 and demolished in 1863

3

Federal Classic

With the establishment of American independence, a new sort of community came into the world. As H. G. Wells observed, "it was like something coming out of an egg...such a clean start in political organization as the world had not seen before." So far as they were able, and they were extremely able men, the signers of the Declaration of Independence had stripped the matter of political relationships down to fundamentals. They had re-examined and eloquently proclaimed the "inalienable rights" of men who must live together in a governed society. Thirteen years later the Constitution of the new nation, although soundly based on the experience of the past, was enlightened with new and courageous thinking. The framers of that historic document cast away the traditional props of state—royalty, aristocracy, and an established national church—and designed its federal structure in the name of all the people, whoever they were. With those two statements Americans made exceptional contributions to political history.

Writing to Benjamin Franklin's English friend, the Reverend Dr. Richard Price, Turgot, minister of finance under Louis XVI, remarked that the new nation was "the hope of the human race. It may become the model. It ought to show the world by facts, that men can be free and yet peaceful and may dispense with the chains in which tyrants and knaves of every colour have presumed to bind them, under pretext of the public good. The Americans should be an example of political, religious, commercial and industrial liberty. The asylum they offer to the oppressed of every nation, the avenue of escape they open, will compel governments to be just and enlightened; and the rest of the world in due time will see through the empty illusions in which policy is conceived. But to obtain these ends for us, America must secure them to herself; and must not become, as so many of your ministerial writers have predicted, a mass of divided powers, contending for territory and trade, cementing the slavery of peoples by their own blood."

The year that the peace was signed formally ending the Revolutionary War, a young Hartford schoolmaster, Noah Webster, pleaded with his countrymen for a brand-new start toward a purely American way of life in social and cultural matters as well. "America must be as independent in *literature* as she is in politics," he insisted, "as famous for *arts* as for *arms*." She must stop "mimicking the follies of other nations" and create her own standards, as Webster tried to do that year with the first issue of his famous blue-backed

Entrance of the Pingree House, built for John Gardner by Samuel McIntire, Salem, Mass., 1804

Inauguration of George Washington

speller—which would become one of the best-selling books of all time.

Webster found a kindred and even more vehemently chauvinistic spirit in Philip Freneau, the warrior-poet of the Revolution and the very model of an Anglophobe. The mere thought of any cultural dependence upon England charged his pen with vitriol. As he wrote in one of his popular verses, composed after the war was over:

> It seems we had spirit to humble a throne,
> Have genius for science inferior to none,
> Yet hardly encourage a plant of our own....
>
> Can we never be thought to have learning or grace
> Unless it be brought from that horrible place
> Where tyranny reigns with her impudent face...?

But however brave and fresh America's experiment in self-government might be, it could not promptly remove the authority of European forms and precedents; nor could it ever abolish the benefits of European experience, which were, of course, such a rich part of the nation's birthright to start with. The very document by which the colonists declared their independence reveals a heavy debt to the political thinking of Locke, Sidney, Harrington, and other English writers.

At the time of George Washington's inauguration, in 1789, the prestigiousness of foreign etiquette became a matter of sensitive debate in high circles. According to the ancient usage of the British Parliament it was proper to frame an answer to the president's inaugural speech. (His address was delivered from the balcony of New York's old City Hall, which had been redesigned in the classical style as the first Capitol of the United States by Pierre Charles L'Enfant, a French veteran of the Revolution. Subsequently, L'Enfant was commissioned to plan the future city of Washington.) But in just what form to address the president with their message tried the minds of Congress. Certain members felt that with a "decent respect for the opinions and usages" of older civilized nations some exalted title of respectability must be used— something like His High Mightiness (a title used by the Stadtholder of Holland), His Serene Highness the President of the United States, His Supremacy, and so on. (There were even those who would have liked to see Washington crowned as King George the First.) However, the senator from South Carolina pointed out that "this spirit of imitation...this spirit of mimicry and apery," instead of lending dignity to such solemn proceedings, would merely expose them to the ridicule of foreign observers. In the end Washington was addressed simply as Mr. President.

Plenty of Americans found nothing incompatible about fighting British troops to a finish and continuing to respect British manners, customs, and fashions. The year after the peace was signed, William Pynchon of Salem, Massachusetts, remarked that "all who can cross the Atlantic seem determined to go and procure their goods from England." About the same time Abigail Adams wrote from London that she saw there so many of her fellow Americans, she hardly felt she was out of her own country. And for those who could not travel overseas to shop, imports of every description from Great Britain were again available in American markets; in greater supply, indeed, than they had been before the Revolution.

Over the decades of dissension and disturbance that had led to the outbreak of hostilities at Lexington and Concord and ended with the surrender of Cornwallis at Yorktown, England had undergone its own separate and peaceful revolution; one that within those few decades brought about radical changes in the style of fashionable English homes. Essentially the new ruling taste was another classical revival, but one that instead of finding its precepts in Palladian versions of antiquity, rather looked directly for inspiration among the ruins and remains of ancient Rome itself. The way had been opened for the new vogue just before the middle of the eighteenth century with the excavations at Pompeii and Herculaneum. In those long-buried cities were discovered unexpected and enchanting revelations of Roman design, as well as evidence of an ancient way of life that had been abruptly and eerily halted in the midst of a daily routine by the heavy fall of volcanic ash. The excitement caused by those remarkable discoveries led to fresh expeditions. Rome, Palmyra, Baalbek, Split, and other ancient sites and ruins were examined with new enthusiasm and interest. Western Europe at large was seized by archaeological fervor. As the century progressed a flow of books published in a number of different languages reported and illustrated the various discoveries that were made. And out of the evidence presented in that growing library of publications evolved the styles of the new classical revival.

One of the earliest exponents, and the most influential, of the new style in England was the Scottish architect Robert Adam, son of the William Adam whose designs had been used in the planning of Mount Airy in Virginia (pages 90–91). The young Adam had toured Italy and Dalmatia and examined their ruins at first hand. In Paris he had studied with the great classicist Charles Louis Clérisseau. Then, in the 1760s and 1770s, with his brother James, he created light and graceful adaptations of Roman forms and ornaments which almost immediately became the fashionable vocabulary for British architecture and design. A few years before the Revolution, in 1773, the two brothers issued the first volume of *The Works in Architecture of Robert and James Adam, Esquires*, a publication that led to widespread copies and modifications of their inventions and that brought those, with different degrees of fidelity, to the attention of a wide audience. Some years later, in a lecture at the Royal Academy of Arts, Sir John Soane, one of Adam's most ardent admirers, quite truthfully remarked that "To Mr. Adam's taste in the Ornaments of his Buildings, and Furniture, we stand indebted, in-asmuch as Manufacturers of every kind felt, as it were, the electric power of this Revolution in Art."

The impact of the new vogue was not felt in America until after the problems of the war and peace with Britain were settled. By then the young nation was also in direct, close communication with the European Continent, where much the same classical "revolution" had taken place. Americans viewed the cultural climate there, as in England, with very mixed feelings.

ADAM, ROBERT. WORKS IN ARCHITECTURE, LONDON, 1779

Design for a house, by Robert Adam

When John Adams joined Benjamin Franklin in Paris as a member of the American peace commission, he noted with grudging admiration—and barely concealed envy—that his elder colleague was the darling of French society. The self-made republican, the tallow chandler's son, the modest printer, the many-sided tradesman, moved with ease and honor among the powdered heads of Europe, quipping with royalty and apparently unscathed by the artificialities of courtly circles. But Adams could not willingly accept the conventions that ruled such a society. There was much to marvel at, he wrote his wife Abigail, "yet...there is everything here, too, which can seduce, betray, deceive, deprave, corrupt and debauch [the heart]." "How much should we deplore that spirit of dissipation, vanity and knavery," he wrote in another letter, "which infects so many Americans and threatens to ruin our manners and liberties in imitation of the Old World!"

In still another letter he wrote his wife that he had no time to luxuriate in such matters as art and architecture, nor did he believe his country just then had need of such accomplishments. However, Adams reflected, if he applied himself to the study of politics and war, and saw to it that his sons followed such practical studies as mathematics, commerce, and agriculture, then he could foresee the possibility that his grandsons might at last be free to cultivate a taste for architecture, painting, and the other arts.

Thomas Jefferson looked at the world, both at home and abroad, with different eyes. "I am an enthusiast on the subject of the arts," he wrote James Madison. "But it is an enthusiasm of which I am not ashamed, as its object is to improve the taste of my countrymen, to increase their reputation, to reconcile them to the respect of the world, and procure them its praise." In France, as he wrote the Comtesse de Tessé, his good friend in Paris, he "fell in love" with one fine example of architecture after another—with the Hôtel de Salm in Paris, the gates of that city designed by the classicist Claude Nicolas Ledoux, and among many others, especially the little Roman temple at Nîmes, called the Maison Carrée, which had been restored by Louis XIV. Everywhere in his travels through that country, he was, as he wrote, "nourished" by the remains of Roman grandeur, and in that ancient building at Nîmes he saw a perfect and precious expression of the classical spirit. "Here I am, Madam," he wrote the comtesse, "gazing whole hours at the Maison Carrée, like a lover at his mistress." And it was with this vision in his mind's eye that he designed, or rather redesigned, the Virginia State Capitol at Richmond.

Jefferson was himself a born classicist, and through his great influence, official and personal, direct and indirect, he was largely responsible for guiding the interest of the American people straight back to the buildings and culture of ancient Greece and Rome. In this he was a major American prophet of the new gospel that would attract a host of faithful followers throughout the land in years to come. He was prophetic, too, when he estimated that the population of the United States, and the need for houses with its growth, would double every twenty years. And he wanted those structures to be both sound and beautiful, because he believed that the world would judge us by the quality of our building.

Franklin's reception at Versailles

Thanks in good measure to his own initiative, Jefferson's wishes were gratified. There had been relatively little building during the war. But during the early years of the republic construction boomed in every state of the federal union. Not only were houses needed to accommodate the growing population, but public buildings as well to serve the state and national governments. And in every part of the land the structures that were rising reflected in one way or another the classical spirit that Jefferson himself so fervently espoused. The new classicism was a national idiom, freely and easily enough used by men who saw in ancient Greece and Rome the models for their own new republic. In other words, the style was not merely an architectural fashion, it was also an expression of social and political purpose. It has been fairly claimed that American building of those years, the so-called Federal period, was at least equal in merit to that of any nation in the world.

In naturalizing the new style, giving it what could broadly be termed a national character, individuals played much more prominent roles than in the colonial period. As the eighteenth century waned, men of truly professional training in architecture now took their place beside the distinguished laymen and amateurs who first launched the style in America. The earliest of them came from other lands, from Ireland, France, England, among other places, bringing with them fresh ideas and ways of realizing them that broke sharply with colonial precedents. And by their example they stimulated native talents to unexpected achievements. Whether or not he was aware of the emigrant architects' work, Samuel McIntire, a carpenter and carver (among other things) of Salem, applied his native skills to the design and construction of a score of buildings in and about his home town and produced personal versions of the Adam style that gave additional and special grace and dignity to the local scene.

New standards of convenience, comfort, and privacy were introduced, features that had rarely been considered in colonial times. The "modern" house of the Federal period was planned with dressing rooms, butler's pantries, closets, and other areas of specialized purpose—even, as at Monticello, with indoor privies. Rooms that had traditionally been rectangular assumed elliptical and octagonal shapes, the better or more agreeably to serve their separate functions as dining rooms, salons, or whatever. The main staircase that in earlier days had almost universally claimed a prominent place in the entrance hallway, was moved to the side to discourage the casual caller from visiting the upper rooms, thus assuring greater privacy. With a similar objective in mind, a second staircase for service gradually became customary.

Those trends toward flexibility and specialization of arrangements within the house at times were modified by the need to maintain a classically symmetrical exterior. But solutions to that conflict were usually found. No contemporary house demonstrates the ideal of classical form and the achievement of creature comfort so thoroughly as Jefferson's own Monticello. That house was equipped with all manner of laborsaving devices and gadgets—double-acting doors, lifts for conveying wine from the basement, self-winding clocks, weather vanes with indoor dials, and the like. The entire service system was placed out of sight below the main floor. Jefferson eliminated

Top: State Capitol at Richmond, Va.
Above: Maison Carrée, Nimes, France

the central staircase altogether, replacing it with two arrangements of stairs, halls, and cupboards for the use of the family and guests and for the servants respectively. He installed both outdoor privies for use in fair weather (each with a view) and, as already indicated, efficiently functioning indoor privies on each floor as retreats during inclement weather. There were other ingenious features to render the house comfortable in all seasons and efficient as a functioning home. With such care and ingenuity Jefferson in a relatively modest way provided himself with conveniences unknown to any of the monarchs of history. For all the classical references of its profile and ornament, Monticello was a house of the future in its successful intentions.

There were houses of more splendid appearance than Jefferson could approve of, either as a thoughtful architect or as a conscientious democrat. When in 1790 the capital was moved from its temporary site at New York to Philadelphia, en route to the barren flatlands of the Federal City, Penn's "green countrie towne" became the seat of the "republican court" and the center of fashion. Jefferson thought the city itself was more handsome than London, or even Paris. There, in 1789, the banker William Bingham built an extravagant town house in the manner of the Duke of Manchester's residence on Manchester Square in London. With her wit, taste, and brilliant worldliness, not to mention her indulgent husband's enormous fortune, Mrs. Bingham (née Anne Willing) became the indisputable leader of American society, and at her home entertainment reached a level of luxury and urbanity hitherto unknown to America. Young Charles Bulfinch, on his way to becoming New England's most prominent and fashionable architect, dined at the Binghams' shortly after the house was finished. With its white marble staircase, valuable paintings, the richest furniture and the utmost magnificence of decoration, Bulfinch thought the house was "far *too* rich for *any* man in this country."

This gracious hostess, whom Abigail Adams conceded was the finest woman she had ever seen—surpassing the celebrated Duchess of Devonshire in charm and beauty—had the name of each guest at her parties called out by a servant at the entrance, to be picked up by another on the stairs, and relayed in a loud voice to a third servant at the door to the drawing room. On his first exposure to this imported formality, James Monroe, hearing his name repeated so insistently, is said to have called back, "Coming—coming, as soon as I get my greatcoat off."

While the capital still remained in Philadelphia, a competition was held for a design for the President's House in Washington. Although Jefferson submitted an entry, the award was given to one James Hoban, a thirty-four-year-old emigrant from Kilkenny County in Ireland. Hoban's design was strongly influenced by a plate from James Gibbs' *A Book of Architecture*, published more than sixty years earlier, hardly a book of "modern" patterns. However, the interior was well planned to accommodate the variety of functions, official and residential, that were called for, with audience rooms, clerks' rooms, as well as a study, library, bedrooms, dressing rooms, and other special chambers. (Both exterior and interior have undergone a succession of changes over the years.) John and Abigail Adams, the first tenants, moved into the building before it was finished, just before Adams' term of office

A portrait of Mrs. William Bingham

expired in the spring of 1801. In a letter to her daughter that is often quoted, Abigail referred to the structure as "this great castle," and outlined a few of the domestic problems her residence there imposed. It was built on such a "grand and superb scale," she wrote, that thirty servants were required to keep it and the stables in proper order; "lighting the apartments, from kitchen to parlours and chambers," she continued, "is a tax indeed; and the fires we are obliged to keep to secure us from daily agues is another very cheering comfort. To assist us..., and render less attendance necessary, bells are wholly wanting, not one single one being hung through the whole house, and promises are all you can obtain. This is so great an inconvenience, that I know not what to do, or how.... We have not the least fence, yard, or other convenience, without, and the great unfinished audience-room I make a drying-room of, to hang up the clothes in...."

However, in a letter written to her sister that spring, Abigail conceded that the house, which was "twice as large as our meeting House" at home in Massachusetts, was "built for ages to come." And John Adams, in again another letter of an almost interminable correspondence among the Adamses, wrote that same time: "Before I end my letter, I pray Heaven to bestow the best of blessings on this house, and on all that shall hereafter inhabit it. May none but wise and honest men ever rule under this roof!" His successor, Thomas Jefferson, was just such a man, and he devoted serious attention to finishing the "palace," as it was sometimes called, and furnishing it to his taste. His taste was clearly more cosmopolitan than that of the Adamses. In 1790 he brought back from Paris eighty-six cases of French furniture; during his two terms in office he spent more than ten thousand dollars for wine to be served at his table. He employed a French chef, and because he loved such alien delights as those wines of France, and macaroni in the Italian manner, Patrick Henry viewed him as "a man unfaithful to his native victuals."

Just what improvements Jefferson and his successor James Madison may have made in the mansion cannot be accurately described, for in 1814 the British put a torch to the building, and to the nearby Capitol. On the day of the burning, before she fled for safety, Dolley Madison wrote her sister that she could hear the sound of cannons. "Two messengers, covered with dust, come to bid me fly." She continued, "...At this late hour, a wagon has been procured; I have had it filled with the plate and most valuable portable articles belonging to the house...." "When I shall again write to you," she concluded, "or where I shall be tomorrow, I cannot tell!" She removed Gilbert Stuart's portrait of Washington from its frame and with it escaped in her wagon. Thereupon the building was gutted.

The design for the Capitol was also opened to a competition, and once again an emigrant, William Thornton, a West Indian Quaker and an architect almost by chance, won the day. "I lamented not having studied architecture," he confessed later, "and resolved to attempt the grand undertaking and study at the same time." Although his design was accepted with Washington's recommendation, the actual building was entrusted to one of his competitors. Then and repeatedly in years to come the original plan for the Capitol was also modified. After the structure was burned, the same day

Top: charred ruins of the Capitol

Above: the reconstructed Capitol

as was the White House, the problem of reconstructing and completing the charred near-ruin was given to Benjamin Henry Latrobe, a gifted British architect who came to America in 1795 and ended his days here. Except for its massive central dome, added in 1865, the Capitol as we know it today is largely Latrobe's building. Rising as it did from the raw landscape of the nascent, unformed city, the new Capitol was more than an imposing building; it was a symbol of the national spirit, a proud reminder of the nation's recovery after the humiliations endured during the War of 1812.

It was the design and construction of such large public buildings that provided the architects with their most exacting challenges. Even the hypercritical Mrs. Trollope was "struck with admiration and surprise" at the successful accomplishment of the Capitol when she visited Washington almost twenty years later. Although conceived and built on a smaller scale, New York's third (and present) City Hall, completed in 1812, was hardly less successful. This elegant marble structure was the joint effort of a native-born builder-architect, John McComb, Jr., and a French architect, Joseph François Mangin. About the latter little is known but to him is credited the French character of the exterior and the especially graceful interior staircase.

As just one further example of the public structures that rose during the Federal period, the Massachusetts State House, on Beacon Hill in Boston, is outstanding. The story of the architect, Charles Bulfinch, will be told elsewhere in this book; it suffices here to remark that as a young man Bulfinch made the grand tour of England, France (he saw Paris with Jefferson as a guide), and Italy, observing "particularly the wonders of Architecture" that he encountered. Upon his return to America he drifted into the architectural profession, and in 1795 his design for the State House was approved by a legislative committee. When it was completed, a group of "southern gentlemen" pronounced it "the most magnificent building in the Union."

By the end of the Federal period the classical style was firmly entrenched in all parts of the United States. In the years to come it would take on new forms that would bring the revival of ancient models to a climax.

An early view of the New York City Hall, designed by Joseph F. Mangin and John McComb, Jr.

PRINTS DIVISION, N. Y. PUBLIC LIBRARY

Homes of the Great

Presidential Places

Three American houses, the building of which was undertaken or completed in the early years of the republic, have, above all others, become revered as national shrines—the White House, Mount Vernon, and Monticello. Each of the three has its own distinctive style, couched in the classical idiom of the period, but each is also so rich in important historical associations that it is almost impossible to think of them other than as symbols, or monuments. Mount Vernon assumed its essential form in the colonial period, but it was not completed until after the Revolution, and some of the last improvements Washington made there recall the neoclassical designs of Robert Adam. Even during his lifetime, Washington's home had become a "tourist attraction" that brought the curious and the interested from all parts. In 1794 he wrote William Pearce that he had "no objection to any sober or orderly persons's gratifying their curiosity in viewing the buildings, Gardens &ct about Mount Vernon." His actual guests and casual callers, including the most distinguished personages of the day as well as many others of little or no rank, were in themselves so numerous that Washington once resignedly referred to his home as "a well resorted tavern." In that long procession came Louis Philippe, the future citizen king of France (but christened Citoyen Égalité during the French Revolution), and his two brothers. When they presented themselves a flustered doorman reported to Washington: "Your Excellency, there are three Equalities at the door!" In what seems to have been an entirely unnecessary caution,

A detail view of Monticello

the American diplomat and statesman Gouverneur Morris once wrote Washington that he considered it "of very great importance to fix the taste of our country properly, and I think your example will go very far in that respect. It is therefore my wish that everything about you should be substantially *good and majestically plain*, made to endure...." There were few visitors at Mount Vernon who found the Father of his Country or his beloved house otherwise.

The construction of Monticello was also started before the Revolution and completed in the Federal period; and that remarkable building also received a long file of eminent visitors from near and far to enjoy Jefferson's presence —and to admire his hilltop home. Among them, in 1782, came the Marquis de Chastellux, who described his host as "the first American who has consulted the Fine arts to learn how to shelter himself from the weather." He was so enchanted by his stay, he wrote, that his four days at Monticello passed like four minutes. Fourteen years later, before the house was finished, the Duc de La Rochefoucald-Liancourt prophesied that Monticello would "deserve to rank with the most pleasant mansions in France and England."

When Jefferson moved into the White House he found it "big enough for two emperors, one Pope and the grand lama." He proceeded to improve it. As the official residence of all presidents, the White House has always had its own very special character. For the same reason, it has been constantly altered and "improved." So long as it stands those changes will continue.

In 1833 John James Audubon dined *en famille* with Andrew Jackson at what, the great "American Woodsman" reported, was then becoming familiarly and vulgarly known as "the White House." At the start, and for years afterward, the building had been called "the President's House" or, by some, the "Palace" of the president. No house in the nation has had such a continuous succession of different residents, and residents of such differing tastes. Inside and out the building has been subject to frequent—almost constant—alteration, with enlargements, to suit the changing needs and tastes of its many occupants. It has twice been damaged by fire and substantially rebuilt. The original structure was far from finished in 1797 when Washington finally retired from public life to spend his very few remaining years at his beloved Mount Vernon. (While he was president he had been obliged to live in rented quarters, first in New York and then in Philadelphia.) The building was still unfinished when John Adams moved in, shortly before his term of office expired in March, 1801. From then to this day it has served as a home, and official residence, for thirty-five presidents. As it stands today, in spite of the changes that have been made, the White House still recalls the original structure from which it has grown over a period of more than one hundred and seventy years to its present size and appearance.

The north facade of the White House. The portico with its Ionic columns was added to the building in 1829.

The President's House as it appeared in an 1825 drawing, after it had been reconstructed following the fire of 1814

A reconstructed view of Dolley Madison as she prepares to flee from the White House during the British advance

Time after time various rooms of the White House have been redecorated by different occupants. The Adamses used some of their own furniture, with pieces from the President's House in Philadelphia. Thomas Jefferson introduced French furnishings. "Queen Dolley" Madison, working with the architect Benjamin Latrobe, favored the English Regency and French Empire styles. In 1811 Washington Irving described her drawing room as a room of "blazing splendor," an unfortunately apt phrase, for all those appointments soon went up in flames. Seventy years later, after many other changes of décor, Chester A. Arthur sold more than twenty wagonloads of furniture at public auction and had Louis C. Tiffany redecorate the mansion in the art nouveau style. Theodore Roosevelt, in turn, had those embellishments stripped away. During recent presidencies, the White House has been given a new and distinctive air of elegance.

The Blue Room, or "elliptic saloon," decorated in 1962 in French Empire style

Above: a view of the Red Room as reflected in an early 19th-century convex mirror hanging on the wall

Opposite: the Yellow Oval Room, designed by Hoban, the original architect, as a private sitting room

The house, built by his father, in which George Washington lived as a boy

"No estate in United America is more pleasantly situated than this," wrote George Washington to an English correspondent. "It lies in a high, dry and healthy Country 300 miles by water from the Sea, . . . on one of the finest Rivers in the world." He was referring, of course, to his beloved Mount Vernon; the land on which he had played as a child, and the house which his devoted attention over the years had transformed from a modest cottage into a substantial and handsome mansion. Washington first came to his future estate (it was then known as Little Hunting Creek Plantation) in 1735 when his father moved there to occupy a small house of one and one-half stories he had built to accommodate his family. The lad was three years old. Four years later the family moved again; and in 1743 Washington's older half-brother, Lawrence, took deed to the Little Hunting Creek dwelling, soon renaming it Mount Vernon in honor of Admiral Vernon, under whom he had served on a Caribbean expedition. When Lawrence died in 1752 George purchased the property from the widow. Seven years later he married another widow, Martha Dandridge Custis. In preparation for his married life he raised the structure to two and one-half stories and largely redecorated it. "I am now, I believe, fixed at this Seat," he wrote a friend optimistically, "with an agreeable Consort for Life and hope to find more happiness in retirement than I ever experienced amidst a wide and bustling World." In 1773 he made plans for further, extensive additions and changes, not only to the main house but to the dependencies and gardens. Although he ardently wished to supervise personally every detail of the work, he was called to war before much progress could be made. For the next eight years while he was in the field Washington kept up a constant correspondence with his manager at home, instructing, advising, and questioning with minute concern. It was only in 1787 that the final enlargement and decoration was completed and the cupola topped with its weather vane in the form of a dove of peace. Again Washington was called away, to the presidency this time, for another eight years. "I can truly say," he wrote wistfully during that period, "I had rather be at Mount Vernon with a friend or two about me, than to be attended at the seat of government by the officers of State and the representatives of every power in Europe." He had but two years to enjoy the peace of his final retirement before his death in 1799.

Mount Vernon as it was enlarged by Washington in 1759 to receive his bride, Martha Custis. A second story was sandwiched between the first floor, with its four rooms and central hall-way, and the attic story. The overall dimensions measured 33 feet deep and 47 feet long.

Mount Vernon as it was further enlarged between 1774 and 1787. The house was first extended to the right during 1774 and then, in 1776, to the left with a similar addition. The pediment and cupola on the roof were added by Washington after he returned from the Revolutionary War.

Upon the occasion of a visit to Mount Vernon, the gifted English-born architect Benjamin Latrobe, who enjoyed Washington's friendship, remarked that the house itself "has no very striking appearance, though superior to every other house I have seen here [in Virginia]." Latrobe concluded that the structure was for the most part "extremely good and neat, but by no means above what would be expected in a plain Englishman's country house of £500 or £600 a year." Other visitors were more impressed by both the dwelling and its surrounding estate. "The General has never left America," wrote a Polish traveler who spent twelve days at Mount Vernon, "but when one sees his house and his home and his garden it seems as if he had copied the best samples of the grand old homesteads of England." When he was in residence Washington was tirelessly in the saddle paying serious and loving care to his farms; and he no less carefully watched over every detail of his house and gardens. "It's astonishing," observed still another guest, "with what niceness he directs everything in the building way, condescending even to measure the things himself, that all may be perfectly uniform." Mrs. Washington was apparently no less conscientious as the mistress of the house. Once she came upon her granddaughter Nelly Custis entertaining a suitor when she should have been practicing at her harpsichord. Upon her approach the youth fled leaving behind a smudge on the freshly painted wall above a settee. "Ah, it was no federalist," exclaimed Lady Washington (as she was generally addressed). "None but a filthy democrat would mark a place with his good-for-nothing head in that manner!" In a milder mood she once described herself as "an old-fashioned Virginia housekeeper, steady as a clock, busy as a bee, and cheerful as a cricket." Most visitors found the physical presence of Washington himself awesomely impressive. "There is not a king in Europe but would look like a *valet de chambre* by his side," reported one London newspaper during the Revolution.

A schoolhouse in the garden at Mount Vernon

The mansion and one of its dependencies with connecting arcade from the North Grove

Colonnaded east facade of Mount Vernon, facing the Potomac River, as it appeared in 1801, from a detail of a drawing by William Birch

Above: the South Piazza of Monticello, where Jefferson's workshop and greenhouse were located

Opposite: Monticello, 1826. The completed house was far different from the one first planned.

Thomas Jefferson's passionate involvement with Monticello was no less constant or ardent than Washington's with Mount Vernon, and his amendments to and improvements of his home were even more numerous. "All my wishes end," he wrote in 1787, "where I hope my days will end, at Monticello." And at another time he is said to have told a visitor, "Architecture is my delight, and putting up, and pulling down, one of my favorite amusements." His first studies for Monticello began when he was twenty-four, in 1767, and some changes and additions in the actual building and grounds continued virtually until his death in 1826 at the age of eighty-three. (Jefferson designed or planned changes in every house he ever lived in, including the Hôtel de Langeac in Paris and the White House, as well as Monticello.) The major and very considerable alterations at Monticello were made after his five-year sojourn in Europe, where he was especially impressed by the subtle interpretations of Roman classicism by French architects under Louis XVI. "We are now living in a brick kiln," he wrote George Wythe in 1794 while new construction proceeded, "for my house, in its present state, is nothing better." Jefferson apparently was the first American to own a copy of Palladio's great work on architecture (as against the numerous available English adaptations of Palladio's original designs), but he used that reference creatively and in the light of his other studies and experiences. His ultimate intention, as he told the Duc de La Rochefoucauld-Liancourt, was to have Monticello appear on the exterior as a one-story house "crowned with a balustrade and a dome." To achieve that appearance, as well as to hide from view the service system of the house, he suppressed such functional elements below the main living floor and at the rear. The various offices—kitchen, smokehouse, dairy, laundry, servants' quarters, and the like—were connected by colonnaded passageways that protected the servants from inclement weather as they went about their daily rounds.

A passageway under the terrace walk, leading along the kitchen, dairy, and servants' quarters

One of the two stairways Jefferson designed for Monticello

Entrance hall, with busts of Jefferson, Voltaire, and Turgot

Jefferson's bedroom. The revolving chair with accompanying table and leg rest enabled him to write in a half-recumbent position.

In 1815 the eminent Bostonian George Ticknor visited Monticello armed with a letter of introduction from John Adams. "You enter," he wrote, "by a glass folding-door, into a hall which reminds you of Fielding's 'Man of the Mountain,' by the strange furniture of its walls. On one side hang the head and horns of an elk, a deer, and a buffalo; another is covered with curiosities which Lewis and Clark found in their wild and perilous expedition." There were also, he added, mastodon bones, Indian maps and paintings, and other oddments. And there was a big clock, possibly made to Jefferson's design, run by Revolutionary War cannon ball weights, some of which controlled the striking (a copper gong on the roof sounded the hour) and others which indicated the days of the week as they slowly moved down the wall. The indications for Friday afternoon and Saturday had to be placed on the basement wall, since there was no room for them on the entrance wall, with holes cut in the floor through which the weights could pass. On Sunday the clock was rewound. With his major redoing of the house Jefferson installed bed alcoves such as he had seen in France. His own bed alcove was open at either side for the sake of ventilation. It also enabled him to retire from and arise into either of two rooms. A clothes closet over the bed could be reached by a narrow stairway entered by a door near the head of the bed. Thoughtful arrangements to increase efficiency and comfort were all but endless. To conceal service traffic within the house, to save space and money, and to increase a sense of privacy for the members of the household, Jefferson did away with central stairs and replaced them with two unobtrusive cores, consisting of stairs, halls, and cupboards. One for the use of the family and guests, the other for servants, these cores served all the rooms of the house.

The housekeeping at Monticello was somewhat less than perfect. Another Bostonian who visited Jefferson with Ticknor in 1815 was struck by the condition of some of the furniture. He noted chairs with "leather bottoms stuffed with hair, but the bottoms were completely worn through and the hair sticking out in all directions...." One broken pane of glass in a door was being replaced with a wooden panel, he continued, because the glass had been procured from Bohemia in a large size not available in the vicinity of Virginia. Books of all descriptions littered a marble mantelpiece. (Jefferson once wrote John Adams that he could not live without books.) Some years later Jefferson's granddaughter remembered the delicious muffins that at times were served at Monticello "when the cook happened to be sober." The constant reconstruction had its perils. One day in 1797 Jefferson's younger daughter Maria (Mrs. John Wayles Eppes) fell through one of the floors of the building and landed in the cellar. Although she received no injuries then, shortly after, she fell out of a doorway and suffered a sprain. Monticello's site was and is one of its most noble and distinctive features. "The house stands on the summit of a mountain," wrote the Duc de La Rochefoucauld-Liancourt in 1796, "and the tastes and arts of Europe have been consulted in the formation of the plan." As Jefferson himself wrote, "where has nature spread so rich a mantle under the eye? mountains, forests, rocks, rivers. With what majesty do we there [at Monticello] ride above the storms! How sublime to look down into the workhouse of nature, to see her clouds, hail, snow, rain, thunder, all fabricated at our feet! And the glorious Sun, when rising as if out of a distant water, just gilding the tops of the mountains, and giving life to all nature!"

An aerial view of Monticello, with the Blue Ridge Mountains rising in the distance

The Urban Scene

City Styles

At the time of Washington's inauguration the new nation boasted only a handful of cities worthy of the name. The population of New York, the country's first capital under the Constitution, numbered barely thirty-three thousand — fewer people than enter a single modern office building in the course of a day. Without its suburbs Philadelphia, the next capital, had even fewer; Boston, Baltimore, and Charleston were considerably smaller. A decade later Washington took incipient form as the permanent capital of the United States, but for years to come it remained, as various observers noted, "a capital without a city," "a little village in the midst of the woods," at best a "City of Magnificent Intentions." In 1803 New Orleans became a city of the Union — a city already over eighty years old, with a colorful history under two other flags and with architectural traditions completely alien to those of the English colonies.

Each of these burgeoning urban communities had grown out of widely differing circumstances and, excepting Washington, each had been shaped differently by its separate colonial experience, and by the nature of its local resources. Visitors were tempted to liken them to one or another European city; Philadelphia was called "the London of America," New York was compared with Liverpool, and so on. But the analogies were superficial, and as the American cities grew at a quickening pace any such comparisons became increasingly meaningless. (Within two generations New York became the third largest city in the world and Philadelphia's population

Carved ornament by McIntire

MARKHAM W. SEXTON

was larger than that of Berlin.)

Even while they were still small and few, cities exercised an influence far out of proportion to their size and the numbers of their people — an influence that was sometimes resented in the hinterland. As early as 1770 "A Connecticut Farmer," railing against New York, wrote the *New London Gazette* that he hoped "the plumes of that domineering city may yet feather the nests of those whom they have long plucked." However, for better or worse, the cultural and economic forces generated within cities would provide the dynamics of the future.

Even in colonial times there were occasional complaints about the noise and congestion in some cities, and there were those who retreated to newly created suburbs to escape such botherations. However, for time still to come there was room enough for individual houses to rise on ample plots of land; albeit they were customarily designed more compactly than their village and rural counterparts, and their height tended to increase. Four-story dwellings were not uncommon, and in 1797 one Boston house rose to five stories, "a height unknown in the town." But as cities continued to grow and become more populous, at least in "downtown" areas of the larger centers, urban dwellings tended to huddle together in continuous rows, building wall against building wall. Whole rows of town houses with identical facades were indeed thus planned and built as a single, unified architectural scheme, as had earlier been done so agreeably at Bath and London in England, at Paris and Bordeaux in France, and in other European cities.

Above: the Pingree House, Salem, Mass., built for John Gardner in 1804

Left: a pair of bellows carved by Samuel McIntire for a Salem cabinetmaker

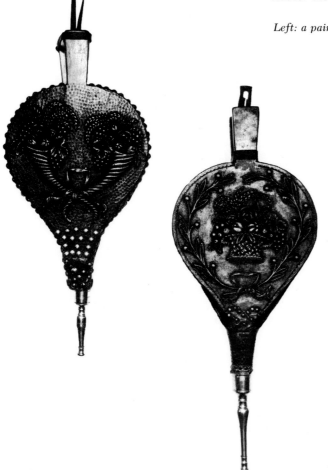

For more than a generation after the Revolution, Salem, Massachusetts, was one of the most celebrated ports of the world. Its sleek ships were known about the seven seas. In some remote parts where they visited in search of markets, it was believed that Salem *was* the United States—an immensely rich and important country. At home its merchant princes built houses whose charm was unsurpassed anywhere in the land. Many of the best of them were designed, built, and decorated by the local self-made architect, wood carver, and Jack-of-many-other-trades, Samuel McIntire. (Among other accomplishments, "directed by an ear of exquisite nicety," he played several musical instruments, and repaired them when they were out of order. "All the instruments we use," recalled one contemporary, "he could understand & was the best person to be employed in correcting any defects.") A visitor from Baltimore considered at least one of his houses—the mansion, long since destroyed, that he built for Elias Hasket Derby—to be

Above: the Peirce-Nichols House, Salem, Mass., designed by McIntire, 1782

Right: a bust of Voltaire carved by Samuel McIntire, probably about 1802

"more like a palace than the dwelling of an American merchant." In 1782 McIntire built a three-story frame dwelling for Jerathmiel Peirce, a Salem shipping merchant. Four-square, its facades edged with bold fluted pilasters, and topped by a balustraded "captain's walk," it is one of the outstanding houses remaining from the early Federal period. The home was partially remodeled in 1801, at which time McIntire added a fence with classical urns capping its posts. A few years later, in 1804, he designed what may well be his finest structure, the brick house commissioned by sea captain John Gardner (and now known by the name of later owners, the Pingrees). The slender columns of its semicircular portico, the slim, reeded pilasters that flank the doorway, and the delicate fanlight above the door (page 116) recall the grace of Robert Adam's designs. When McIntire died in 1811, the obituaries agreed that on all counts he was "one of the best of men." It was mournfully agreed that no one could take his place.

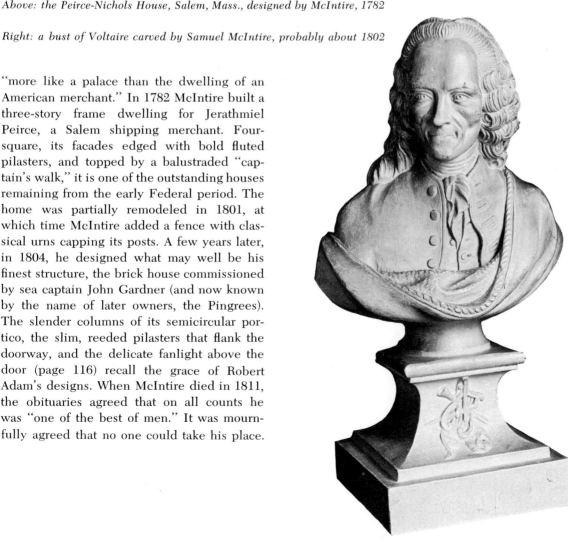

The city block composed of buildings of uniform design was a wholly new development of the Federal period. Having been inspired by the beauty of the town planning in England and France, Charles Bulfinch imposed architectural harmony on Boston to a degree unknown in other parts of the nation. The first of several splendid groups created by the architect was the curved row of connected houses known as the Tontine Crescent, which in its day was acclaimed "the most improved of modern elegance." Bulfinch's plan for making the upper slopes of Beacon Hill into an exclusive residential area, dominated by a garden square, never materialized. However, much of his original conception is preserved on a smaller scale in Beacon Hill's Louisburg Square, featuring a central park that was jointly owned by the occupants of the bow front houses of red brick. Federal New York lacked the urban charm of the Massachusetts capital. Even on Broadway, a wide thoroughfare lined with stylish homes, hogs still rooted for garbage. Despite such filth, James Fenimore Cooper, in 1828, wrote that "Broadway . . . is the fashionable mall of the city, and certainly, for gaiety [and] the beauty and grace of the beings who throng it . . . it may safely challenge competition with most if not any of the promenades of the old world."

A view of lower Broadway in New York City, from an 1826 water color by William J. Bennett

Bulfinch's elevation for Boston's Tontine Crescent, erected in 1794 and demolished in 1858
Federal style town houses, completed in the 1840s, surrounding Louisburg Square in Boston

State Street, Boston, and the Old State House, a seat of government until 1798, as it appeared in 1801
Charleston, shown below in 1831, retained its earlier character more faithfully than other cities.

A winter scene in Brooklyn, 1817–20. A predominantly rural nation lay just beyond the limits of the little cities of the newborn republic.

In 1800 the combined populations of the five major cities of the United States totaled barely two hundred thousand persons. They were, however, destined for rapid growth, along with other, smaller cities throughout the land. As it was somewhat later remarked, the nineteenth century was to be "the century of cities." At the start of the century each of the major urban centers still clearly revealed the distinctive character and appearance that had developed from the colonial experience. Although it grew less rapidly than some of the others, Boston was expanding at a pace that caused comment. "The great number of new and elegant buildings which have been erected in this Town, within the last two years," remarked one returning visitor in 1808, "strike the eye with astonishment, and prove the rapid manner in which the people have been acquiring wealth." And Boston ever remained the capital of New England, a region, claimed one of the Cabots in 1804, where there was among the people "more wisdom and virtues than in any other part of the world." Brooklyn was a city in its own right (it did not officially become a part of New York City until 1898), although New Yorkers were led to include its population with their own in order to win out in the race among rival cities for size — as Philadelphia claimed the citizens of Northern Liberties and Southwark to swell its figures. Charleston also grew at a slower rate than New York or Philadelphia. However, wrote Jedidiah Morse in his *American Geography*, "in no part of America are the social blessings enjoyed more rationally and liberally than in Charleston." Northern visitors were delighted by the city's gaily colored, verandaed mansions standing within gardens of orange trees, palmettos, and magnolias. It seemed more like a scene in southern Europe than a part of the New World.

145

Right: exterior detail of the Nathaniel Russell House, Charleston, S.C., with recessed window embrasures

Below: oval music room of the Russell home. The mirrored windowpanes reflect garden windows opposite.

The free-flying staircase curves up to the third floor without ever touching the walls.

Several days after he arrived at Charleston in 1777 the Marquis de Lafayette wrote his wife a long, rhapsodical letter expressing delight at his reception there. Everything about Charleston and its people seems to have enchanted him. In the following years the city suffered at the hands of British troops, and in 1778 a fire destroyed two hundred and fifty houses—a disaster that led to a great rebuilding during the Federal period, from about 1790 to 1808. It was at that time that Nathaniel Russell built his sumptuous house in the Adam style on Meeting Street; he was living there in 1809. Russell, son of a Rhode Island chief justice, had come to Charleston from Bristol in his home state. Following the Revolution there were others who came from New England (as well as from England, the West Indies, and elsewhere). Russell was apparently nicknamed "The King of the Yankees," and became president of the Charleston New England Society. (Many Charlestonians habitually passed their summers in the relatively cool neighborhood of Newport.) He spared no expense on his new house (something over eighty thousand dollars) and made it one of the most elegant in a city of elegant houses.

Top: profile portraits of Dr. William Thornton (left) and Col. John Tayloe (right) drawn by Saint-Mémin
Above: the Octagon House in Washington, D.C. It was completed in 1800 before the White House was finished.

The frame house built in Augusta, Ga., in 1818 for Nicholas Ware

Although row houses were a successful innovation in a number of cities, throughout the Federal period and for years afterward there remained a conspicuous amount of individual assertion in the design of urban dwellings. One outstanding example is the so-called Octagon House (actually it is hexagonal in form) in Washington, D.C., designed by Dr. William Thornton for Colonel John Tayloe. Thornton was the designer of the national Capitol, and one of the most urbane and witty ornaments of Washington society. Tayloe, who also owned Mount Airy (pages 90–91) with its three thousand acres and private race track, was himself a sophisticated and wealthy man of the world with a wide acquaintance among the celebrated figures of his day. The house, planned in 1797 when Washington was still virtually a wilderness, was built on a plot of ground formed by an acute angle between two converging streets, which determined its unique shape. In 1818 at Augusta, Georgia, Nicholas Ware built a highly individual house. With its horseshoe entrance stairs, its double porch, and its flanking octagonal bays. Ware's house is a unique native variant of the Adam style. Another Georgia house, the Owens-Thomas House, as it is now called, was designed in England by a young British architect, William Jay, for Richard Richardson of Savannah. When the structure was completed in 1819 it incorporated a singularly handsome, unusual balcony resting on cast-iron supports in the form of acanthus leaf scrolls and further graced by cast-iron columns, pilasters, and railings.

Cast-iron balcony of the Owens-Thomas House, Savannah

149

Charles Bulfinch, Architect

During the three decades between the Constitutional Convention of 1787 and the end of the War of 1812, Charles Bulfinch transformed his native Boston from a provincial town into an orderly and elegant New England capital, planned after the model of neoclassical London. Although Bulfinch the architect designed the most important public and residential structures that arose in the city in the Federal period, his achievements extended beyond the mere beautification of Boston. Bulfinch was even better known among his contemporaries as the tactful and devoted public servant—the chairman of Boston's Board of Selectmen and chief of police—who totally involved himself in every aspect of community life including politics, social reform, and education.

There was little in the Brahmin background of this fourth-generation Bostonian to indicate that he would someday become America's first native-born professional architect. His maternal grandfather, Charles Apthorp, was reputed to be Boston's richest citizen, and it seemed unlikely that Bulfinch would ever have to earn a living. Apthorp did serve as a stimulus to his grandson's early architectural interests: he not only helped finance the construction of King's Chapel in Boston, but he induced his friend Peter Harrison to design it; and Apthorp owned a well-stocked architectural library containing editions of Vitruvius, Palladio, and their interpreters, which was presumably at the disposal of the young Charles. One or another of these academic authorities probably provided the inspiration for Charles' schoolbook doodle, executed at the age of ten, of a fluted column with a Corinthian capital. By the time he entered Harvard in 1778, Bulfinch was as well prepared to pursue architecture as a gentlemanly avocation as

Mather Brown's 1786 portrait of Bulfinch

any young dilettante in the land. In college he first became acquainted with neoclassicism through such archaeological source books as Robert Adam's *Ruins of the Palace of the Emperor Diocletian at Spalatro.* After receiving a Master of Arts degree in 1784, Bulfinch was undecided as to his calling. He later wrote in his autobiography that "My disposition would have led me to the study of physic, but my father [a doctor] was averse to my engaging in the practice of what he considered a laborious profession." Instead, Bulfinch went to work in the counting rooms of the merchant Joseph Barrell. The job was apparently so undemanding that the would-be accountant spent most of his time "at leisure to cultivate a taste for Architecture." In a belated token of gratitude, Bulfinch, in 1792, designed a rural retreat for his former employer and "intimate friend." This mansion achieved practically instant renown for its beauty and novelty, and evoked rapturous responses of the sort composed by a local poet: "A goodly sight in sooth it is, to stand/ On Bos-

tons banks, where western breezes play,/. . . One house there is midst groves of poplars gay,/ To know whose owner, strangers oft desire;/ When Phoebus downward winds his westering way/ They see its windows look like crimson fire;/ Whose that conspicuous roof they then enquire?"

In 1785 Bulfinch embarked on a grand tour of England and the Continent. Thomas Jefferson, who at the time was minister to France, received Bulfinch in Paris and arranged for him to stay at the recently completed Hôtel de Langeac. Here Bulfinch experienced at first hand the French method of designing rooms for function and convenience. The structure embodied such features, later identified with Bulfinch's domestic buildings, as carefully laid out service areas, variations in the size and height of rooms according to their use, and the placement of a suite of rooms, centering on an oval salon, along the garden side. Of all the places the young graduate visited, London left the most lasting impression. There, Bulfinch was captivated by the neoclassicism of the brothers Adam and their followers. He saw infinite decorative and spatial possibilities in the style, which could easily be adapted to the standard wood construction of New England.

The Boston to which a more worldly architect returned in 1787 was, in its building styles, at least two generations behind London. One British traveler rudely but accurately described the Massachusetts capital at this time as "heavy, antique, and incommodious." Even the newest, most pretentious residences in the area were designed in the academic style of the mid-eighteenth century. The Federalist rulers of Boston, however, were generally eager to make amends with England and developed an acute Anglomania, in the throes of which they tried to remodel their town into a little London. It was in this atmosphere that Bulfinch spent the next several years. He married his wealthy cousin Hannah Apthorp, and passed what he described as that "season of leisure, pursuing no business, but giving gratuitous advice in Architecture." The products of his drawing table included designs for a triumphal arch, erected on the occasion of George Washington's visit to Boston in 1789, two state capitols, three churches, the nation's first Revolutionary War memorial, twelve private houses, a hotel, and a theater. In addition to designing the latter, Bulfinch played an important role in securing the repeal of a long-standing Boston statute banning dramatic performances. This prolific activity also resulted in much favorable publicity: the *Massachusetts Magazine* in 1793 touted the architect as a young man who "to a good natural genius and a liberal education, having added . . . a tour through Europe, has returned to adorn his native town and country."

Bulfinch doubtless would have continued his "gratuitous" public services had it not been for an overly ambitious attempt to introduce monumental town planning to Boston. Begun in 1793, the project was referred to as the Tontine Crescent, after its method of financing, invented by the Italian Lorenzo Tonti. The plan called for two curved rows of houses of uniform design on either side of a small enclosed park. The crescent of sixteen houses, comprising half the projected ellipse, and completed in 1794, was universally praised: Bulfinch's disciple, Asher Benjamin, wrote that the Tontine Crescent "gave the first impulse to good taste [in] architecture in this part of the country." The second of the two crescents was never built. Bulfinch, who had undertaken the project in the midst of an economic recession, assumed the tremendous

financial burden himself, and in so doing sacrificed both his and his wife's fortunes. However, the loss proved to be the catalyst that led the architect from aristocratic amateurism to professional achievement. As Mrs. Bulfinch succinctly put it, "My husband . . . made Architecture his business, as it had been his pleasure." Bulfinch soon discovered that his professional practice was less than remunerative, mainly because people were unaccustomed to paying for services they formerly had received for nothing. He fell heavily into debt trying to support a wife and seven children on an income of less than one thousand dollars a year, and was rescued from his dilemma only when concerned Bostonians, in 1799, devised a means by which they "might extricate, from immediate dif-

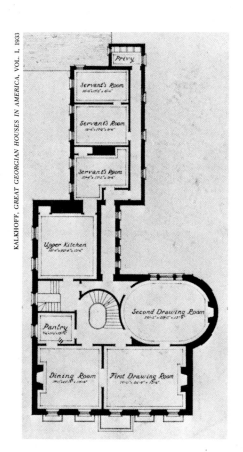

KALKHOFF, *GREAT GEORGIAN HOUSES IN AMERICA*, VOL. 1, 1933

A plan of Harrison Gray Otis' town house

ficulty, that liberal protector, that noble patron of the arts." Bulfinch was duly appointed chairman of the Board of Selectmen and chief of police, positions which along with design fees supported architect and family for nearly twenty years.

In his dual capacity as Boston's principal official and architect, Bulfinch directed a second venture in town planning that gave Boston Common a border of harmoniously designed houses. Other accomplishments during the first decade of the 1800s included developing Beacon Hill into Boston's choicest property, laying out Indian Wharf, Boston's largest commercial district to date, and designing the state prison at Charlestown. Solidly constructed of Chelmsford granite, the prison, with its rows of single cells, conformed in plan with the prevalent penal philosophy of rehabilitation through solitary confinement. Of the institution, a contemporary wrote: "Competent judges pronounce this to be one of the strongest and best built prisons in the world. It has these advantages over many other buildings of this kind, it can be neither set on fire by the prisoners nor be undermined." Bulfinch's most important public commission was, perhaps, the one for Massachusetts General Hospital, originally conceived by its trustees as a hundred-bed establishment for the use of the urban poor. Today, the much enlarged hospital is considered to be one of the finest in the country. Among the building's "Various modern improvements in domestic economy, conducive to cleanliness and comfort," was a stepped dome ceiling, providing light for the operating theater below. This clinical amphitheater was also equipped with tiers of chairs for medical observers. Another improvement was a version of the new English heating system that eliminated the need for fireplaces in individual rooms by supplying heat via air flues from furnaces in the cellar.

Bulfinch's years in public office came to a climax in 1817 when President Monroe visited Boston. In anticipation of the event, Harrison Gray Otis, a prominent Federalist lawyer and politician, offered the President the "accommodations and felicitations of my house," a magnificent Beacon Hill residence and, incidentally, the third dwelling designed by Bulfinch for Otis. Although the president elected to stay at the "superb apartments" chosen for him by Bulfinch, he attended a ball at the Otis', and may have inaugurated the "era of good feeling" between Federalists and Republicans there on the dance floor. Stephen Greenleaf Bulfinch took note that the president "was pleased with the public buildings . . . and found that the architect of them was the gentleman at his side." Monroe was probably equally impressed with Bulfinch's extraordinary tact, a virtue that had enabled him to administer Boston and improve its architecture during years of bitter party strife. The mild-mannered architect seemed, to the president, to be the ideal man to replace Benjamin Latrobe as the architect of the Capitol.

The work had been carried on under five presidents and five architects, and it had caused so much dissension of late that its progress had come to a virtual halt. Bulfinch accepted the summons to Washington, along with an annual salary of twenty-five hundred dollars, moving expenses, and wages for a draftsman. Rather than suggest any major changes, Bulfinch preferred "to follow in the prescribed path," and thus won the "complacency" of his employers, and completed the Capitol in 1828. The Herculean task had occupied most of his middle age, but Bulfinch considered the time spent in Washington "the happiest years of my life in pursuits congenial to my taste, and where my labors were well-received." He lived in Boston in retirement from 1830 until his death in 1844. A few years later, Josiah Quincy, a former mayor, commemorated Bulfinch's unique place in the history of Boston: "Few men deserve to be held . . . in more grateful remembrance. . . . During the many years he presided over the town government, he improved its finances, executed the laws with firmness, and was distinguished for gentleness and urbanity of manners, integrity and purity of character."

Bulfinch's elevation of the Massachusetts State Prison at Charlestown, built in 1805

Town and Country

The Ample Land

The inexorable and accelerating drift of people from the countryside into the cities of America had barely begun in the early days of the republic. In Washington's time, nine out of ten American families still lived in rural areas, and most of them practiced husbandry—as Washington himself did. There seemed to be ample room in the new republic to accommodate Thomas Jefferson's vision of a largely pastoral nation, a land of farmers who, he firmly believed, were "the most vigorous, the most independent, the most valuable citizens" of any country.

That was a sentiment worthy of Vergil, altogether consonant with the feelings of those who chose to compare the newborn nation with the glorious Roman republic of ancient times. To such eyes Washington bore a stirring resemblance to that ancient Roman dictator and patriot Cincinnatus, who in the fifth century B.C. left his farm to lead his countrymen to victory over invading forces, and who, when the battles were won, renounced his dictatorship and returned to the quiet, pastoral life of his farm—much as Washington had done in resigning his commission in the Revolutionary Army and returning to his Mount Vernon plantation. Both Washington and Jefferson were the very models of country gentlemen, whose virtuous and sober lives, led in more or less idyllic surroundings far from the hubbub of cities, gave their fellow Americans noble examples to emulate.

In the Federal period, while city dwellers were learning to accustom themselves to living on relatively small plots of ground (and to

Fence post detail, Litchfield

living close to their neighbors), the vast majority of Americans knew no such limitations in designing their rural retreats and village houses. With ample ground space there was little or no need for such houses to rise to any great height, and they were typically built with no more than two stories (and attic). To give an expression of local truth to a country house, wrote one contemporary observer, "it should always show a tendency to spread out and extend itself on the ground, rather than to run up in the air. There is space enough in the country." As already noted, Jefferson carefully designed the layout of Monticello so that it appeared to be a one-story house.

There were country houses certainly of greater pretension than either Mount Vernon or Monticello, and innumerable examples of a more modest nature. It was in the Federal period that the first original architectural book produced in this country appeared, *The Country Builder's Assistant: Containing a Collection of New Designs of Carpentry and Architecture*, by Asher Benjamin, published at Greenfield, Massachusetts, in 1796. In this, and in a succession of other popular illustrated works of similar nature, Benjamin provided local craftsmen with complete instructions for the building and designing of houses in the current styles. He included everything from elements of carpentry to details of the various classical orders. All in all his publications ran to forty-five editions over the first decades of the nineteenth century, and they had a profound influence on the development of architecture throughout much of New England.

Boscobel, an unusual and graceful American adaptation of the Adam style. The house was dismantled and re-erected near Garrison, N.Y.

Above: the Taft House, a dwelling in the Federal style that was originally known as Belmont, built at Cincinnati, Ohio, in 1820
Opposite: the columned entrance hall and stairway of Boscobel, designed for States Morris Dyckman and completed shortly after 1800

During the Federal period, as in colonial times, the waterways of America remained the principal avenues of travel and communication. (Even after railroads and improved highways had begun to ease problems of transportation, fresh eggs were for a time still delivered to markets in Providence, Rhode Island, by sailing sloops.) Two of the major routes of the nation were the Hudson and, as the years passed, the Ohio river valleys. Through these channels flowed back and forth great tides of people, goods, and ideas. It was along the banks of the Hudson, on Montross Point, that, shortly after 1800, States Morris Dyckman began construction of Boscobel, a house designed in the manner of Robert Adam. (One of Dyckman's British advisors was a nephew of Adam.) With its large expanse of windows, its tall, delicate porch columns, and its carved wooden swags, the house is a model of classic grace that has no counterpart in this country. In 1820 at Cincinnati Martin Baum built a house, originally known as Belmont, now as the Taft House, that recalls the refinement of the Federal style as it was developed slightly earlier in Virginia and Maryland. Emigrants from those states — and from almost everywhere else — were drifting down the Ohio River, the "Beautiful River," in ever-growing numbers during the early decades of the nineteenth century, and enough of that westward drift settled at Cincinnati to convert the little village founded in 1788 into a shining ornament of the new country. It had just been nominated a city when Baum built his handsome home there.

White Hall, a Mississippi River plantation in Louisiana, as it appeared about 1800

Montpelier, the Virginia home of President James Madison, as illustrated in 1818

The Pennsylvania country house of Genera

The countryseats that were everywhere to be seen throughout the new nation displayed a great and pleasing variety clearly manifest in the four contemporary views shown on these pages. White Hall, the Bringier plantation house in Louisiana, was veneered with light gray marble; the ground floor was paved with marble tiles; and the first story was enclosed by arcades. William Claiborne, then governor of the Mississippi Territory, described it admiringly in a letter to Thomas Jefferson. That house stands in sharp and exotic contrast to James W. De Peyster's neatly formal countryseat in the Federal style at Bloomingdale, New York, overlooking the Hudson River in the neighborhood of what is now Columbia University. In 1817, at the end of his second term as president, James Madison returned to his Virginia home, Montpelier, a house dominated by the massive classical portico Madison had added to an earlier structure in 1809. The view illustrated was drawn by the Baroness Hyde de Neuville, wife of the French minister to the United States, who earlier had sketched the Pennsylvania home of her compatriot General Jean Victor Moreau. Moreau, an able general, had been exiled by Napoleon for his dealings with factions opposed to the emperor. After his sojourn in America Moreau returned overseas and lost his life fighting for Napoleon's enemies. His American home was a social rendezvous for his friends, and it too was admired by visitors. The De Neuvilles had also been refugees from Napoleon's absolutism.

Jean Moreau, sketched in 1809

METROPOLITAN MUSEUM OF ART, GIFT OF LIVINGSTON L. SHORT, 1961

A view of the country house of James W. De Peyster at Bloomingdale, N.Y., in 1800

Nothing more clearly distinguished the rural life of New England from that of the South than those tidy villages that were essentially centers for the surrounding farm lands. Shaped by the vital community interests they served, such villages and their houses recall the complete and intelligent partnership between earth and man that once prevailed. "New-England may justly glory in its villages!" wrote James Fenimore Cooper. ". . . In space, freshness, an air of neatness and comfort, they far exceed any thing I have ever seen, even in the mother country. . . . I have passed, in one day, six or seven of these beautiful, tranquil and enviable looking hamlets, for not one of which have I been able to recollect an equal in the course of all my European travelling." The pages of Asher Benjamin's various books helped local craftsmen to develop the Federal style in simplified ways suitable to the demands of their neighborhoods. By the 1800s the outsides of houses were usually painted and white became a popular color.

A portrait by Ralph Earl of Chief Justice and Mrs. Oliver Ellsworth, 1792, in their home at Windsor, Conn., with a view of the house itself beyond the open window.

Above: Nickels-Sortwell House, a provincial version of the Federal style, Wiscasset, Me., 1807–12
Opposite: a street in Litchfield, Conn., one of New England's finest surviving old villages

The colorful variations in the architectural style of countryseats in the Federal period are expressions both of individual taste and regional traditions and circumstances. As the nation expanded, incorporating people and places of still different background and character, those variations increased in measure. Following the Louisiana Purchase and with the swelling prosperity of the Deep South, a building boom transformed the banks of the Lower Mississippi River. In 1810 Lewis Evans, first sheriff of Adams County, Mississippi, built a relatively plain, square, and commodious mansion, Elms Court, south of Natchez. A subsequent owner, Frank Surget, one of the first Natchez millionaires, added substantially to the house and presented it to his daughter as a wedding gift. The original appearance of the structure was attractively modified by the addition of double galleries, front and rear, and side porches trimmed with delicate iron lace-work designed and made in Europe. Andrew Jackson, Lafayette, Thackeray, and Jenny Lind were a few among the many who enjoyed the hospitality at Elms Court. Shortly after 1810, with the proceeds of a fortune realized from the culture of Sea Island cotton, William Seabrook built a plantation house on Edisto Island, South Carolina, that survived the misadventures of the Civil War and remains one of the outstanding nineteenth-century mansions of the Carolina Low Country.

Seabrook Plantation, built on Edisto Island, S.C., in 1810, served as an elegant prototype for other neighboring plantation houses.

Elms Court, built in 1810 at Natchez, Miss. Its double galleries, added in 1830, are trimmed with imported wrought-iron tracery.

Opposite: landscape design for an estate at Richmond, Va., drawn by the English-born architect and engineer Benjamin Henry Latrobe

OVERLEAF: Gore Place, the countryseat of Christopher Gore, seventh governor of Massachusetts, built at Waltham, Mass., in 1809–10

In September, 1793, the Reverend William Bentley noted in his diary that he saw "rising on our right a splendid seat belonging to Gore. The right wing was not compleated but the whole formed a fine object." Bentley was referring to "the young, beautiful, and excellent Christopher Gore," as a female contemporary described him, whose estate at Waltham, Massachusetts, at one later point comprised four hundred acres. In 1799, while Gore was in England on a government mission, his "splendid seat" was destroyed by fire. He promptly had a new mansion designed, and this was ready for occupancy in 1804 when he returned to America fully prepared to live in the style of an English country gentleman. Sir Augustus John Foster, a visiting British minister, conceded that Gore Place (pages 162–63) was "a very handsome comfortable house." Actually it remains one of the finest country houses built in New England during the Federal period. Gore then became Massachusetts' seventh governor. However, his conservative constituency was disconcerted by his frequent public appearances in an orange coach with brilliantly liveried footmen and outriders, and shortly turned him out of office. The exquisitely studied design of Gore Place contrasts remarkably with the strictly traditional character of such a house as Home Place. With its steep-pitch roof spreading over the galleries surrounding the structure to provide a cool, dry outdoor area, its main floor ventilated by tall French windows and raised above the earth by a ground floor of full height as a protection from dampness, and its complete reliance on native materials, it is a direct outgrowth of local need, tradition, and habit—a successful solution, developed in French colonial times, to the special problems presented by the climate and geography of the region.

Home Place, St. Charles Parish, built in 1801; a typical Louisiana plantation house

Cabins and Cottages

Less Stately Mansions

Over the years from the seventeenth century through the nineteenth and beyond, as one style and fashion in building succeeded another, two very modest but highly distinctive types of dwellings flourished continuously—the log cabin and the Cape Cod cottage. Completely unpretentious in design, both varieties enjoyed widespread popularity, and their derivatives are still with us today.

Log cabin construction detail

While visiting Cape Cod in 1800, the president of Yale, Timothy Dwight, observed that nearly all the homes of this whaling and shipbuilding center were of one and one-half stories, with central chimneys, small windows, and gabled roofs. He referred to these dwellings as "Cape Cod houses," a type which originated with the Pilgrims, and which today can be found everywhere from Palo Alto to Provincetown. The shingled exteriors of these cottages usually weathered to a silvery gray. In Cape communities, where pretension was abhorred, and where the homes of captain and crewman were undifferentiated, even painted clapboards were considered "showy." As one Bostonian put it, "Cape Cod residences have a peculiarity. . . . The houses and their surroundings seem of an unsuitable inferiority of style to those who live in them . . . [men] whose sons and daughters visit and marry in the best circles. . . . There is . . . a remarkable republican simplicity in the style of buildings; little distinction that betokens wealth; an equality that extends to everything."

The log cabin, along with the coonskin cap and Kentucky rifle, conjures up images of rugged pioneer days. Simple, one-room dwellings of logs, notched together at the corners, were introduced to America around 1638 by Swedish settlers in Delaware. Subsequently, German and Scotch-Irish immigrants, as well as Russian explorers along the western coast and in Alaska, introduced their own forms of log construction. During the great westward expansion that began in the late 1700s, the log cabin was practically ubiquitous in timber-rich frontier areas; it could be built with only the aid of an axe, and required no costly nails. Intended to serve merely as way stations in the wilderness, cabins rarely became permanent homes. When families desired better housing with more amenities, they either abandoned their cabins—often to be occupied by new transients—incorporated them into larger dwellings, converted them into storage facilities, or in the South, used them as slave quarters. The myth of the log cabin as the sacrosanct birthplace of leaders, renowned for their honesty, humility, and other virtues, was inaugurated during the presidential campaign of 1840, when William Henry Harrison was touted throughout the country as a hard-cider swigging bumpkin who lived in a log cabin. His landslide victory over Martin Van Buren set a precedent for future presidential aspirants, but only a few such as "Honest Abe" Lincoln had bona fide claims to their humble origins. In the present day, the log cabin appears on such memorabilia as coins and postage stamps, and it is also the brand name of a popular syrup. The cabin is perpetuated architecturally in resorts, camps, inns, and restaurants along byways and highways.

A double Cape Cod dwelling of the 1770s near Cohasset, Mass., is attached to part of an earlier Indian structure on the right end.

Beginning about 1670, on the stormy, windswept peninsula of Cape Cod, a local dwelling type developed that became a continuing feature of the landscape into the nineteenth century and beyond. Inhabitants of small fishing villages transformed the one-room-and-loft house of the Pilgrims into snug, ship-shape cottages. Generally facing south to catch the winter sun, and nestled against a hill for protection against the hostile elements, the structures rested on wooden sills without foundations in order to ride the shifting sands the same way that schooners rode the waves. If a site happened to blow away, the sturdy house could be trundled across the dunes, or even floated to a new location. A recognizable type by the late 1700s, the Cape Cod cottage persisted with minor variations through the first half of the 1800s. Newlyweds commonly erected a three-quarter house, intending to enlarge it with the arrival of children. Thrifty families occasionally built double houses in order to share an end wall. Some cottages sported bowed or gambrel roofs, and details that reflected the influences of the Federal and Greek Revival styles. The era of the authentic Cape Cod cottage ended around 1850 when the advent of the stove eliminated the massive chimney block that had previously anchored the house to its site. At that time, home builders also had to import precut lumber from Maine. Thoreau explained the reason, "The old houses . . . are built of the timber of the Cape, but instead of the forests in the midst of which they originally stood, barren heaths . . . now stretch away on every side."

The Peak House, built in the late 1600s at Medfield, Mass.

Constructed about 1720, this Cape Cod house at Wilmington, Mass., characteristically has an ell addition in back and a barn nearby.

A Cape Cod cottage with a gambrel roof at Duxbury, Mass., is believed originally to have belonged to Alexander Standish, Miles' son.

Were it ever so humble, the log cabin figured prominently in the winning of the West by serving as temporary shelter for the legions of hardy pioneer families who crossed the continent in the early decades of the nineteenth century. Its unique role in the nation's history was celebrated in local legend, as well as in the art and literature of the era. On a visit to America in the 1830s, Alexis de Tocqueville observed that Shakespeare's works could be found in many a wilderness hut, a dwelling he ennobled to the level of an "ark of civilisation lost in the middle of an ocean of leaves a sort of oasis in the desert." Not everyone, however, eulogized log cabin life. Charles Dickens viewed the log structures he had seen in Virginia as "squalid to the last degree." If indeed his disparaging remark referred to the run-down, vermin-infested hovels used as slave quarters, Dickens was a mite closer to reality than Harriet Beecher Stowe, who depicted Uncle Tom's cabin as a cozy little cottage bedecked with bignonias and multiflora roses, or than Stephen Foster, who waxed nostalgic over young folks rolling "on the little cabin floor, all merry, all happy, and bright." Such romanticization of the log cabin actually contributed to the making of the ninth president of the United States. William Henry Harrison, the lackluster Whig candidate of 1840, was caricatured as the product of a lowly log cabin. Although a plantation-born aristocrat whose cabin connections were remote—a one-room log dwelling had been the nucleus of his sixteen-room Ohio farmhouse—Harrison gained so much grassroots support that he did nothing to dispel the untruth. In fact, the nominee even exchanged his high silk hat for a broad-brimmed one and dressed in the plain fashion of his backwoods constituents. Songs, slogans, buttons, banners, and floats carrying miniature cabins completed the task of selling the homespun hero of Tippecanoe to the nation's voters.

A trapper, laden with pelts, returning from the forest to the warmth and security of his cabin, from an 1810 engraving

Above: an 1847 painting by Linton Park, depicting inhabitants of a log cabin community working at a flax-scutching bee

Right: a contemporary representation of a parade during the campaign of 1840, with a log cabin scene mounted on a wagon

4

Greeks, Goths, and Tuscans

When George Washington delivered his farewell message to the American people in 1796, he looked forward to that day when they would be strong enough as a nation to repel any threat to their peace and security from abroad. As he well knew, ever since the time of King William's War in the seventeenth century America had repeatedly been drawn into the major conflicts between European powers. Earlier in his life, he himself had fought with the English against the French in the American wilderness, and he had later fought beside the French against the English, each time because America was too weak to stand alone in protection of its own interests. Even as he spoke, Napoleon was on the rise and overseas new wars were brewing that once again would involve this country, in the War of 1812 this time. America's participation in that long struggle came to its bloody anticlimax in 1815 with Andrew Jackson's slaughter of the British troops at the Battle of New Orleans, two weeks after the Treaty of Ghent formally ended the war. When the United States next took up arms against a European nation it was because this country was strong and felt called upon to exercise its strength —and the wars were fought on foreign soil.

When news of the peace treaty reached America early in 1815 there was general rejoicing. Later that same year, following the defeat of Napoleon at Waterloo, the war-weary European nations laid down their arms and looked forward to an interim of peace on land and sea. For the first time in many years Americans could go about their business both at home and around the globe without interference from belligerents in any quarter. The War of 1812 has been called the second war for American independence, and it is true that with its conclusion the country faced the future with a new spirit of freedom and of confidence. That future opened in all directions. American ships, so long pent up by British blockades, thronged back on the seven seas of the world in greater numbers than ever; and they were larger, better, and faster ships. It was epic seafaring; the dream of adventure on salt water and in exotic places lured a new generation of youths from the farm to the forecastle. A fair number of them returned with a fortune made while life was still young, to build such handsome homes as would reflect their improved station in the world.

The lure of the land was as great for some as the lure of the sea was for others; there, too, the adventurous and the bold might look for new fortunes.

Opposite: doorway to the dining room at Lyndhurst, Tarrytown, N.Y., designed by A. J. Davis

Along roads leading to the West where the land seemed rich and inexhaustible the flow of vehicular traffic at times resembled a continuous parade. "Old America seems to be breaking up and moving westward," wrote one British traveler. "We are seldom out of sight, as we travel on this grand track [the Great Cumberland, or National, Road, completed as far as Wheeling, West Virginia, by 1818] towards the Ohio, of family groups, behind and before us. . . ." The Americans, he concluded, were "a migrating people" by nature. And as they moved on, they dotted the land with log cabins that, for the most part, marked their brief pauses on the way to finer and more permanent houses to be built still farther west. In places like Cincinnati, Chillicothe, Louisville, and elsewhere, mansions were already rising that vied with those in the older settled communities of the East.

Viewing that swelling exodus with alarm, Timothy Flint, a Harvard missionary, complained that the older sections of the country might soon be depopulated. "Our dwellings, our schoolhouses, and churches will have mouldered to ruins," he wailed, "our graveyards will be overrun with shrub oak; and but here and there a wretched hermit, true to his paternal soil, to tell the tale of other times." However, the end of the Napoleonic wars released a new flood of emigrants from abroad who added substantially to the population of the eastern cities and countryside alike. In addition, the war and the blockades had stimulated domestic manufactures to a new and rising level. Even Thomas Jefferson, ardent champion of an agrarian society, conceded that under the circumstances America must develop its own manufactures or Americans would go clad in skins. By the time peace arrived and great cargoes of long-delayed European goods were dumped on American markets, too much capital had been invested in native factories to abandon them. In 1816 a protective tariff passed Congress—surety that the nation was preparing for an industrial future. Partly because of the abundance of convenient water power new factories for the most part did not mass in existing cities but rather sought points along the swifter streams of the countryside. In these beginnings of the industrial revolution in America, there were no such grimy congested manufacturing centers as those of England; rather the American counterparts had an almost idyllic aspect. In Connecticut, wrote Tenche Coxe, the traveler's eye was "charmed with the view of delightful villages, suddenly rising as it were by magic, along the banks of some meandering rivulet; flourishing by . . . the protecting arms of manufactures." Such water-powered mills apparently initiated American mass production. The mills at Lowell, Massachusetts, according to a visiting English manufacturer, produced "a greater quantity of yarn and cloth from each spindle and loom (in a given time) than was produced by any other factories, . . . in the world."

The emergence of the factory as a new and special type of architecture had a decided and lasting influence on the development of American building in all its phases, home building along with the rest. A successful manufacturer demanded a much more efficient performance of his structure than a householder did of his. The colonial craftsman could and did perform his tasks in his own home or the equivalent. Mass production required greater facilities and more precise control of environmental factors. The Lowell

New England mill town, about 1830

enterprise, for example, for the first time brought all clothmaking processes within one mill. There was need for greater spans to cover such expanded operations, stronger floors to support heavier machinery, and this called for better building materials and techniques. For efficiency's sake, improved lighting and heating were necessary; greater fire resistance was demanded than in the ordinary home. All these conditions were met in time, and in further time were applied to the design and building of houses as well.

Thomas Jefferson lived on to witness changes in the American scene that he had not anticipated, although in some cases they were changes that had germinated in the light of his own genius and influence. His plans for an architectural school in this country, where professionals of sound knowledge and technical competence would be trained, were not realized until 1866, long after his death. However, men with such training, largely the products of European universities, were working in America during the latter part of Jefferson's lifetime. These were full-time architects who increasingly found commissions enough to keep them more or less profitably employed at their specialty; the long day of the gentleman-dilettante was past, or fast passing. In more senses than one Benjamin Henry Latrobe, who has already been mentioned, was an early, leading representative of this new breed. Latrobe held an engineering degree from a German university and had been apprenticed to a prominent English engineer (the engineer of the Eddystone Lighthouse) and then to an eminent English architect when he arrived in the United States in 1796. He was befriended by Jefferson, who understood and appreciated his qualifications, and he remained in America until his untimely death in 1820, rich in accomplishment.

Latrobe's major achievement, and one of the most ambitious building projects of the new nation, was the Philadelphia Water Works, completed in January, 1801. If cities were to grow and survive, an adequate supply of good water was an elementary and pressing necessity—for fire fighting, street cleaning, cooking, drinking, and even, for a progressive few of the population, for bathing. To provide such a service for Philadelphia Latrobe installed steam pumps by far the largest ever built in America to that date, to distribute water from the Schuylkill River through hollowed pine logs. The plan was fiercely criticized as being hopelessly visionary when it was projected. The night before the inauguration of his system, Latrobe himself—with a few close friends—nervously kindled the fires that would set his machines in motion, fearful that the boilers might burst as so often happened in such early engines. The next morning the city awoke to find clear water abundantly flowing from the new hydrants, and there was rejoicing.

To house his large and cumbersome machinery, Latrobe designed a pumping station of impeccable classical style. Thus, combining the functions of both a competent engineer and a sensitive architect, he provided an early, neat solution to a problem that would grow larger with time—how to accommodate the discipline of the new machines to the traditional disciplines of architecture. In more time to come engineering and architecture became distinct professions, but so long as the problems remained relatively simple ones man could master both, as Latrobe did.

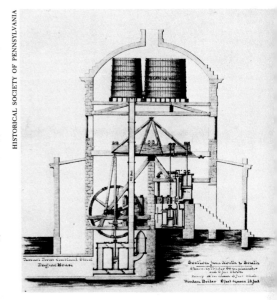

Top: steam pump designed by Latrobe
Above: Center Square water works

Top: portrait of Benjamin Latrobe
Above: the Bank of Pennsylvania

During the course of his somewhat abbreviated American career, Latrobe's accomplishments were more generally and more strictly architectural in character, and in this field he was without a peer until his death. Among his many other notable achievements he rebuilt the Capitol after the fire of 1814, as previously remarked. As early as 1798, shortly after his arrival in this country, he provided a new accent in American architecture with his design for the Bank of Pennsylvania in Philadelphia. This was the first structure in the New World to look to ancient Greece for its source of inspiration, and with this innovation he set in train a long series of developments that quite transformed the look of this country. In an address to a Philadelphia audience in 1811, he looked forward to a time when "the days of Greece may be revived in the woods of America." And so, in a sense, it came about, although he did not live to see the realization of his vision.

The Greek Revival style had an earlier history abroad, a history stimulated by the publication at London in 1762 of the first volume of Stuart and Revett's *Antiquities of Athens*. Latrobe himself was undoubtedly impressed by the beautiful plates of those books, reproducing the actual ruins that could then still be seen in Greece. But it was in America that the style sank its deepest roots and flourished in a distinctively native manner. In the generation following Latrobe's death the entire country, from Maine to the farther western outposts, sprouted with buildings of every description—city mansions and banks, farmhouses and wayside stores, state capitols and outhouses, prisons and saloons—that in one way or another borrowed their forms and ornament from the vocabulary of ancient Grecian architecture and decoration. The rapid spread of the Greek Revival style was spurred to a degree by a number of American publications providing illustrated instructions in the mastery of the new fashion. Indefatigably, Asher Benjamin revised his earlier books to keep abreast of the times. "Since my last publication," he wrote in 1830, "the Roman school of architecture has been entirely changed for the Grecian"; and he proceeded to advise his readers in the practical and ornamental nature of the style. Some part of the widespread popularity of that style stemmed from America's sympathy for the contemporary Greeks who in the 1820s were engaged in their war of independence from Turkish domination. Those were the years, also, of ascendant democracy in this country, leading to the election of Andrew Jackson as president in 1828, and Americans were eager to identify their own civic and political virtues with those of classical Greece. "*Greece was free,*" Latrobe had once remarked, adding that in Greece every citizen considered himself an important part of his little state. And thus every white American could be persuaded to consider himself, including the southern plantation owner in his porticoed mansion who saw the perfect democracy based on a system of slavery, as ancient Greek society had been.

In time the extraordinary popularity of the Greek Revival style waned and other fashions found high places in public favor. When Samuel F. Smith wrote "My Country, 'Tis of Thee" in 1832, he referred to America's "templed hills" that were then so characteristic of the native landscape—hills dotted with generally temple-like buildings of wood or brick painted "the whitest of white," as Dickens observed, to suggest the gleaming marble of ancient

Greek originals. However, the very next year James Fenimore Cooper, returning from Europe, complained of the "mushroom temples" that lined the banks of the Hudson River and marred the landscape with their whiteness. Not long after, in 1846, Andrew Jackson Downing, America's leading landscape architect and one of its most discerning critics, exulted that "The Greek temple disease has passed its crisis. The people have survived it."

Downing agreed with Cooper that white was a "vulgar" color for a house. Rather, he urged the readers of his books and the clients he served, the natural colors of stone, grass, and moss—colors that would blend harmoniously with the landscape—should be used. He passionately believed "above all things under heaven, in the power and virtue of the individual home," truly built and rightly placed in its proper setting, to preserve and support the dignity of man. A good house—"a fitting, tasteful, and significant dwelling"— was, he wrote, a "powerful means of civilization," and he felt it was his mission to guide his fellow Americans in this right direction. Downing's influence was enormous. The last book he lived to see published, *The Architecture of Country Houses*, which first appeared in 1850, went through nine printings within a relatively short time. This along with his other books on horticulture, landscape architecture, and architectural and furniture design won him an international reputation. In appreciation of his writings the Queen of Denmark sent him a "magnificent ring." When the popular Swedish spinster author Frederika Bremer arrived in New York in 1849 to observe this growing world across the seas, Downing was among the first to greet her. That perceptive lady was deeply impressed by his "noble and acutely discriminating mind" and, she wrote her sister, by his "dark eyes and dark hair, of a beautiful brown, and softly curling...quite a poetical appearance!"

It was a romantic age and both in his appearance and his talents Downing was ideally cast in his role as arbiter and promulgator of the advanced tastes of his day. His own preference in architecture was for the Gothic Revival style. "Those who love shadow, and the sentiment of antiquity and repose," he claimed, "will find most pleasure in the quiet tone which prevails in the Gothic style." From his Gothic cottage on the shores of the Hudson River he issued such preachments as this in its favor, and they were taken up and repeated by a host of other writers on domestic architecture—as he in turn had borrowed from others. Like the classical revivals, the Gothic Revival had much earlier antecedents in England. There, indeed, a "Gothic" strain in architecture, decoration, and furniture had lingered through the centuries since the Middle Ages. And there as well medieval survivals and medieval ruins were constant reminders of a distant past that continued to stir the imagination and breed nostalgia. The full tide of the revival there in the nineteenth century coincided with the restoration in France of such hallowed monuments as Sainte-Chapelle and Notre Dame, as well as of the walled city of Carcassonne and other historic structures. In both countries the Gothic style took on national patriotic overtones. When Westminster Abbey and the House of Parliament, the most important nineteenth-century building to be constructed in the British Empire, were rebuilt in that style the revival had its ultimate realization.

DOWNING, A. J., THE ARCHITECTURE OF COUNTRY HOUSES, 1850

A design for a "bracketed cottage"

The American scene had no such reminders of an ancient past, a point that concerned Nathaniel Hawthorne in writing his novels. "No author, without a trial," he wrote, "can conceive of the difficulty of writing a romance about a country where there is no shadow, no antiquity, no mystery, no picturesque and gloomy wrong, nor anything but a commonplace prosperity, in broad and simple daylight, as is happily the case with my dear native land." Sir Walter Scott's medieval romances, and his other tales, were at the time a raging fashion among the reading public of America as well as of England, and elsewhere. More than one reverent American made a pilgrimage to the great man's home, Abbotsford, near Melrose on the Tweed. Audubon took his drawings of American birds to show to Scott, hoping for words of high praise that were not forthcoming. Washington Irving, on a happier visit, spent four memorable days with Scott, walking and talking with the older man.

Years before, in a letter to Thomas Jefferson, Latrobe had written that his "principles of good taste are rigid in Grecian architecture." Yet it was this "bigoted Greek," as Latrobe called himself, who in 1799 designed the first Gothic Revival house in America—a countryseat for the Philadelphia merchant William Crammond. Jefferson himself had toyed with the thought of having a little Gothic "folly" for his family graveyard at Monticello. However, it was not until Downing's day, helped by his influence, that the vogue became firmly established. By the middle of the nineteenth century the style was endemic in America. "The ambition of almost every person in the country," Downing wrote in 1850, was to build and live in a Gothic cottage. Before his tragic and untimely death in a steamboat explosion in 1852, the American landscape from Maine to the Blue Grass and beyond did, in fact, abound with structures of many varied designs that by a stretch of imagination could be associated with the spirit of the Middle Ages.

In America as in England the Gothic style and its revival in various forms was associated with honesty, morality, and religion. It was, wrote one contemporary critic, "the architecture of Christianity, the sublime, the glorious Gothic." A number of the most ambitious and successful realizations of the style were such ecclesiastical structures which bore some apparent relation to medieval prototypes (the Manhattan diarist George Templeton Strong thought, nonetheless, that the use of "cheap ornamentation in iron" would "surely rock [St. Patrick's] to pieces by expansion and contraction of its incongruous materials"). Although the cottages and "castles" that were built in the style also were vaguely associated with Christian virtues, few of them showed any respect for historical accuracy or archaeological nicety. It was enough for most builders and homeowners that an indistinct but mysteriously romantic past could be recalled by such structural and ornamental elements as crockets and cusps, towers, turrets, and trellises, pointed arches and oriel windows. It was in much that spirit that Idlewild, the countryseat of the author and editor Nathaniel P. Willis, was planned for just such a site "as a medieval knight would have selected for his stronghold...a little imagination may easily transmute the simple domestic cottage into the turreted and battlemented castle." It hardly needs mention that a confection of that description would have utterly bewildered people of the Middle Ages.

MUSEUM OF THE CITY OF NEW YORK

St. Patrick's Cathedral in New York

The romantic nostalgia that bred and sustained the Gothic Revival went ever farther afield for its satisfactions. Whatever was remote in time or space appealed to the sensibilities of a generation that was beginning to face the unsettling realities of the industrial revolution. "It was no accident," wrote Lewis Mumford in *Sticks and Stones*, "that caused romanticism and industrialism to appear at the same time. They were rather the two faces of the new civilization, one looking towards the past, and the other towards the future; one glorifying the new, the other clinging to the old; industrialism intent on increasing the physical means of subsistence, romanticism living in a sickly fashion on the hollow glamour of the past."

Downing's own books, along with his recommendations for houses in the Gothic style, included designs and commentaries on a wide variety of other possibilities. In preparing those publications he had the collaboration of Alexander Jackson Davis as illustrator and occasional mentor. Davis, twelve years older than Downing, was probably the most prominent, influential, and prolific architect of the time. His versatile genius led him to design houses and other buildings in virtually all the popular contemporary modes. "With the passion for novelty," as his friend Downing observed, "and the feeling of independence that belong to this country, our people seem determined to *try everything*"—and Davis was prepared and equipped to serve every variety of client. At one point in his diary Davis recorded that he had planned structures in fourteen different styles, including ancient Etruscan, Greek, Lombard Italian, Oriental, and still others.

No style was too bizarre or too exotic to be denied a place in the American landscape of the 1830s and 1840s. In 1831 an impressive gate in the Egyptian manner was raised at the entrance to Mount Auburn Cemetery at Cambridge, Massachusetts—to be followed by analogous constructions in other cemeteries. There were those who objected to such pagan symbols before Christian graveyards, but the practice was rationalized quickly enough by those eager to plunder the distant past for forms rich in occult associations. Critics more easily agreed that the style was appropriate for prisons, such as The Tombs in New York City, which should be "pleasing and at the same time imposing, not gloomy and terrific" as Gothic buildings tended to seem. And along the Mississippi River, "the American Nile" as it was sometimes called, towns were given such names as Cairo, Karnak, Thebes, and Memphis.

The arts of every age have been more or less derivative, especially since the Renaissance. But the nineteenth century was finding wider opportunities than any earlier period to gather evidence from other cultures and other times. As archaeological adventures became increasingly far-reaching, travel and trade about the globe more extensive, and printed reports and reproductions of other places more abundant, an ever greater vocabulary of design was available for architects to draw upon. That they often did so with limited understanding or unbridled imagination is clearly evident.

Yet along with what appears to us to be the stylistic anarchy of those decades of American building went some more positive contributions. The rigid formalism of the classical styles was abandoned, and that had a healthy, liberating effect on the planning of houses. Books like Downing's placed

Design for Egyptian-style gateway

WAYNE ANDREWS

a new emphasis on the outdoors and that too was wholesome. Fresh attention was also paid to proper heating, ventilation, and other aspects of domestic mechanics, whatever the style of the structure. Occasionally such experimentation led to eccentric solutions to traditional problems of homemaking; as in the case of Orson S. Fowler, the author of *A Home For All*, who advocated the octagonal house as an architectural panacea. Fowler was a phrenologist and socialist of sorts as well as a home counselor, and he claimed his designs would eliminate the ill-lighted corners in a house, save steps between rooms, and improve the space economy of the furnace. The triangular areas that resulted from his plan could efficiently be used for closets and water tanks. The octagon house would be a cheap, efficient dwelling for "the people."

Amid the extravagance of novelties that were raised about the countryside, the various Shaker communities stood out in quiet protest to the follies of excess and pretension. Those frugal, industrious, and celibate people eschewed every non-essential element in the principle and practice of building, reduced their architecture—and everything else they contrived—to fundamental values, and worked their skills with such conscientious care that in our machine-tooled world their houses and their artifacts remain models of functional efficiency—stark, but clean lined and flawless. Their frame dwellings, wrote Miss Harriet Martineau, were the finest she had seen in America, "finished with the last degree of nicety, even to the springs of the windows and the hinges of the doors." Whereas much of the "elegant" embellishments of mid-nineteenth-century structures today seem quaint, if not meretricious in spite of the highly principled claims of their builders, the Shaker accomplishment served as a model in its way for designers of a later day. In the mid-1920s when America explored its past in search of a viable tradition that would accord with the newly developed aesthetics of that period, stemming from the Bauhaus in part, that Shaker accomplishment was recognized as the purest American statement in the spirit of modern design.

A group of Shakers dancing to "trample sin underfoot" at a meeting held in New York, 1873

Old Wine in New Bottles

Some Grecian Modes

In the years between its first florescence in Benjamin Latrobe's 1798 design for the Bank of Pennsylvania, and its farewell appearance eighty years later in the Crystal Palace Saloon at Tombstone, Arizona, the Greek Revival dominated American architecture to an extent unparalleled by any style, before or since. Americans everywhere not only saw in the chaste symmetry of the Grecian temple the embodiment of their cultural ambitions, but related the temple's rectangular form to their own architectural traditions. A simple addition of a Greek portico to the pitched-roof houses that dotted the American landscape was generally all that was needed to imbue the structure with new meaning.

The buildings of the best architects of the period rarely reflected archaeological exactitude. To these designers, classical Greece served as an inspiration that allowed enormous variety in personal expression, and could be modified to suit the needs, native materials, and tastes of the American people. The illustrations on the following pages indicate that it was the very adaptability of the temple form, whether in the monumental authority of a public building, the tight geometry of a northern manufacturer's Doric domicile, or the open, diffused grandeur of a southern plantation house, that gave the Greek Revival its extraordinary diversity and strength. As Thomas U. Walter, the Philadelphia architect whose achievements included the colossal colonnade on Nicholas Biddle's farmhouse at Andalusia, and the cast-iron dome of the nation's Capitol, pointed out,

Design for a Grecian ornament

LAFEVER, THE MODERN BUILDER'S GUIDE, 1833

"The popular idea that to design a building in Grecian taste is nothing more than to copy a Grecian building is altogether erroneous;—even the Greeks themselves never made two buildings alike. . . . If architects would oftener *think* as the Greeks thought, than to *do* as the Greeks did, our columnar architecture . . . and its character and expression would gradually conform to the local circumstances of the country and the republican spirit of its institutions."

By the 1840s, however, people were beginning to question the validity of Grecian forms for modern purposes. "We compose better copies of Grecian temples and other structures than our ancestors; but do these copies satisfy the real wants of the present age, or correspond with the general advancement of art?" wrote one contemporary. Diatribes against the Greek Revival came from such distant sources as the London *Builder*: "The Americans seem to be affected with an absolute mania for Greek temples. . . . Public and private buildings are all dressed up and disguised in that uniform, and the greater part in a bungling manner." And, on the eve of the Civil War, Walt Whitman decried the inappropriateness of the temple form on Wall Street. Archaeology had by this time opened a Pandora's box of knowledge about historical epochs other than the Greek. Egyptian, Gothic, and Renaissance styles of architecture provided a long-sought escape from the enclosed box of the Grecian temple, and could express the internal needs of a house in ways which the simple rectangular shape could not admit.

Above: colonnaded portico of Nicholas Biddle's Andalusia, added by Thomas Walter in 1836
Left: Hiram Powers' "Greek Slave," modeled upon a girl in chains in a Turkish slave market

The "alabaster cities" immortalized in Katharine Lee Bates' "America the Beautiful" doubtless included Philadelphia, the nation's first metropolis to don the mantle of the Greek Revival. In the early 1800s this rapidly growing town, whose very name is Greek, attracted architects—beginning with Latrobe—who erected public and private buildings in the new fashion. Even the municipal water works on the banks of the Schuylkill were housed in Grecian temples, based on designs by Robert Mills. Popular enthusiasm for antiquity was generated in part by Nicholas Biddle, Philadelphia's social, cultural, and financial leader, who had traveled to Greece in 1806, and had become so enamored of its ancient structures that he confided in his diary, "The two great truths in the world are the Bible and Grecian architecture." Biddle subsequently promoted Grecian forms as models for an American architecture, and at his estate of Andalusia had a colossal Doric portico appended to the Delaware River side of his eighteenth-century farmhouse. During the 1830s and 1840s, the Greek Revival style spread to other cities, where it was adapted to the conditions peculiar to each. In a typically narrow New York dwelling, for example, the front and back parlors on the main floor were commonly separated by folding mahogany doors flanked on either side by Ionic columns, thus permitting the rooms to be used together *en suite* for large-scale entertaining. The furniture and fine arts of the period also reflected Grecian inspiration. Unveiled in 1847, Hiram Powers' statue of a Greek slave became a smashing success as far west as Cincinnati. Victorian prudery notwithstanding, the nude nymphet drew praise even from such pillars of society as the clergyman who observed, it was "clothed all over with sentiment, sheltered, protected by it, from every profane eye."

Above: Greek Revival interior with "double parlor" in New York, in a drawing by Alexander Jackson Davis

Left: Nicholas Biddle, Philadelphia banker, dilettante, traveler, and ambassador, in a portrait by Thomas Sully

181

Constructed between 1811 and 1819, the stately Greek Revival structures along the Schuylkill River house Philadelphia's water system.

Erected a century later, the Philadelphia Art Museum above the water works is the world's largest edifice in the Greek temple style.

Oak Alley, built from 1832 to 1836 for Jacques Roman III, a wealthy Creole planter

'Way down upon the Mississippi, in the cotton kingdom, a colorful and gracious society flourished briefly and brilliantly during the ante-bellum era. Frock-coated planters and hoop-skirted belles entertained in stately splendor at their pillared plantation houses, which were Greek Revival in feeling, yet made allowances for the local Creole culture, the hot humid climate, and such available building materials as cypress wood and brick. Romantically situated at the end of an avenue of giant oaks, Oak Alley, with its square mass, encircling columns, and wide, shaded galleries, typifies the architecture that arose along the Louisiana levees in the 1830s. In mid-century Natchez, Mississippi, a town grown rich from a fortuitous combination of cotton and steamboat commerce, wealthy citizens like Frederick Stanton, whose mansion contained a seventy-two-foot ballroom, spared no expense in furnishing their high-ceilinged, airy interiors. The Civil War put an abrupt end to the balls, soirees, and pretensions of a would-be aristocracy. Among the plantation houses seized and occupied by invading Union troops was The Shadows on the Bayou Teche. According to an eyewitness, its elderly mistress, "a lady . . . accustomed not only to the conveniences, but the elegancies of life, was driven . . . to the upstairs apartments where . . . she died—imprisoned in her own dwelling, deprived of the comforts she would have bestowed upon the humblest of her servants."

Reflecting mirrors in the lavishly fitted double salon of Stanton Hall in Natchez enhance its sense of spaciousness.
Begun in 1830 at New Iberia, La., The Shadows on the Bayou Teche is depicted in an 1861 water color by Adrian Persac.

Although Minard Lafever ran an architectural drafting office in New York during the building spurt that followed the opening of the Erie Canal in 1825, his influence extended far beyond Manhattan. Of all the builders' guides that conveyed the gospel of the Greek Revival to Middle America, Lafever's were pre-eminent. In his handbooks, Grecian ornament—volutes, rosettes, frets, bands, and moldings—was freely applied in fresh and personal ways. Much of the crisp, imaginative wood and plaster trim in houses of the period from up-state New York and as far west as Michigan and Kentucky stems directly from Lafever's plates. His first book, *The Young Builder's General Instructor*, of 1829, contained such illustrations as the plan and elevation of a four-story town house. Here, in an inventive but crude way, Lafever tried to improve upon the prevalent New York house type that had developed with the standardization of the twenty-five- by one-hundred-foot building lot. Instead of placing the front door at the side, as was customary, Lafever curved his stair-hall to meet a central door, and thus gave the parlor a somewhat awkward shape. Within four years, Lafever's maturing taste led him to replace his first book with *The Modern Builder's Guide*. The new manual projected a complete set of plans, including a section of an elegant stairway for a "Country Residence." This temple-type structure, with its Ionic portico, and side wings, was widely reproduced throughout the country. Ironically, Lafever personally designed only one edifice in the Greek Revival style—the Reformed Dutch Church in Brooklyn. His subsequent experiments were in the Gothic, Renaissance, and eclectic modes. A new point of view is implicit in Lafever's last book, written in 1856: "The inquiry is often made, what architecture must a nation, situated as ours is, adopt? It has no indigenous architecture; it is not, therefore, a matter of religion with us, but a matter of taste . . . we are not by the force of circumstance or example, bound to build in this or that particular way, but all ways are before us to choose."

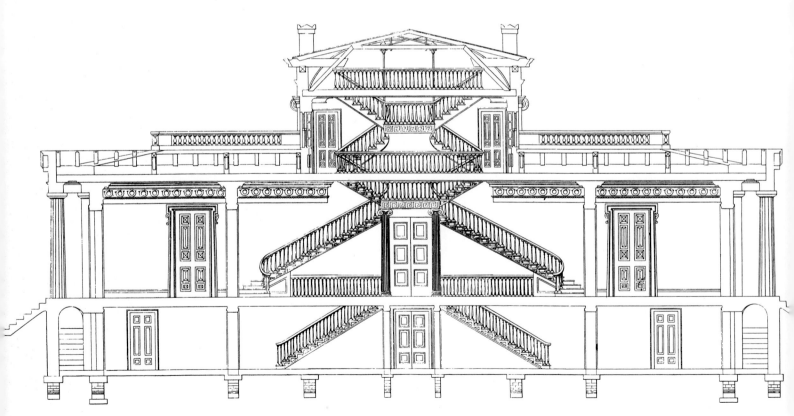

LAFEVER, MINARD, *THE MODERN BUILDER'S GUIDE*, 1833. AVERY LIBRARY, COLUMBIA UNIVERSITY

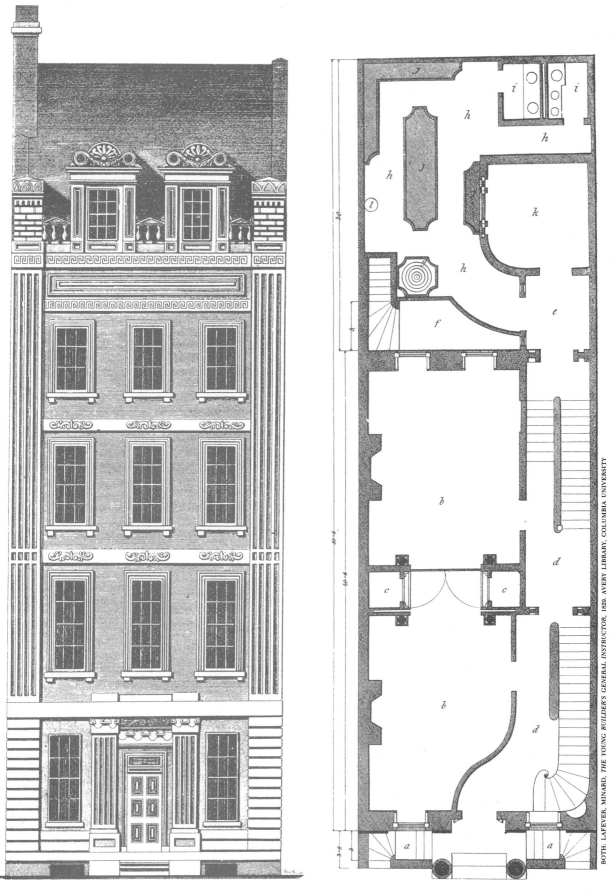

Above: the elevation and plan for a town house with Grecian decoration, in The Young Builder's General Instructor
Opposite: a longitudinal section of the central hall and stairwell of a country residence in The Modern Builder's Guide

During the 1830s, when Alexander Jackson Davis was designing Gothic and Tuscan villas alongside Grecian temples for his proposed development of Ravenswood, at Astoria, Long Island, the Greek Revival was just reaching remote, newly settled parts of the nation. On a provincial level, hundreds of classically inspired residences arose, which were as varied as the numerous regions, towns, and individual builders who brought them into being. In western New York State, Grecian forms underwent bold and imaginative modifications, as seen in the diminutive Tousley House at Albion, with its low-pitched roof, horizontal lines, and low frieze windows embellished with Greek fret grilles of cast iron. Overlooking the Champlain Valley, the more monumental Wilcox-Cutts House of Orwell, Vermont, seems to be a traditional temple-type dwelling with wings. Yet, although its Ionic components were faithfully copied by a local carpenter from the books at hand, its relatively steeply pitched roof was more likely a concession to Vermont snows than antique prototypes.

Erected in 1844, the Tousley House gives the Greek Revival style a fresh, vivid interpretation.

Despite its imposing formality, the Wilcox-Cutts House of 1843, in detail, reveals the unsophisticated work of a rural carpenter.
A. J. Davis' view of Ravenswood, projected in 1836 along the East River water front, indicates his wide range of domestic designs.

At a time when Society, in the North at least, centered primarily in cities, the Greek Revival town house provided a dignified and fitting framework for the genteel gatherings and formal entertainments that took place with ever increasing frequency. Stylish homes in the nation's metropolises contained drawing rooms with ceilings eleven to fourteen feet high, large expanses of window, broad wall surfaces, and concentrated ornament, generally confined to the mantelpiece, moldings, cornice, and doorways. The overall effect of austere simplicity conveyed by the interior architecture was mitigated by such rich accents as thick carpets in classical patterns, long silk draperies with tassled and fringed lambrequins, and sparse though elegant furnishings in the American Empire style of Duncan Phyfe and his contemporaries. A New York cabinet-maker par excellence, Phyfe would charge his affluent clients the then sizeable sum of one thousand dollars to outfit a drawing room with delicate mahogany pieces. The convivial and ubiquitous stag dinner notwithstanding, receptions like the one held at the Broadway mansion of Dr. John C. Cheesman, illustrated below, were apt to be decorous, if not dull, affairs, peopled by strait-laced women in narrow-waisted dresses with leg-of-mutton sleeves and abbreviated bodices displaying that portion of the anatomy euphemistically referred to as the "neck," and by men in frock coats and tight-legged trousers. A mid-afternoon dinner party in such fashionable establishments was customarily followed by music and polite conversation. However, as that inimitable critic of American manners, Mrs. Anthony Trollope, caustically observed, such rigid rules of decorum prevailed that "whatever may be the talents of the persons who meet together in society, the very shape, form, and arrangement of the meeting is sufficient to paralyze conversation. The women invariably herd together at one part of the room and the men at the other. . . . The gentlemen spit. . . . The ladies look at each other's dresses till they know every pin by heart."

A reception at the fashionable New York home of Dr. J. C. Cheesman, depicted in 1840

Crockets, Cusps, and Gables

Gothic Romanticism

By the middle of the nineteenth century the long vogue of classical forms in architecture and in the decorative arts had passed its climax. Over more than a century and a half it had gone through various phases; first the Palladian styles of the later colonial period, then the more delicate and refined stage that owed much of its character to the books and models of Robert Adam, and finally a culmination in the immensely popular fashion of the Greek Revival. Now, different styles of nonclassical inspiration were competing for favor. In 1854 Benjamin Silliman, Jr., the eminent Yale professor, reviewing the American scene of the generation just past, referred critically to "ponderous and frigid monstrosities" of the classical style. "The solemn affectation of Greek and Roman forms was so ridiculous," he remarked, "that only the inherent vitality and grand simplicity of the classic motives [*sic*] enabled them to survive 'the deep damnation of this *taking off.*'" What Silliman was really saying was that tastes were changing as they periodically do.

The classical style had endured longer than any other styles that were to follow. Its declining authority opened the way for experimentation with a variety of other, shorter-lived historical revivals. During several decades around mid-century the Gothic Revival won wide, popular acceptance, with enthusiastic endorsement by leading architects and critics of the day. It was a style that encouraged inventiveness and led all too easily toward such architectural caprices as may still be seen about the countryside.

Roof detail of a Gothic pump

SLOAN, S., HOMESTEAD ARCHITECTURE, 1861

In 1850 Andrew Jackson Downing, who played such a prominent role in popularizing the style, warned his readers against excesses of decoration and whimsy. He had small use for what he called the many-gabled "cocked-hat cottage," and he deplored that "frippery or 'gingerbread' look which degrades, rather than elevates," the beauty of a structure.

By the same token, however, in its free interpretations and imaginative renderings the style did result in a wider variety of accommodations than those suggested by classical formulas.

The balanced order and formal restraint that had given the classical style its essential character were completely rejected in the Gothic Revival, and were replaced by asymmetrical designs and picturesque arrangements of almost endless variety. Obviously, in their studied irregularities and their ornamental "Gothicisms," houses built in this style were a far cry from those seventeenth-century structures in America, discussed in the first chapter, which were true survivals of a medieval tradition of building and of housing. The utter remoteness of the idealized image from drab historical realities, which were so conveniently obscured by the mists of time, was a positive asset. In architecture as in the literature of the period, the medieval world that was reconstructed was a more or less poetic creation, mysterious but fresh. At their best, Gothic Revival buildings in America were charming yet quite practical innovations, their picturesque romanticisms happily combined with sensible and careful planning.

A view of Lyndhurst, near Tarrytown, N.Y., with additions made in 1864–66, as it appears today

Front view of Lyndhurst. Jay Gould bought the house from Merritt's widow in 1880 and kept it intact.

Davis' drawing of the original structure he designed as a summer retreat for Paulding

With the passage of time and changes of taste most of the finest buildings designed in the Gothic Revival style have long since disappeared — except for the churches which by their special nature and function have more often been spared. One of the best and most impressive dwellings that have survived, Lyndhurst, stands on a magnificently landscaped slope overlooking the Hudson River near Tarrytown, New York. Lyndhurst was originally planned in 1838 by Alexander Jackson Davis as a summer "villa" for General William Paulding and his son, Philip. Paulding was a wealthy lawyer who married an heiress of the Rhinelander family who was richer than he was. In 1841, as the house was still rising, Philip Hone, the witty and urbane one-time mayor of New York (and an old political rival of Paulding) observed the scene and noted his impression in his diary. "In the course of our drive we went to see Mr. Paulding's magnificent house, yet unfinished, on the bank below Tarrytown. It is an immense edifice of white or gray marble, resembling a baronial castle, or rather a Gothic monastery, with towers, turrets, and trellises; minarets, mosaics, and mouse-holes; archways, armories, and air-holes; peaked windows and pinnacled roofs, and many other fantastics too tedious to enumerate, the whole constituting an edifice of gigantic size, with no room in it; . . . which, if I mistake not, will one of these days be designated as 'Paulding's folly'. . . ." However, Paulding faithfully relied upon Davis' judgment while the building was growing, and there were others who shared his confidence in the architect. A. J. Downing had already written Davis that on a visit to Tarrytown he saw the progress of Paulding's mansion and was "exceedingly pleased" with it. "I think it does you great credit —," he continued, "indeed I have never seen anything to equal it, as I conceive it will be when finished." In 1864–66 the second owner of the property, George Merritt, employed Davis' services in the same spirit, when he commissioned the architect to add a new wing to the original structure, also in the Gothic Revival style. (It was Merritt who named the place Lyndhurst.) Later in the century Jay Gould, one of the greatest of American "robber barons," purchased the house and, with similar respect for Davis' creation, made no significant alteration in its style or structure, although furnishings of various later styles were introduced.

Above: the library at Lyndhurst, converted into an art gallery by George Merritt
Opposite: view of a gable with crocket from one of the tower windows at Lyndhurst

Paulding's trust in Davis, and the relationship between the two men, is indicated by letters that passed from one to the other. In 1841, as Lyndhurst was being built, Paulding wrote the architect: "Make designs for all the windows of the library. . . . Rich colors will tell well in the small window above the big one. . . . Here expense may be excused. The big window must be a nonpareil. . . . I leave this entirely to your taste." At another point Paulding asked Davis to look over some mantels he had designed before they were delivered for installation. "If you see anything offensive. . .," he wrote, "put your veto on it. They are extremely elegant and I wish them to be correct examples of the style. How the ladies will *dote* on them." When George Merritt enlarged the building he converted the library into an art gallery to house his collection of paintings, although he kept the interior architecture intact. Davis also designed furniture for Paulding and had it made to his specifications by his cabinetmaker Richard H. Byrnes. The two chairs silhouetted against the windows in the accompanying illustration (the windows mentioned in Paulding's letter quoted above) are part of the original furnishings of the library as it was planned by Davis. In 1965 Lyndhurst was bequeathed to the National Trust for Historic Preservation by Jay Gould's youngest daughter, Anna, Duchess of Talleyrand-Perigord.

To the romantic imagination the prospect of a Gothic ruin was enough to arouse "sublime" meditation. As early as the eighteenth century in England, where none existed such "ruins" were sometimes carefully constructed to catch the eye and stir the mind to sentimental reveries. In the next century they were copied or recreated on canvas by artists in various countries, including America. Such scenes and other more purely decorative Gothic motifs were used in abundant variety and for all manner of purposes within mid-century homes—in the design of furniture and furnishings, to embellish windows and window screens, as well as to add interest to interior architecture. Very few of those forms—cast-iron stoves, whatnots, bookcases, and so on—were known to the Middle Ages and had to be created from imagination and with ingenuity to accommodate the needs and desires of a generation becoming increasingly concerned with the comforts and conveniences of life.

Above: a couple reading in the presence of the ruins of a Gothic castle
Left: a 19th-century cast-iron, base-burning stove with Gothic decoration

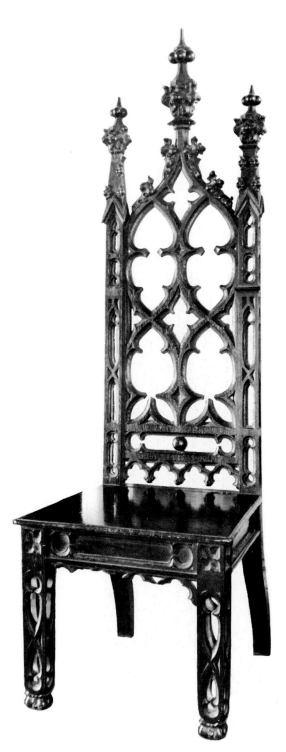

Above: a painted window with representations of Gothic buildings
Right: detail of a side chair carved with various Gothic motifs

Top: a "Gothic" park guard shelter in Fairmount Park, Philadelphia, with pointed-arch door and windows and quatrefoil ornament
Above: the frame Gothic Revival cottage at Strafford, Vt., built for Senator Justin Morrill in 1848–51 from his own designs

In 1845 Davis designed the "Pointed Cottage," happily still standing in New Bedford, Massachusetts, for William J. Rotch, a wealthy mill owner. Building in that city, it was explained, was more expensive than in New York, and Rotch's house cost him about six thousand dollars. "The character expressed by. . .this design," wrote A. J. Downing, "is that of a man or family of domestic tastes, but with strong aspirations after something higher than social pleasures." A few years later Senator Justin Morrill designed and had built in Strafford, Vermont, his own version of a Gothic cottage. (Morrill was the author of the famous Land-Grant College Bill enacted into law during Lincoln's presidency.) The unusual battlemented entrance porch was enclosed to provide cupboards on either side of a window to accommodate Morrill's huge hand-painted dinner service; the painted designs related to the particular kinds of food for which the plates were used. As Downing related in his book, already discussed, the Gothic Revival style was epidemic in America by the mid-nineteenth century, and was used for every conceivable type of structure from university buildings to garden houses, from churches and penitentiaries to park shelters, and from railroad stations to clubhouses. The whimsical little clubhouse shown at right, now removed to Mystic, Connecticut, was formerly used by the New York Yacht Club at Hoboken, New Jersey, for its celebrated turtle dinners. Its sloping eaves are trimmed with pendants.

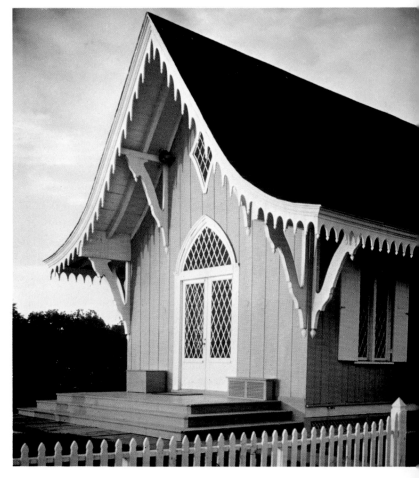

Top: the "Pointed Cottage" designed by Davis for William Rotch
Above: bracketed clubhouse formerly used by the N. Y. Yacht Club

Alexander Jackson Davis

Alexander J. Davis in an 1852 portrait

From the 1820s until the Civil War, Alexander Jackson Davis led the revivalist movement in American architecture, establishing the Greek, Gothic, and Tuscan styles on a national basis, and ending, once and for all, the "little England look" that had characterized our towns and cities since the seventeenth century. The architect, who at the end of his long career claimed to have designed more buildings than any of his contemporaries, conducted most of his revivalist experiments in and around his native New York, a city that in 1825 was already the commercial center of the young republic, and one that was about to embark upon an era of unprecedented prosperity and expansion. Here, with Ithiel Town, he founded this country's first architectural firm of any duration and influence, and laid the foundations for a national organization to regulate the conduct of the profession — in 1857 this body materialized as the American Institute of Architects.

Davis was born in 1803 to middle-class parents whose forebears had figured prominently in the settlement of New York and Connecticut. Although Cornelius Davis, theologian and publisher, provided his son with a classical education hoping that he would pursue an intellectual career, his prayers went unheeded: at an early age, Alexander revealed a considerable aptitude for drawing, either from life or from the imagination. After leaving school at the age of sixteen, he ventured to Alexandria, Virginia, where he worked as a typesetter for his older brother, Samuel, who published a weekly newspaper. There, Alexander also created costumes and sets for local amateur theatricals. One design for a proscenium with Egyptian columns was prophetic of Davis' 1835 excursion into the realms of ancient Egypt, when he projected a Hall of Detention and Justice (The Tombs) for New York, which was to be modeled upon the temples of Karnak and Philae, and appropriately adorned with massive ball and chain motifs, keys, and whips. From the midst of this fantasy world of the stage, Davis wrote his Aunt Hetty in Florida, New York, "I do not intend to trouble myself much about what business to follow as a livelihood; but jog along . . . without cares and at my ease. It's the best way!!!"

Upon returning to New York at the age of twenty, Davis was abruptly confronted with the reality of earning a living, and decided to become an artist. However, Colonel John Trumbull and Rembrandt Peale, both prominent painters, persuaded the youth that architecture might be a more rewarding vocation for the times just ahead. Although Davis exchanged his palette for a drawing board, he always referred to himself as an "architectural composer," implying that he was as much a painter as a draftsman. Trumbull not only taught Davis the rudiments of perspective, but he introduced him to New York's leading artistic and literary figures — James Fenimore Cooper, Washington Irving, William Cullen Bryant, and Samuel F. B. Morse — and secured his membership in the exclusive Antique School, where Davis learned to draw from plaster casts. The budding architect concurrently mastered the art of lithography, and began recording on stone New York's public buildings and streets for a local guidebook. These vignettes, as well as later lithographs, etchings, book illustrations, and architectural delineations, were meticulously rendered in painstaking detail, and accomplished for architecture what Currier and Ives accomplished for American folkways before the camera became a commonplace. While working for Josiah Brady, a contractor-architect, in 1826, Davis learned the practical side of his craft, preparing elevations and floor plans, writing specifications, judging materials, and estimating labor. The next year, Davis and one James Eddy hung their shingle on Wall Street and opened a drafting office that catered to the city's increasing horde of speculative builders.

Having become acquainted with Ithiel Town, a renowned architect, bibliophile, engineer, and inventor of the Town Lattice Truss, a patented device that greatly increased the span of wooden bridges, Davis decided to collaborate in the partnership that was literally to lift the face of America. On February 1, 1829, Davis wrote: "Since Town . . . is so pleased with my drawings in perspective . . . he kindly proposes an Association to practice Architecture professionally in New York, opening an office at 32 Merchants Exchange [on Wall Street] for the transaction of business." Town subsequently moved four thousand volumes on architecture and engineering from his prodigious home library in New

Haven to these offices, and the architects began to gather about them young apprentices from different parts of the nation, who formed something of a school. Soon, the firm accumulated honors and distinctions, and was flooded with commissions for civic, commercial, academic, and domestic structures. Although Ithiel Town's purist tastes, and especially his preference for the Greek Revival, dominated the firm as long as he lived, the junior partner was not totally eclipsed. His invention, duly called the Daviséan window, of a vertical shaft of casements in two or more stories, spaced at intervals to suggest an order, became the hallmark of the firm's products.

Among the architectural "firsts" Davis claimed for the firm in his diary were the "FIRST Greek Temple buildings, public or private," in the country. The state capitols of Indiana, Illinois, North Carolina, and Ohio were patterned after the Parthenon, which served as the prototype for similar legislative piles from Connecticut to California. Realizing the architectural potential of metal, Town and Davis designed the "FIRST iron shop front in New York" for the Athenaeum of Natural History, a truly advanced form of expression for 1835. The firm was also the first to take a serious approach to urban problems in New York, and created several blocks of multiple dwellings with uniform skylines and facades. The most magnificent residential row New Yorkers had yet seen was La Grange Terrace on Lafayette Place, built by Town and Davis in 1832. The block-long, two-story structure of marble featured a Corinthian colonnade, rusticated basement, and a roof terrace enclosed with a delicate wrought-iron screen. A quarter of a century later, Davis projected a similar scheme in the Gothic mode. Located on Fifth Avenue at Forty-

Top: Davis' 1836 drawing of a "pointed" Gothic villa with brackets and an oriel window, erected at New Bedford, Mass.

Above: the monumental Greek Revival "palace," completed about 1846 for John C. Stevens on College Place in New York

Below: a rendering of the New York Athenaeum of Natural History, built in 1835, displays vertical Daviséan fenestration.

Second Street, the House of Mansions appeared to be a gigantic Gothic castle, bounded by towers, but it was actually eleven separate dwellings grouped under one roof. Town and Davis also designed the United States Patent Office in Washington, D.C., the New York Customs House, and the Pauper Lunatic Asylum, situated on Blackwell's Island in the East River and laid out with separate recreation yards for male and female inmates.

At a time when the Gothic fever was highly contagious, Town and Davis were among the earliest architects to acknowledge this popular taste. They produced houses with pinnacles, towers, oriels, traceried windows, and ribbed ceilings by the gross. One of their most spectacular Gothic designs was for a castellated country house, erected in 1844 on Manhattan's Murray Hill for William Coventry Waddell, a man whom Davis astutely noted had "been twice married and each time to *great pecuniary advantage*." Although the edifice stood a brief twelve years before it was razed in the name of urban progress, it was a thoroughly familiar sight to New Yorkers. The mansion even figured prominently in a saccharine romance of the day by Mrs. Anne Sophia Winterbotham Stephens, entitled *Fashion and Famine*: "This dwelling so graceful in its architecture—so fairylike in its grounds—had risen as if by magic among those old trees. Lavish was the cost bestowed on it, rich and faultless was the furniture.... Grand, imposing, and unsurpassed for magnificence by anything known in our city, it was nevertheless filled with a sort of gorgeous gloom that fell like a weight upon the beholder. . . ."

After Town's death in 1844, Davis was freed from his former restraints, and for the next three decades practiced mainly in the Gothic and Greco-

Tuscan styles. He fell increasingly under the spell of Andrew Jackson Downing, and began to spread the landscape architect's gospel with a missionary zeal. Between 1852 and 1870, Davis and Llewellyn P. Haskell, a wealthy chemist from Orange, New Jersey, put Downing's precepts into practice on an idyllic tract of land on the side of Orange Mountain. Intended to be an exclusive residential area combining rural solitude with suburban conveniences, Llewellyn Park, as it was named, was the first development of its kind in America. Davis not only preserved the natural beauty of the landscape, with its rushing brooks, woodland glades, and sweeping meadows, but enhanced it with rustic bridges, arbors, gatehouses, and lookouts in the most romantic manner. For the spacious building lots, Davis produced a fanciful array of rural abodes. A list of some of the specific houses designed by the architect indicates the wide range of his styles: Glen Rest, "an entrance lodge in Italian"; Trap Rock, "in Gothic"; Virginia House, "an arcaded villa"; Eyrie (Haskell's house), "in rustic"; and, Wildmont, Davis' own Gothic retreat.

In post-bellum days, revivalist architecture was gradually outmoded in favor of eclecticism. Although Davis made occasional excursions into the eclectic, his architecture never completely merged with the international potpourri. Besides, Davis seemed to be going against the currents of the day by preaching simplification, while everyone else preached elaboration. And, a forgetful public no longer accepted the ideas and designs that had won so much acclaim in the 1840s and 1850s. Davis retired from practice in 1874. The architect spent his declining years sorting out his voluminous collection of notes, papers, journals, and drawings, and pouring forth bitter invectives against what he considered to be the "degraded," "depraved," and "barbarous" state of contemporary architecture. He died at Wildmont in 1892. An obituary printed shortly thereafter recognized his contribution, and concluded, "His work bears the stamp of marked ability and genius, and never fails to arrest attention by the exactness of its proportions and beauty."

An elevation of the Tuscan style Pauper Lunatic Asylum, begun in 1834 off Manhattan

Homes Away From Home

Release from Domesticity

To some foreign visitors to this country it seemed that the American's home was quite literally where he hung his hat. The typical American, in short, appeared to be constantly on the move, either up in the world to some higher station in life or to some other place where the prospect of doing just that seemed brighter than where he happened to be. In the larger cities the prevailing restlessness came to a peak on moving day. In 1840 an English guidebook to emigrants headed for the United States warned them that "the year in New York begins on the first of May . . .," a day when "the whole population appear in confusion as if alarmed by some extensive conflagration." House rents, the publication added, were continually on the advance, and all places were at a premium for each successive year.

In those larger cities, also, where the concentration of travelers was greatest, the temporary residences provided in hotels was a matter for further astonishment. The city hotel burgeoned into a peculiarly American institution where every need and convenience of the guest was anticipated, including many with which he was not always familiar. In the land notorious for its everlasting "servant problem," visiting Englishmen were surprised to learn that at some of those public palaces they could have their shirts washed and ironed while they enjoyed the pleasures of a hot bath. And in all seasons the strange delight of ice water was available for those who fancied it.

Even while actually on the move the traveler

A hotel ballroom chandelier

could enjoy the comforts and conveniences of an elegant home on the increasing number of steamboats that plied the inland waterways. Early in the century the Russian artist Paul Svinin marveled at the accommodations provided by one of Robert Fulton's boats, which he likened to "a whole floating town!" Here, he reported, "the most fastidious person of the most refined taste can find . . . everything to his liking." Its dining saloon served one hundred and fifty passengers a day meals that were cooked by steam.

The competition between rival steamboat companies later became so fierce that, on the New York to Albany run, rate wars led to reducing the fare to ten cents. However, by 1840 there were more than one hundred steamboats on the Hudson alone. Rates were considerably higher in any case at a growing number of resorts where those who could afford it fled on occasion to relieve the monotony of money-grubbing at home. "All the world is here," wrote Philip Hone in 1839 from Saratoga, New York's most popular spa. "Politicians and dandies; cabinet ministers and ministers of the gospel; officeholders and office-seekers; humbuggers and humbugged; fortune-hunters and hunters of woodcock; anxious mothers and lovely daughters."

Without going so far afield for a retreat from home, gentlemen of standing had their clubs where they could manage to escape from prying female eyes, the hurly-burly of business matters, and the bumptiousness of democratic society, as they did in such comfort at the Union Club in New York City.

The advent of first-rate hotels, hotels that could be called modern in their concepts of service and accommodations, coincided with the rise of the Greek Revival style in America. Among the finest early examples on all counts were the Tremont House in Boston and the Astor House in New York City, both designed by Isaiah Rogers (in 1828 and 1832 respectively). The Tremont House, with its numerous water closets and its basement bathrooms with running water and other more elaborate appointments, was one of the first buildings in the world in which mechanical equipment constituted an important consideration in architectural design. "It has more galleries, colonnades, piazzas, and passages than I can remember, or the reader would believe," wrote Charles Dickens in amazement. The mechanical equipment of the Astor House, and its luxurious interior design and skilled architectural planning were even more impressive and caused a sensation when the hotel was opened. Here every floor was provided with baths and toilets, fed with water raised by a steam pump, conveniences still not common in private dwellings. Beyond such entirely practical features, the Astor House was famed for its sumptuous cuisine.

At the same time, steamboat architecture and decoration also reached a level of elegance that caused wonder in some quarters and evoked criticism in others. Downing thought that the decor of hotels and steamboats alike was often more opulent than even the wealthy could afford in their own homes, ostentatious to the point of vulgarity. "The only resort for a gentleman who wishes his house to be distinguished by good taste," counseled that popular author, "is to choose the opposite course, viz. to make its interior remarkable for chaste beauty, and elegant simplicity." However, those accommodations away from home continued to grow in popularity for years to come.

Section of a bathroom with shower and other conveniences in the Greek Revival style

The Tremont House in Boston, Mass., one of the first "modern" hotels to be built in America

The Ladies' Saloon aboard the Long Island Sound S.S. Atlantic *as it appeared in the 1840s*

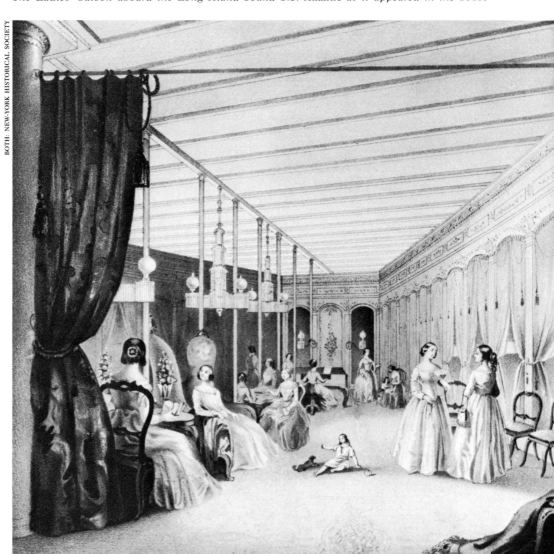

Highrock-Iodine and Empire Springs at Saratoga, N.Y., one of the more fashionable spas, in 1848
Refugees from domestic responsibilities; a scene in an upper-class 19th-century boardinghouse

For those Americans who could not face the problems of housekeeping, aggravated as they were by a perennial shortage of servants, for those whose restlessness discouraged them from putting down roots in a home of their own, and for those who sought relief from loneliness, boarding-houses offered a convenient haven. They existed at every level of luxury and shabbiness. It has been estimated that, in the course of the nineteenth century, more than 70 per cent of the population lived in boardinghouses at some time in their lives. And from that general experience stories and legends grew that found their way into the literature of the land. Until leisure attained a more respectable status in the hard-working society of democratic America, those who could afford it in conspicuous fashion either traveled to Europe where, as Tocqueville observed, idleness was still held in honor—or they disguised their indulgences at "health" resorts that profited by the trade in valetudinarianism, real or affected, and costly. "The worthy, fashionable, dashing . . . people of every state . . . flock to the Springs," remarked the *Salmagundi Papers* as early as 1807, ". . . to exhibit their equipages and wardrobes, and to excite the admiration, or . . . the envy of their fashionable competitors." Ladies from the South, the report continued, would invest the whole proceeds from a rice plantation on costumes and new liveries for such occasions, "while a lady of Boston or Salem will wrap herself up in the net proceeds of a cargo of whale oil, and tie on her hat with a quintal of codfish." Closer to home—but away from it—men could find sanctuary in saloons where the problems of domestic routine were pleasantly forgotten. At the Gem Saloon in New York the mayor of that city and other well-known citizens met to discuss their opposition to a state prohibition law.

Conviviality amidst the gilt, mahogany, and cut-glass setting of the Gem Saloon in New York, with the largest mirror in the city

As the nineteenth century advanced the proliferation of steamboats and railroads made it ever more easy to quit the city for a fresh-air holiday elsewhere, even for those on slender budgets. On a summer day in 1845 one editor reflected that so many vacationists were leaving New York for the cool delights of the country that the city, it seemed, would soon "be abandoned to the dog-killers, cabmen, and police justices at The Tombs." In 1823, high in the Catskill Mountains but within less than a day's journey of that city, construction was started on what was to become one of the most phenomenal of the early resort hotels that lured city dwellers away from their workaday haunts and into the very bosom of nature. This huge Greek Revival structure (it grew larger over the years), perched on a rock that projected "like a circular platform beyond the regular line of the ridge," immediately attracted an enthusiastic clientele. In its perfect natural setting overlooking "all creation," and with its great columned facade, its gigantic piazza, its haute cuisine, its elegant rooms, and its other delights, the Catskill Mountain House was an ideal base for those who sought to commune with nature in style and comfort. For scores of years it served as a favored retreat for a long line of illustrious men and women, among them William Cullen Bryant, Washington Irving, James Fenimore Cooper, Thomas Cole, Jenny Lind, Oscar Wilde, Henry James, and a host of others. The doors were finally closed with World War II and the structure demolished in 1963.

Catskill Mountain House, about 1844, with additions made to the original structure

Hands to Work, Hearts to God

Shaker Simplicity

Of the various utopian societies that proliferated in this country during the first half of the nineteenth century, the Shakers alone produced a distinctive style of architecture that reflected their particular beliefs and customs. Shunning what they considered to be the corrupt world, this pious and celibate sect practiced a form of Christian communism in secluded agricultural settlements

Out-of-the-way Shaker chairs

whose unconscious architectural beauty, even in that day, deeply impressed visitors and passersby. James Fenimore Cooper rhapsodized that he had never seen "in any country, villages as neat, and so perfectly beautiful as to order and arrangement, without, however, being picturesque or ornamented, as those of the Shakers."

Shaker communities were precisely planned in accordance with the rules and regulations known as the *Millennial Laws* of 1845, which expressly prohibited "Odd or fanciful styles of architecture," as well as "Beadings, mouldings, and cornices, which are merely for fancy." Villages were customarily divided into four "families" of thirty to one hundred individuals each. These families occupied amply scaled dwellings which had their stylistic basis in the simple homes of rural New England, but were adapted to a communal order of housekeeping, with gathering rooms for united worship, retiring rooms or dormitories, and commodious kitchens, bakerooms, and storerooms. Interiors, reduced to bare essentials, were characterized by the ubiquitous pegboards along walls, and built-in drawers and cupboards. A sense of order and

cleanliness was all-pervasive, because the sect's founder and spiritual leader, "Mother" Ann Lee, had stated, "There is no dirt in heaven."

Since the Shakers regarded the sexual act as the seed of all evil, elaborate precautions were taken to keep the mingling of the sexes to a minimum within their communal living arrangements. Brethren and sisters were provided with equal but separate facilities, including a segregated system of halls, stairways, retiring rooms, and entrance doors. Men and women ate at separate tables, and were forbidden to pass one another at close range, exchange gifts, shake hands, or touch during their highly spirited religious dances. The only permissible intercourse were weekly social visits between well-chaperoned groups for some elevated purpose.

Despite the repressions, regimentation, and seemingly Spartan existence, the eloquent simplicity of Shaker architecture and furniture denies unhappiness or frustration. Instead, fulfillment and repose seem to emanate from Shaker work, qualities that many of their worldly analogues, with their tortured forms and grotesqueries, clearly lacked. For nearly a century, the Shakers successfully held their own against the forces of sin. At their peak of prosperity in the 1850s, they boasted six thousand members in eighteen societies, from Maine to Kentucky. About the time of the Civil War, however, the order began to disintegrate. Fewer converts replenished the ranks, and many Shakers were lured away by opportunities in the outside world. Today, only two Shaker communities survive.

Guided by the precept "Whatever is fashioned, [let] it be plain and simple, . . . unembellished by any superfluities, which add nothing to its goodness or durability," the Shakers purified their interiors of nonessentials and concentrated instead on restrained but useful detail. Built-in cabinets, delicately turned banisters, pegboards, which held everything from bonnets and cloaks to spare chairs, and woodwork on which "not a knot, blemish or nail head was anywhere visible before painting," all reflected flawless, unhurried workmanship. Cabinetmakers religiously heeded Mother Ann's dictum against "costly and extravagant furniture," and many of their pieces, untainted by the "deception" of worldly decoration, have now become collectors' items. A small chamber might have only a few homemade rugs, a candlestick and stand, and a stove of Shaker design, whereas a gathering room characteristically contained several straight-backed chairs and benches to serve group needs.

A typical Shaker interior, featuring a stove with a narrow, elbowed tin pipe

Above: a spacious, neat gathering room, fitted for sedentary Shakers at Hancock Village, a society founded in 1790 near Pittsfield, Mass. Below: spindled settee, made at Enfield, N. H., 1856, is a traditional form adapted and simplified by the Shakers for communal life. **OVERLEAF:** *Hancock Village, with its geometrical houses and round stone barn, evokes an otherworldly sense of order and harmony.*

PHILIP LIEF

By engaging in agriculture and light manufacturing, the Shakers maintained economic self-sufficiency and earned a reputation in the outside world for the exceptional quality of such products as garden seeds, medicinal herbs, brooms, and baskets. It was perhaps without exaggeration that a traveler in 1844 pronounced the sect's "beautiful and well cultivated kitchen and flower gardens, vineyards, orchards, and farms, the very best that are to be seen in the United States." Farm structures, like houses, were carefully designed according to utilitarian principles, and as an observer noted, "every building whatever may be its use, has something of the air of a chapel." In the round stone barn at Hancock Village, for example, a framework pillar soared from the manger to the cupola, and not only supported the roof, but formed an air shaft to ventilate the hay piled around it. Only after laboring the greater part of the day could brethren and sisters return to their communal dwellings. A rule stipulated that "NONE shall go thither only for the purpose of eating, sleeping, retiring for evening worship, and spending the Sabbath, unless for short errands." Once at home, the sexes had to "walk softly and open and shut [their respective] doors gently, and in the fear of God . . . [and] spend the time allotted . . . mostly in their own rooms."

Opposite: the interior of the round stone barn, built in 1826 at Hancock, Mass.

Below: separate doors for men and women flank a hallway at Pleasant Hill, Ky.

The meetinghouses where the Shakers conducted their devotional services were generally the most dignified, imposing buildings in their respective neighborhoods. Like dwellings and workshops, churches provided separate, hooded entrances for men and women, yet at the same time they were set apart from the rest of the community architecture by their white exteriors—painted thus to symbolize purity—and their gambrel or rainbow roofs. Inside these simple structures, worshipers could experience the sublime, as well as sublimate their repressed sexual drives, in the spirited marching, singing, dancing, clapping, and shaking that formed an integral part of Shaker ritual. Religious meetings, especially in the early days of Shakerdom, had a distinctively orgiastic flavor. One Thomas Brown, who witnessed a service at the beginning of the nineteenth century, wrote of an entire congregation being caught up in "Trembling, shaking, twitching, jerking, whirling, leaping, jumping, stamping, rolling on the floor or ground, running with one or both hands stretched out and seemingly impelled toward the way one or both pointed; some barked or crowed, and imitated the sound of several other creatures." Gradually, over the years, formalized ritual supplanted the physical ardor of an earlier era. Furnishings in the great rooms of the meetinghouses were regulated according to principles of economy. As a Shaker elder explained, "If sacred places are abandoned to secular uses, cumbered with the truck of trade, papers, books, literature of a worldly character, or needless furniture inappropriate to a place of retirement and worship, there is unavoidably added much labor of obtaining, in those retreats, a heavenly, devotional, worshipful spirit; because of the sensitiveness of the human soul to surroundings." Suffused with sanctity, these halls contained only movable benches for the devout and rows of stationary seats along the walls for the "world's people," who considered the Shakers sightseeing curiosities.

A Shaker meetinghouse with a rainbow roof, completed in 1826 at New Lebanon, N. Y.

Styles for All Regions

A Continental Range

In the eighteenth century Benjamin Franklin, America's most sanguine prophet and apostle of expansion, supposed that it would take ages to fill the western continent. At the time and until years later no one was quite sure what did lie to the west. From the East it appeared to be an interminable, dense, and dark forest. But beyond that, wrote French scholar and adventurous traveler Constantin Volney, around the time of the Louisiana Purchase, was "a world of unexplored deserts and thickets." Still farther west rose the Rocky Mountains, standing "like a Chinese Wall," as a congressman observed in 1828. Beyond that lay "inhospitable" Oregon.

Yet, as one proverb put it, if hell lay to the west Americans would cross heaven to reach it. The prospect of greener pastures, blacker soil, more golden hills, gave express purpose to those who searched for one. "Every sunset which I witness," wrote Thoreau in the name of a multitude of wondering Easterners, "inspires me with the desire to go to a West as distant and as fair as that into which the sun goes down. He appears to migrate westward daily, and tempt us to follow him." Americans did indeed seem hell-bent to follow the sun. By mid-century gigantic chunks, any one of them as large as a good-sized European country, had been added to the national domain—the Louisiana Territory, Texas, California, the area of present-day New Mexico. Just a few generations after Franklin's remark the continent was not only spanned but beginning to fill up rapidly.

During the years when all America seemed to

Design for cast-iron grille

be moving westward, more people were actually moving into the cities of the land at every point of the compass. The urban movement would become the greatest of all migrations. It did not fire the imagination as did the slow march of covered wagons, but it involved more people and had consequences quite as profound in the shaping of the nation.

The continental sprawl and the larger concentration of people in cities alike involved new conditions and new experiences, as indeed did the accelerating growth of industry that was so emphatically demonstrated by the "mighty exhibition," held at the Crystal Palace in New York in 1853. The increasing variety of circumstances, from one end of the land to the other, found expression in a greater diversity of building than had been known in the American past. The cast-iron structures that were rising in major eastern cities stood in strong contrast to the low adobe dwellings that spread over the semi-arid country in the Southwest and Far West where Yankee and Spanish traditions jostled and mingled. In any case, the romantic mood lingered over the entire scene.

Meanwhile, with the decline in popularity of the Greek Revival, other styles emerged to compete with the Gothic Revival for public favor. The past was hunted with increasing intensity for models of design and ornament that would appeal by their novelty, their far-ranging historical association, and any practical application that could be made of them to the needs of the time. As the century advanced an ever-larger population of homeowners had to be satisfied.

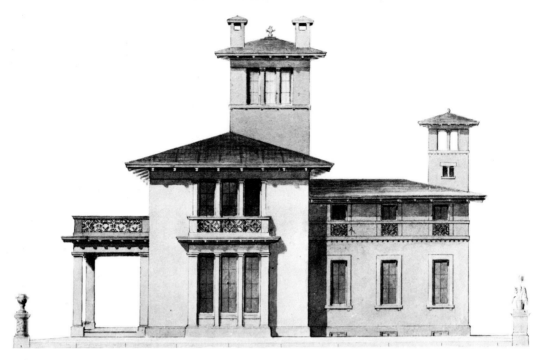

Top: a drawing made in 1835 by the architect Alexander J. Davis of a house that he labeled as in the "Etruscan or American Style"
Above: a lithograph of a Tuscan villa with tower, balcony, and bracketed eaves appearing as background for happy outdoor family life

The Italian villa designed by Richard Upjohn for Edward King in Newport, R.I.

One of the most flexible of the styles that competed for popularity with the Gothic was the Tuscan Revival, a composite style ultimately derived from the timeless domestic architecture of the Italian Campagna—of Tuscany, Umbria, Lombardy, and the Veneto—but interpreted here with unrestrained freedom and with endless improvisation. "As in music," wrote one commentator, "the original melody can be rendered more attractive by a great number of harmonious variations"; and, he continued, "a little foresight leaves everything in a favorable state for additions, with, at the same time, an appearance of present completeness." That remarkably inventive "architectural composer," Alexander Jackson Davis, played a number of variations on the Tuscan theme, although, like others among his contemporaries, he defined the style with different terms at different times. A "Roman and Tuscan Villa," according to Davis, might also be called Lombard, Italian, *Roman of Pliny* and *Palmyra*, Vitruvian, Etruscan, *Suburban Greek*, or Norman. (His drawing here illustrated was labeled "Etruscan or American Style.") Typically, however, such houses featured low-pitched, projecting roofs, square towers, and occasional piazzas, as could be seen in popular prints of the period that celebrated the delights of a home in the country. Although it is customarily designated as an "Italian villa," the house planned by Richard Upjohn in 1845–47 for Edward King in Newport, Rhode Island, is actually a composition of freely developed masses organized asymmetrically around a central entrance loggia. Upjohn, an English-born cabinetmaker turned architect, designed Trinity Church in New York, the third church of that name, at the end of Wall Street. That church, Downing observed, "will stand as far above all other Gothic structures of the kind in this country, as a Raphael's madonna before a tolerable sign painting."

Ornamental cast-iron tracery of a garden house, Mobile

Starting around the middle of the last century the use of cast iron as a building material—and indeed for almost everything else from furniture to street lamps—became a raging fashion. "The needs of the time call for it [now]," as one contemporary remarked. The metal could be cast in virtually every conceivable design, and since the foundry molds which gave the casting their shapes could be used endlessly, forms could be reproduced repeatedly at a comparatively moderate cost. Cast-iron structural columns and facades were employed primarily for commercial buildings, but dwellings throughout the land flowered with ornamental tracery in a rich variety of designs used on porches, balconies, fences, gates, and railings. As one nineteenth-century builder observed, cast iron had a "happy adaptability to ornament and decoration," and with an occasional coat of paint it could, "at a very small expense, be made to endure for a thousand years unaffected by the winds or the weather." Among other advantages, that builder wrote, was the fact that such ornaments would retain "their original fullness and sharpness of outline long after those in stone have decayed and disappeared."

Detail of ornamental cast-iron work on the Richards House, Mobile, Ala.

New Orleans balconies with cast-iron ornament. Much of such metalwork was cast in northern foundries and shipped about the country.

A

Cast- and wrought-iron ornamental details of varied designs. A. Gate B. Porch tracery C. Fence D. Detail of railing E. Grave marker F. Gate post. All the examples are from houses in Brooklyn Heights, N.Y., except D, which is in Manhattan, and E, which is in a cemetery in Mobile, Ala. Although much of this kind of decorative work was originally painted in dark colors, white, gray, and cream were also popular.

B

C

D

E

F

Two-story house of Thomas Larkin, completed 1837 at Monterey, Calif.; an adaptation in adobe of a New England merchant's house

Along the farthest edge of the continent, when East met West with the arrival in California of New England traders, new strains in architecture developed in a fusion of native and imported styles and methods of building; at least until a vast influx of easterners, bent on retaining their own inherited culture, overwhelmed local traditions. To eastern eyes the existing native dwellings seemed hardly more than heaps of mud, without the "smallest pretensions to architectural taste or beauty." Few of them used glass for windows or wood for flooring, and there rarely were fireplaces or chimneys. Nevertheless with the scarcity of wood, adobe was a convenient and practical building material, durable so long as it was protected from the weather by broad, overhanging eaves. In 1835 the Boston merchant Thomas Larkin planned to reproduce a kind of New England dwelling in Monterey but, obliged to use adobe, he ended with a wide-eaved structure with a double porch. He did introduce shingles for roofing and an inside fireplace. The resulting compromise with local conditions has been termed "Monterey colonial." One of the largest of adobe domestic structures was the so-called Petaluma Adobe, built by Mariano Guadalupe Vallejo about the same time as Larkin's house went up. It served as a combined hacienda, workshop, and storehouse.

Opposite: the garden court corridor of the Mission of San Juan Capistrano
Below: the Petaluma Adobe, built in 1834–44; one wing has been destroyed.

Writing of Monterey, California, in 1835, Richard Henry Dana observed, "The houses here, as everywhere else in California, are of one story, built of clay." For him, as for most other early visitors and settlers from the East, neither the rude adobe dwellings of the Spanish-Mexicans nor the decaying Catholic missions had much appeal. Before Larkin introduced them in his Monterey home, the use of shingles in roofing was unknown. Thus, too, the indoor fireplace and chimney of Larkin's house were innovations, as was glass for windows that was introduced about the same time; houses of the Spanish-Mexicans were heated with pans of coal placed on the floor, and cooking was done outdoors. Houses with a second story were another novelty introduced from the East Coast.

Dana's observations were made before the impact of such novelties had been felt. "In the hands of an enterprising people," he wrote, "what a country this might be." Shortly afterward New England ships were peddling everything from "Chinese fireworks to English cart-wheels," and settlers came in their wake. "These emigrants will change the face of California," remarked one American naval officer in 1846. "We shall soon have not only the fruits of nature, but of human industry." And soon this happened. Later in the century a romantic interest in "the good old times" before the American invasion had changed things drew a colorful and inaccurate picture of the Spanish-Mexican culture and its architecture. In her novel *Ramona*, Helen Hunt Jackson described a scene where "the representative house of the half barbaric, half elegant, wholly generous and free-handed life . . . under the rule of the Spanish and Mexican viceroys" was a pastel-colored hacienda with carved woodwork, cantilevered balconies, tiled roofs, glazed galleries, and other picturesque attractions that would have astonished those viceroys.

Santa Manuela Rancho, a typical one-story adobe California dwelling, drawn in 1851

Homes for the Dead

Tomb Architecture

In the course of the nineteenth century the romantic spirit found its most poignant and liberated expression in graveyard architecture and its associated monuments. The "homes of the dead" fashioned in those years were often melancholy caricatures of the homes of the living—somber and sometimes extreme architectural fantasies that could be indulged in such segregated areas where reverence for the dead hushed any breath of criticism from the living. Such conspicuous memorials were remarkably different from the burial sites of the first generation of Pilgrims whose "graves were leveled and sown with grass" lest the Indians should learn of the Pilgrims' weakened condition after more than half their number had been carried off by illness and weakness; or from the modest tombstone art of the eighteenth-century churchyard, or graveyard, adjoining church or meetinghouse.

By the nineteenth century those parochial graveyards were becoming overcrowded and, it was increasingly felt, constituted a menace to public health. Steps were taken, in New Haven as early as 1796, to remove them to a secluded area. Aside from such practical considerations this removal to some spot away from the center of town was also prompted by a sentiment, expressed by Timothy Dwight, that a grave placed close to "the current of daily intercourse . . . speedily loses its connection with the invisible world in a gross and vulgar union with the ordinary business of life."

In 1825 the Massachusetts Horticultural Society bought some seventy acres of land over-

Drawing of a cast-iron tomb

looking the Charles River in Cambridge and pleasantly landscaped it with various types of terrain—marsh, forest, rock and hill, valley and meadow—as a botanical garden to accommodate a wide variety of flora. When it became evident that the garden could not use or afford so much ground, fifty acres were laid out as the Mount Auburn Cemetery, inaugurated in 1831. It was the first large-scale example of romantic landscape design in this country. Although there were some who felt that tombs should not be permitted to intrude on the picturesque, unspoiled woodland setting, their objections were not heeded. The cemetery, tombs and all, proved an attractive retreat not only for the dead but for the living urbanites who came to visit the departed and who also used it as a verdant and quiet escape from the noise and congestion of the workaday city. As Lewis Mumford has observed, life came back to the town by way of the graveyard, just as the removal of graves and tombstones converted a number of churchyards into small but welcome open spaces in crowded areas of towns and cities. In fact the development of landscaped public parks within the limits of larger cities, such as Central Park in New York, was in a real sense an outgrowth of the "romantic" cemetery. The attraction of open space, carefully designed to preserve an effect of natural landscape and apart from the growing congestion of city blocks and streets, was at least first clearly demonstrated in such places as Mount Auburn, in spite of its associations with death. Typically, the city park also has its monuments to departed heroes.

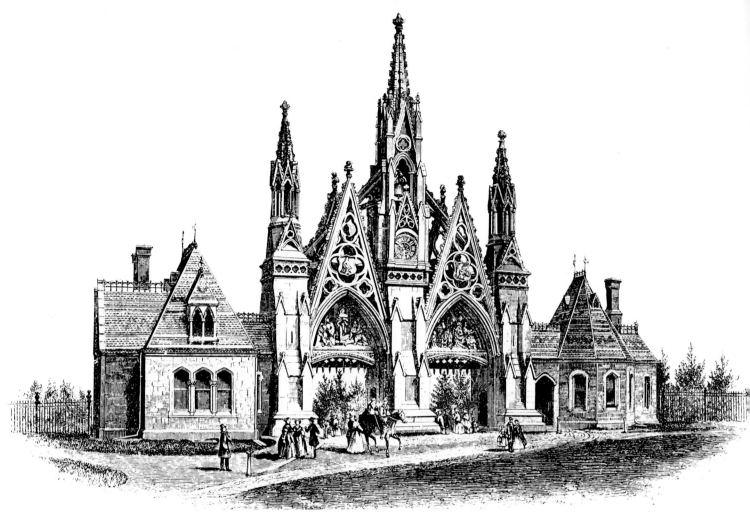

The main gateway and gatehouses in the Gothic Revival style designed by Richard Upjohn and Son, 1861, for Green-Wood Cemetery
CLEAVELAND, NEHEMIAH, GREEN-WOOD CEMETERY, 1866.

A design in the Egyptian Revival style by Alexander Jackson Davis, 1828, an early model for a popular type of cemetery gateway
METROPOLITAN MUSEUM OF ART, HARRIS BRISBANE DICK FUND, 1924.

In 1840 the Green-Wood Cemetery was opened in Brooklyn, New York, and in the course of the years since has become the final resting place for more than one-half million souls, including such prominent figures as Currier and Ives, Samuel F. B. Morse, Lola Montez, "Boss" Tweed, Henry Ward Beecher, Peter Cooper, and still others. It also has become studded with an extraordinary variety of mausoleums and monuments representing, among other things, a wide spectrum of architectural styles. At the entrance, its remarkable main gate house, designed by Richard Upjohn and Son in 1861, and built of brownstone with a polychrome slate roof, has justly been called the culmination of the Gothic Revival style in New York. It was Upjohn, as already noted, who designed Trinity Church at the end of Wall Street, considered by some to be one of the greatest churches built in America. Somewhat earlier Alexander Jackson Davis drew a design for another entrance gate in the Egyptian Revival style, a design that was approximately realized in the gate for the Grove Street Cemetery in New Haven, Connecticut, in 1844–48. At least fifteen Egyptian cemetery gates were designed or built in the score of years between 1830 and 1850, including one for Mount Auburn. Quite aside from the architectural features of those "grave gardens," as one contemporary called these newly designed cemeteries with their elaborately carved memorials, they also constituted outdoor sculpture galleries of a sort.

Top: the model for the funerary statue of the American mathematician Nathaniel Bowditch by the sculptor Robert Ball Hughes

Above: a view of the memorial to Bowditch in Mount Auburn Cemetery, Cambridge, Mass., the first rural graveyard in America

Above: tomb with Christian and Egyptian motifs
Left: a domestic scene of parting, with horsecar

Below: a representation of a fatal train wreck
Opposite, left: tomb of President James Monroe
Opposite, right: a memorial of eclectic design

The Gothic style was by its historical associations with Christian faith and practice considered altogether as appropriate for graveyard architecture as for churches. Rationalizing the use of Egyptian styles and motifs was more complicated. These were, after all, pagan forms, as was pointed out by some grumbling ministers in their sermons and tracts. However, they could be construed as symbols of ultimate wisdom (an attribute conceded to the ancient Egyptians by an old and persistent mythology), and as such they could be interpreted in the light of Christian theology and thus justified as proper funerary expression. Sculptured representations of the deceased or anecdotal reminders of the circumstances of his death were beyond thought of controversy.

5

In Search of a Style

War generally releases unsuspected forces, generates unprecedented circumstances, and wreaks vital changes in men and their culture. The Civil War did all this on a massive scale. Very few living Americans had ever given serious thought to military matters before the day Fort Sumter was fired upon. In 1860 those who would do the fighting were civilians in an overwhelmingly civil society. Five years later, as Denis Brogan has remarked, those same Americans, if they had survived the interval, were again civilians in a society as civilian as ever, a society in which it was possible to live for many years without ever seeing a professional soldier. But for the intervening period they were in the ranks, on one side or the other, engaged in one of the most sanguinary wars in history.

Probably no less than two and a half million men were involved in the conflict; more than six hundred thousand of them lost their lives during its course, not to mention hundreds of thousands who were wounded or crippled. For the number of men who took part, the area covered, the materiel produced and consumed, and the results achieved, the Civil War surpassed all the wars of history up to that time.

When, following the infinitely sad scene at Appomattox, the long, desperate struggle came to an end and the titanic forces that had been brought so suddenly into play were converted to peacetime enterprises, America underwent a major transformation. In the South a colorful, distinctive civilization had been all but destroyed. But in the North new energies and methods of applying them had been discovered. Self-confident, exuberant, and prosperous almost beyond credence, the triumphant North surged forward with reckless haste to fresh conquests. The hostilities were barely over when *Harper's Weekly* reported that the reaction from the tension of war showed itself "in a certain public frenzy. Enormous speculations, losses, and consequent frauds; an increase of crime; a curious and tragical recklessness in the management of railroads and steamers; a fury of extravagance in public watering places are all observable." Great schemes were launched. To the saviors of the Union all things seemed possible; at least they seemed worth trying.

In retrospect those postwar years resemble a mammoth treasure hunt in which people found or lost their way often by chance as much as by careful direction. With so much apparently at stake the frightful waste involved could hardly be counted. Fresh hordes of immigrants crossed the ocean to

Opposite: central hall and staircase of Olana, built for the artist Frederick Edwin Church

lend their brawn and talent, their energy, and their patient courage to the national adventure. As population figures soared per capita wealth increased apace. Millionaires seemed to grow as abundantly as paupers. Men at least talked as confidently of millions of dollars as earlier they had talked of thousands. (It came to the point, later in the century, when one of the Astors could explain that "a man who has a million is almost as well off as if he were rich.") One contemporary observer suggested that to recall what had been achieved before the war in contrast to developments that immediately followed was like reviewing "ancient history." Years later Henry Adams wrote that in 1868, after spending ten years abroad, he returned to a world strangely, almost unrecognizably different from the one he had left. The postwar generation, he concluded, was in fact creating a new world to match its incessantly rising needs and expectations.

These were the years that Mark Twain labeled the Gilded Age in a novel of that title he produced with Charles Dudley Warner in 1873. By extension the phrase has commonly been used to denote much of the rest of the century, with reference to the increasingly extravagant and conspicuous self-indulgence of the rich, the newly rich, and the passing rich. Shortly after the war, *Harper's New Monthly Magazine* noted that there existed, among those with great amounts of money to spend, a passion for building large and showy houses whose costs reached far beyond the bounds of prudence; a passion that reached a climax in the luxurious "cottages," Fifth Avenue "châteaux," and other remarkably ostentatious structures built in the latter part of the last century.

For all this the rather whimsical experimentation with architectural forms in historical styles that preceded the war years was but a modest beginning. In those earlier houses, however freely they were designed, some deference was usually paid to a dominant theme—first the Greek, then the Gothic, Tuscan or Etruscan, Egyptian, and so on. Immediately following the war such themes and others of curious and often dubious origin were as like as not combined in a single structure of no describable "style," unless it be called eclectic or, as vaguely, Victorian. Such was Armsmere, the remarkable house built for Samuel Colt in Hartford, Connecticut, and finished in 1862. It was, reported *The Art Journal* in some confusion, a "long, grand, impressive, contradicting, beautiful, strange thing . . .," something like an Italian villa "yet not carrying out any decided principles of architecture," but with Turkish domes and pinnacles, among other Oriental features, and yet, with its substantial homelike and comfortable aspects, English in feeling. As that journal concluded, it was in the end a "characteristic type of the unique."

Armsmere may have been an extreme manifestation, but by that very token it eloquently expressed the eclectic spirit of the times. It was in much that same spirit that the notorious showman Phineas T. Barnum built Iranistan in an extravagant attempt to domesticate the Taj Mahal in Bridgeport, Connecticut. There were those who lamented the wholesale and often confusing pillage of the past for styles that could be adapted one way or another to modern building. Leopold Eidlitz, the Vienna-trained architect responsible for Iranistan, was one of them. In a moment of disenchantment he concluded

Grand hall of the Stewart mansion

that American architecture seemed to be "the art of covering one thing with another thing to imitate a third thing which, if genuine, would not be desirable." However, as one contemporary periodical justly pointed out, "the vast accumulation of historical precedents, and the convenient publication of them in books, prints, and photographs, so that they are accessible to every student," had opened new vistas to architects and designers. If the abundance of such novel references fired the imagination, it also tended to boggle the mind with possible alternatives that were not always clearly understood. "All we can do," conceded one architect, "is to combine, using bits here and there, as our education affords more or less acquaintance with the models from which we steal our material."

The words *eclectic* and *Victorian* are often confused, or equated, with one another, although during that good queen's long reign there were clearly many different and more defensibly creative trends in building and design. Even while Victoria still ruled her great empire, however, the term *Victorian* had already taken on the pejorative connotations that it still has for most people. Yet, from the perspective of a century later, we can recognize in the undisciplined exuberance of the so-called Victorian mansion a restless energy that spoke for its times and that sought in all directions to reach some more promising end. Household engineering was in a stage of rapid development, and the confusing mixture of styles and nonstyles overlaid progressive advances in the basic standards of living, even in houses of modest pretention.

Iranistan, built for P. T. Barnum

One of the most remarkable commentaries on those changing standards appeared in 1869 with the publication of *The American Woman's Home* by Catharine E. Beecher and her sister Harriet Beecher Stowe. Their book was dedicated to "the women of America"; it was subtitled "a guide to the formation and maintenance of economical, healthful, beautiful, and Christian homes"; and it was advertised as "the cheapest and most desirable book of the year," priced $2.50 in cloth covers. The authors were not particularly interested in "style" as such. They preferred to claim that their model houses with their vaguely Gothic character might properly be called "Christian," implying that the design of such homes was for the good of all and would bring out the best in all who lived and worked in them.

What concerned them principally was that a house should function efficiently, agreeably, and economically—in the disposition of rooms and stairs to avoid unnecessary steps and climbing, the utilization of facilities to avoid waste of time and movement, the design of space-saving furniture, and such essential matters as heating, lighting, and ventilation. Kitchens were arranged with scrupulous regard for convenience and utility. New urban services were exploited, sanitary facilities, gas for lighting, and the like, and absorbed into the fabric of the house. In principle the ideal house they envisioned was the progenitor of the modern American house.

While the Beecher sisters were planning their relatively modest and elementary "machines for family life," engineers and inventors continued to develop a technology of formidable power and complexity. Quaint as they may seem when measured by later accomplishments, the exhibits of the Crystal Palace at the world's fair in New York in 1853 had called attention

The Crystal Palace, New York, 1853

to the industrial revolution that would as rapidly change the course of human affairs, and had served notice that man was freeing himself from conditions of life that had remained relatively fixed since the dawn of history. At a rate and to a degree unknown to any previous age he was gaining new mastery of the materials that framed his existence. The Crystal Palace itself was made of ore and sand that had been scraped from the earth, melted, cast, and wrought into girders of iron and panels of glass, and then daringly flung in soaring domes and light, glittering arcades far above the stalls beneath. It was a symbol of the new control man was assuming over the materials of nature and the audacity with which he transformed the elemental nature of those materials.

The same year that *The American Woman's Home* was published John A. Roebling started work on the Brooklyn Bridge, a much more spectacular demonstration of inventive engineering. Roebling, to be sure, was not an architect, but in structural terms he had revealed potentials which architects would explore for their own purposes. As one element in the transformation of industry and of construction, steel, which in 1864 had been a rare, costly metal restricted in use to small appliances, within barely a score of years became a basic commodity used on a colossal scale. With the evolution of the telephone, electric power, elevators, and numerous other devices, materials, and contraptions, the character of both American buildings and the landscape on which they stood was rapidly transformed. Out of that combination of circumstances, among other things, came the high-rising buildings, and all the special services they depended upon, that were to become such sentinels of American progress, or achievement. With each new development technological obsolescence, hitherto an inconsiderable matter, became an increasingly important factor in the fate of buildings.

Residential building was, of course, not immediately or so largely affected by those novel and massive developments. Nevertheless technology had its impact on the home as well. Little by little new advances in household engineering—matters of heating, lighting, sanitation, and other contrivances that raised the optimum standard of living (of creature comfort at the least) —were becoming organic parts of domestic architecture, whatever the style. There was, as always, some resistance to the inexorable march of progress. In June, 1881, *The New York Times* editorialized that the application of electricity to domestic science would exert no better moral influence than had gas. "We know," the paper opined, "that when a number of reasonably Christian men form themselves into a gas company, they immediately become pirates of the most merciless and extortionate character. Why should we look for better things from electric light companies. . . . We shall have electric meters in our cellars that will be as mendacious as the gas meters. . . ."

Elsewhere, however, the promise of technological improvements released luminous visions of the future. In 1887, Edward Bellamy, journalist and novelist, published his extraordinarily perceptive *Looking Backward* in which he presaged the world (or that part of it that was Boston) of A.D. 2000, as it would appear to someone who awakened from a sleep of more than a century. It was a socialistic community, a kind of utopia in which technology had been refined, organized, and tamed to accommodate the decent needs of mankind. Electric power was ubiquitous and inexpensive. Pollution from combustion was altogether eliminated; chimneys had completely disappeared. Indirect lighting and air conditioning were commonplace; all housework was mechanized; human drudgery was done away with. All interiors were wired for sound and a twenty-four-hour-a-day broadcasting system provided musical programs that could be selectively received and could be controlled in volume.

Bellamy was not concerned with specific styles of architecture, but rather with the good life that could be projected if man seriously studied and engineered his environment, indoors and out. In the year 2000 Boston would have "broad streets, shaded by trees and lined with fine buildings, for the most part not in continuous blocks but set in larger or smaller enclosures. . . . Every quarter contained large open squares filled with trees, among which statues glistened and fountains flashed . . . the public buildings [were] of a colossal size and an architectural grandeur unparalleled." Every city ward was serviced by a branch department store fed by pneumatic tubes from a central warehouse. The typical store was "a vast hall full of light, received not alone from the windows on all sides but from the dome, the point of which was a hundred feet above. Beneath it . . . a magnificent fountain played, cooling the atmosphere to a delicious freshness . . . walls and ceilings were frescoed in mellow tints to soften without absorbing the light. . . . Around the fountain was a space occupied with chairs and sofas."

Bellamy was a visionary who foresaw what his contemporaries, engineers, architects, and social planners together might accomplish if they firmly joined in a high, common purpose. In his book Victorian optimism reached a touching climax. One of his close contemporaries took a dimmer view of the current prospects. "Engineering had monopolized whatever real progress was being made in building," he lamented in the *Architectural Record*. ". . . architects were so preoccupied with their mistaken efforts to resuscitate historic styles that they wholly failed to discover the possibilities of the new material, and scornfully abandoned it." He was writing of the employment of metal in construction, but he might well have included other technological improvements. Years before, as already told, an individual could combine the functions of engineer and architect, as Benjamin Latrobe so conspicuously did. But in this more complicated world the two professions had separated. "What may we not hope from the union of modern engineering with modern architecture," wrote one prominent critic of the day, "when the two callings, so harshly divorced, are again united!"

Meanwhile, even as some builders and architects of domestic structures were piling up extravagant assortments of battlements and towers, crenelations and domes, crockets and gables, to satisfy the taste of the wealthy and wayward, others were working to different and more conservative standards. The Centennial Exhibition held at Philadelphia spurred on interest in what, for rather vague reasons, was called the Queen Anne style, a term applied to some of the English buildings seen at the fair. Those buildings with their open halls and large fireplaces recalled Elizabethan and Jacobean structures

The Brooklyn Bridge, opened in 1883

Capping a New York skyscraper, 1902

rather than those of Queen Anne's own time. Thus it was a sort of revival of elements of those earlier English styles on which colonial American builders had based their practices and designs. The style was soon transformed into an American vernacular characterized by light frame construction, irregular outlines, verandas and balconies, steep-pitched roofs, and large, open interior spaces—spaces that could more comfortably be opened up with the advent of central heating; spaces, what is more, that were extended to the inevitable porches covered by sloping eaves, which served, in effect, as outdoor living rooms in clement weather. Indefinable though it was, the Queen Anne was generally considered a style for the times. As one appreciative critic pointed out, a house in the Queen Anne style offered "a delightful insurrection" against monotony. For reasons that have to be taken on faith, the designs it incorporated were alleged to be "sincere," "artistic," and "practical," words that had been endowed with an almost mystical authority by such reformers as John Ruskin and Charles Locke Eastlake and their American disciples. Since those designs could be adapted to almost every level of architectural pretension, the Queen Anne style became widely popular "not only among the educated, but even among the rustic populations."

Frame construction, in the meantime, had undergone a significant change. For hundreds—even thousands—of years men had framed their wooden buildings of heavy timbers, often more than a foot square, that were mortised, tenoned, and pegged together and then raised into position by group labor. In the middle years of the century a radical new method called "balloon framing" was evolved; a method of construction using light two-by-four studs nailed rather than joined together in a close, basket-like manner, the studs rising continuously from foundation to rafters. Uninjured by mortise or tenon, with every strain coming in the direction of the fiber of some portion of the wood, the numerous, light sticks of the structure formed a fragile-looking skeleton that was actually exceptionally strong. As one contemporary observed, since no mysteries of carpentry were involved in such construction, houses could be thrown up by relatively inexperienced labor in quick time. The method had had to wait until cheap, machine-made nails were available in quantity, which they generally were as early as the 1830s. Balloon-frame houses were more than makeshifts; the method had been generally used throughout the country ever since it was first conceived. In passing, it should be remembered that without its time- and labor-saving advantages the mushroom cities of the West could never have risen as fast as they did.

As always, wood continued to be the favorite building material for housing in America, and the most progressive trends in domestic architecture were reflected in frame constructions. In the 1870s and 1880s about the suburbs of Boston and along the New England seacoast, those trends reached a climax of sorts in homes that were at the same time uniquely American and significant achievements in architecture. This development of design, which has been dubbed the "shingle style," was in effect a sensitive and graceful refinement of Queen Anne style. It was influenced as well by a new appreciation of early colonial architecture that also had been sparked by the exhibits

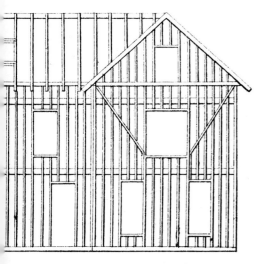

Top: balloon-frame construction
Above: detail of balloon-frame house

at the Philadelphia Centennial, as well as by the demonstrations of exquisite architectural woodwork in the Japanese section of that fair. (One observer judged that the Japanese building erected to house the displays from that country was the best-built structure on the fairgrounds.)

However, in the best of the shingle style buildings those various elements were completely and happily assimilated into a regional expression of originality, integrity, and charm; buildings that were, in the words of one critical authority, "paradigms of domestic felicity." In them was little or no trace of academic pretension. Their interior plans were conceived with an amazingly free use of interconnecting spaces at several levels; their shingled exteriors reflected the interiors in flowing, continuous contours; and interiors and exteriors were joined by sweeping and spacious covered porches. It was such features that prompted one German visitor to the United States in the late nineteenth century to remark that "in contrast to Germany, the modern American house is built entirely from the inside out. It not only corresponds to particular individual demands but above all to the peculiarities, customs, and needs of the Americans. That these customs are pronounced and distinctly marked gives domestic architecture in the United States a great advantage over our own German architecture."

In its pure form the shingle style was native to eastern New England. It has been suggested that in that social and cultural milieu the architect's patrons enjoyed an easy, sure self-confidence that was not shared by those who pretended to rule the world of high fashion and great wealth and who depended upon conspicuous display to prove their ascendancy.

If any one person could be held responsible for the development of an indigenous American architecture during these latter years of the nineteenth century, major credit would go to Henry Hobson Richardson. More surely than any other architect of those decades, he came to terms with his times and with American circumstances. Richardson designed buildings of every purpose from houses in the shingle style to tall, commercial structures of solid masonry. Trinity Church in Boston is just one of the many outstanding monuments with which he adorned the New England landscape. His mature work was freshly conceived in terms of function and graced with a sense of fitness. Beyond that, with the authority of his talent and his person, he endowed the social function of the architect with a prestige and dignity that it often had sorely lacked. It was through Richardson, also, that the new American vernacular was transplanted to Chicago, where it spread its roots and came to fresh flowering in the advanced work of Louis Sullivan and his pupil Frank Lloyd Wright. He was, wrote Lewis Mumford, "the primitive source of modern architecture."

Richardson's Trinity Church, Boston

Richardson died in 1886 at the early age of forty-eight. Ironically, it was the influence of two of his pupils, Charles Follen McKim and Stanford White, that set off a trend back toward the formal historical revivalism which Richardson himself had spurned in his quest of a living architecture. McKim and White were men with a Beaux-Arts background, and the buildings they, with other architects and artists of similar vision, designed for the World's Columbian Exposition held at Chicago in 1893 were a direct return to the classical ideal—the "pure ideal of the ancients," to use a contemporary phrase applied to their taste. To impose those standards on the raw and lusty Midwest seemed to Henry Adams a "rupture in historical sequence" and an "inconceivable" display. As already fully told, Thomas Jefferson was at the same time a fervent admirer of classical architecture and an advanced modernist. He once stated that he preferred the dreams of the future to the history of the past. However, even his educated and enlightened imagination could not have previsioned the monumental extravagance of the White City on the shores of Lake Michigan, with its glittering facades of plaster of Paris. Louis Sullivan, whose steel-framed skyscrapers were already rising in Chicago, lamented those products of "the pallid academic mind, denying the real, exalting the fictitious and the false, incapable of adjusting itself to the flow of living things." And with these sentiments Jefferson would no doubt have concurred.

However, revivalism was given new impetus, and it took new forms. The firm of McKim, Mead, and White had designed trim structures in the shingle style well before the Chicago fair. They had also developed a strong antiquarian taste for colonial architecture, among other earlier forms, that led them back to the Georgian modes of the eighteenth century with their references to classical prototypes. Buildings in the colonial revival style, it was claimed, were distinguished by their "symmetry, restfulness, and good proportions"; but they hardly represented an advance in architectural principles or practices.

A more spectacular and extreme form of revivalism took shape in the luxurious "cottages" modeled after French Renaissance châteaux and other monuments to the historic past that were sprouting along Fifth Avenue in New York, at Newport, and elsewhere in precincts favored by the very rich. In Newport alone, one French visitor was told, there were "more millions of dollars represented . . . than in all London and Paris altogether"; and in that exclusive enclave, built upon its cliff within the space of a few years by the caprice of millionaires, who vied with one another to see who should excel in splendor, he counted scores of different styles of construction, most of them carefully and extravagantly designed in the image of English or Continental models. "In this country, where everything is of yesterday," he wrote, "they hunger and thirst for the long ago." The need of such lavish homeowners to capture some sense of stability and timelessness by borrowing and buying from the past, he concluded, was so sincere it was pathetic.

The Art Palace at the World's Columbian Exposition, Chicago, Ill., seen from across the lagoon

A Medley of High Styles

Victorian Eclecticism

As he walked about the streets of New York in the post-Civil War years, the architect Alexander Jackson Davis was appalled at the buildings that had recently risen in the city. One of them he thought was "barbarous," another "depraved," and still another "a broken heap of littleness." Davis was aging and no longer active in his profession. In the decades before the war he had designed houses and other structures in a multitude of different styles, each of them owing its debt to some historic style that pleased his own or his client's fancy. The modern buildings that caught his critical eye also looked to the past for models to copy or adapt. But a new generation of architects and builders were assembling their borrowed notions in what seemed to Davis impure and indiscriminate mixtures. In 1881, as he approached eighty, he noted in his diary: "Engaged upon my paper entitled 'Abuses in Architecture.'"

The world in which Davis had enjoyed his great successes had died with the war; the new world born of that struggle both enjoyed the benefits and suffered the consequences of rapid, chaotic growth. No one could guess what direction architecture was to take while all groped for some form of expression that would best suit the rapidly changing circumstances. "The world has seen so many mutations of style . . .," concluded one architect, "that it is almost impossible to construct a new character without combining a number of those in use before." Such an approach led to results that were at best highly picturesque—a word, incidentally, that enjoyed

Detail of a tower at Olana

CERVIN ROBINSON, HABS

a very popular vogue during the decades before and after the war.

Rationalizing the eclecticism of those years was not difficult for the theorists and practitioners who guided public taste. Calvert Vaux, who came from England to pursue a distinguished career in America, voiced a prevailing outlook when he wrote: "Webster and Clay were orators of originality, but their words were all old. . . . Any desire on their part to invent a brand-new language would have been, of course, absurd, and any wish to produce a brand-new style of building is without doubt, an equally senseless chimera. . . . All previous experience in architecture is the inherited property of America, and, should be taken every advantage of . . . but the past should always be looked on as a servant, not as a master." The mixing of styles, in short, could be a positive virtue that had not been apparent to earlier generations with their devotion to the Greek, Gothic, and other more specific revivals.

One novelty introduced in the postwar years, and often used on public as well as domestic structures, was the high mansard roof—a roof with a double slope, the lower being longer and steeper than the upper. That feature had first been used by François Mansart, a seventeenth-century French architect, and its use spread outside France when the so-called Second Empire style became an international fashion two centuries later. The mansard was originally developed as a practical device for providing usable attics, a function it served as well in its later adaptations as it had when Mansart introduced that feature at the grand château at Blois.

The Cameron House, built in Waco, Texas, 1879, burned in 1965
The home of Charles Crocker, possibly built by Raun and Taylor

During the 1870s the mansard roof in one variation or another was prevalent, if not ubiquitous. It appeared in modified form on the house in Waco, Texas, designed in 1879 by the Larmour brothers for William Cameron, an immigrant Scot who made his fortune in the lumber business. For the rest, with its sawn brackets and miscellaneous other ornaments applied to the clapboard background, its protuberant, two-story bay, its oddly designed window openings, and its octagonal mansardic tower topped by an inexplicable glittering crown, Cameron's house epitomized the stylistic mixture that A. J. Davis so roundly criticized. The railroad magnate and banker Charles Crocker also topped his own "splendid piece of renaissance building" on San Francisco's Nob Hill with a mansard roof and tower. It is said that this massive pile, with its twisted crestings, bay windows, and columned porch cost Crocker $2,300,000. It was demolished during the fire of 1906. Another conglomeration of motifs capped by mansards was designed in 1875 by G. B. Groff, who described his creation as "an elegant and picturesque Villa prepared for execution on a sightly bluff at Saratoga Lake."

A "villa" designed in 1875 for a site at Saratoga Lake, N.Y., and published in Progressive American Architecture, *by G. B. Groff*

Olana's turreted gazebo commands a superb panoramic view of the Hudson River and the Catskills.

Above: from all views Olana presents different aspects.
Opposite: the main tower and south facade of Olana.

Among the most picturesque and most unusual of surviving houses from the post-Civil War decade is the "Persianized" mansion Olana, built by the prominent landscapist Frederick Edwin Church on a hilltop overlooking the Hudson River near the town of Hudson, New York. Church was widely traveled, and eminently successful in his profession—he received as much as $10,000 for a single canvas. Acting as his own architect and decorator, and taking advantage of his ample resources, he wove into the design of his exotic home (page 232) ornamental themes drawn particularly from Near Eastern sources—"so far as the climate and the requirements of Western civilization permitted." Construction started in 1870 and the Church family moved in two years later, although for years to come the artist continued to develop his decorative schemes with details and furbishings of all manner. "I can say," he remarked at one point, "as the good woman did about her mock turtle soup, 'I made it out of my own head.'" Boldly perched on its lofty site, the exterior walls of its towers, porches, gazebos, and other elements brightly ornamented with tiles and painted brick, Olana presents an exotic and colorful spectacle from all angles. The spacious grounds were magnificently laid out by the eminent landscape architect Frederick Law Olmsted. The spectacular views of river and mountains (the Catskills) seen from its windows recall such great panoramic vistas as Church painted on his large canvases. To Church, Olana was "the Center of the World." And, he added, "I own it."

A view of the Hudson River and the Catskill Mountains as seen from the west porch of Olana

The walls of Olana were virtually covered with Church's own canvases and those of his numerous artist friends. For the rest, the furnishings included almost everything from reproductions of American colonial chairs and tables to actual colonial metalwork, from contemporary kerosene lamps to the stuffed and mounted heads of wild beasts. As in the design of the interior architecture, however, Near Eastern motifs appeared repeatedly among the highly miscellaneous artifacts that he chose to live with. Some such objects were no doubt trophies of his own travels. But there were dealers in New York who could supply the real things or approximations of them. The Oriental bazaars of the firm of A. A. Vantine in that city specialized in creating "highly artistic effects" with "everything that belongs to a genuine Moorish interior," from imported hookahs and Moorish fretwork screens to Persian carpets and art metalwork, all "in bewildering variety." Also, the artist Lockwood De Forest, Church's friend and his wife's relative, actually set up a shop in Ahmadabad, India, whose ninety craftsmen in various media supplied De Forest's studio-salesroom with exotic creations for the American market.

246

Left: facilities of Olana's paneled bathroom in a wing of the building that was completed by Church in 1891

Below, left: the fireplace in the studio at Olana. Actual Persian tiles of the 1870s were used for ornamentation.

Below, right: a close-up of the wash basin in the bathroom at Olana, with decoration simulating Persian tiles

The Hale House, a version of the Queen Anne dwelling, built in Los Angeles, Calif.

While discerning critics were beginning to grumble ever more audibly about the desirability, the vital need, of developing a distinctively American architecture, popular taste did not easily or quickly yield its preference for borrowed motifs in mixed combinations. Both practical and picturesque as it was, the mansard roof was persistently grafted onto structures of otherwise miscellaneous styles. In his painting "House by the Railroad" the American artist Edward Hopper has recorded a haunting image of such a structure as it survived in the 1920s. With or without a mansard, houses in the so-called Queen Anne style continued to enjoy public favor in one form or another. Queen Anne was a label so variously construed as to be almost meaningless. As one highly critical author wrote in 1883, it was a name "which has been made to cover a multitude of incongruities, including indeed, the bulk of recent work which otherwise defies classification, and there is a convenient vagueness about the term which fits it to that use." In its more common forms, with all their irregularities of shapes and outlines, the Queen Anne house did constitute "a delightful insurrection" against monotony. When the concept of freedom of plan and design associated with the Queen Anne style was tamed and naturalized, it led to fresh, indigenous developments of exceptional charm.

Left: design for a hall and staircase, typical of a Queen Anne open plan, from Henry H. Holly's Modern Dwellings, *1878*

Below: "House by the Railroad," painted by Edward Hopper in 1925; a nostalgic view of a house with two mansard roofs

Above: the mansion built for LeGrand Lockwood at Norwalk, Conn., in 1869, designed and decorated by Detlef Lienau and Léon Marcotte
Opposite: interior detail, with inlaid, carved, gilded, painted, and other decoration; both architect and decorator were Paris trained

In 1866 Edwin Lawrence Godkin, founder and editor of *The Nation*, wrote that plenty of Americans knew how to get money, but not many knew what best to do with it. One obvious exception to that pronouncement was LeGrand Lockwood, who had made his fortune in railroad investments, shipping, and trading in stocks and bonds. He was the first millionaire of Norwalk, Connecticut, an area in which his family had settled in the seventeenth century. As Godkin made his observation Lockwood was building one of the costliest and most elaborate mansions in America at the time. He had commissioned Detlef Lienau and Léon Marcotte, both Paris-trained architects and designers, and Frederick Law Olmsted, the distinguished American landscape architect (who subsequently laid out New York's Central Park), to plan and complete his new mansion and its grounds. Lockwood himself scoured the Old World in search of marbles, rare woods, metal, stone, and objects of art to embellish the house. He imported Egyptian porphyry and Florentine marble carved to his order in Italy. The finest of exotic and native woods—dark oak, black walnut, brazilwood, rosewood, satinwood, boxwood, ebony, and cedar of Lebanon—all carved, inlaid, and gilded, were used for the interior trim and furnishings. Murals, wood sculptures, marble statues, and contemporary paintings added to the princely setting. With its fourteen bathrooms, two billiard rooms, bowling alley, theater, library, art gallery, and other accommodations (including a dry-cell burglar alarm system), the house was equipped "with every convenience that ingenuity can suggest or the most generous expenditure procure." The structure itself was an ingenious invention in the manner, broadly speaking, of a French Renaissance château with both mansard and gabled roofs, a turret, and interlacing ironwork trim. The plan was in the form of a Greek cross, with first- and second-floor rooms radiating from a monumental octagonal rotunda. In 1873 the *New York Sun* reported that it was, perhaps, "the most perfect and elegant mansion in America."

A detail of the architectural ornament

251

In 1883 one acid critic observed that the Queen Anne style had still, "after nearly ten years of almost complete sway among the young architects of England and the United States, all the signs of a departure—we might say of a hurried departure—and gives no hint of an arrival, or even of a direction. It is, in fact, a general 'breaking-up' in building, as the dispersion of Babel was in speech." Yet, arguments used by architects to justify the style often sound very much like a rationale for modern functionalism. For example, in a little publication issued in 1878 and entitled *Old Homes Made New*, William M. Woollett, an admirer of the style, set down the principles to be observed in building in this manner:

"*First:* That the convenience of the plan, its best distribution, and adaptation to the wants of the particular individuals by whom it is to be occupied, and the site on which it is to be placed, should in all cases be the paramount consideration.

"*Second:* That the exterior should grow naturally from the plan, its outline being fixed and determined by that . . . that it should also be a consistent following out of the proper and natural uses of the materials of which it is built; each material being fully acknowledged.

"*Third:* That the architectural effect should be obtained by the natural combinations and workings of the constructive portions of the structure, and not by adding or planting on these features: and again by the natural variety of the outline rather than by the richness and variety of the detail.

"*Fourth:* That the proportionately greatest work of art in architecture is that which produces the most effective result at the least expenditure of labor and detail in design, which, in the practical mind of the American, is also money."

With these considerations in mind he explained how a no longer fashionable Greek Revival house could then be transformed into an up-to-date Queen Anne model. As other more "advanced" styles passed into favor the Queen Anne lingered on the landscape as a highly flexible fashion that defied definition.

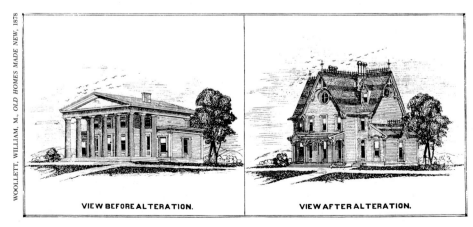

VIEW BEFORE ALTERATION.   VIEW AFTER ALTERATION.

An old Greek Revival house converted into a "modern" structure in the Queen Anne style

Architectural Follies

Styles Unlimited

In all lands and all times men of eccentric bent or strong personal preference have broken with established convention and built themselves houses of such unusual character that they have been dubbed "follies." During the post-Civil War decades in America, it was not always easy to determine at what point exuberance, eclecticism, and inventiveness gave way to what could be considered sheer folly. Extravagance of design, or so it appears to us, was itself a conventional expression of those years, as the examples illustrated on the preceding pages clearly demonstrate. Nevertheless, at times even those extravagances were carried to extremes that constituted parodies of the prevailing taste, "follies" by any standard.

In some areas of American society the sudden increase of wealth led the newly rich to architectural excesses which they fondly hoped would conspicuously signal their prominent station in life. Thus, in Chicago in 1882 the rising tycoon Potter Palmer commissioned a house that was to be larger than any of the Vanderbilt mansions in New York and that, his architect asserted, for size would have no equal "among private residences except some two or three Pacific slope houses of the bonanza kings."

One of those two or three Far Western houses was the country home of James C. Flood, completed at Menlo Park, California, in 1879. The house itself, called Linden Towers, covered almost two acres of land and, as was soberly reported, "no royal or ducal house in Europe excels it." Flood had been a carriage maker and

Carved ornament, about 1890

© CLARENCE LAUGHLIN

a saloonkeeper, among other things, but he became known as the Bonanza King. Once his all-but-indescribable construction was finished, with its gingerbread turrets, its luxurious stables for a score of horses, and its vaulted conservatory, Flood's social security was enhanced by a visit from General Ulysses S. Grant. However, as a bit of an anticlimax, plans to wed the daughter of the house to General Grant's son did not prove successful.

As has been the lot of so many early American houses of more formal design, a large number of these architectural extravaganzas have disappeared from the scene. However, one of the most fanciful examples, the octagonal Moorish castle of the cotton planter Haller Nutt in Natchez, Mississippi, was neither completed nor has it been demolished. "Nutt's Folly" was to have been "a remembrancer of Eastern magnificence which few will judge misplaced as it looms up against the mellowed azure of a Southern sky." As it still stands it is a remembrance of an enchanting byway in American experience.

It was in the heyday of such confections that Catharine Beecher and her sister Harriet Beecher Stowe promulgated their eminently sensible, down-to-earth doctrines on home design, household economics, and family welfare. They were not, to be sure, addressing an audience of the newly very rich, but they were concerned with a growing public of improving circumstances who welcomed counsel in adapting their habits to new or larger homes, in matters of housekeeping and etiquette as well as the planning and decorating of the house itself.

Above: Linden Towers, built in 1879 at Menlo Park, Calif., for Flood, the "Bonanza King"; demolished in 1934

Left: a design for an Oriental villa from Sloan's Homestead Architecture, *published at Philadelphia, Pa., in 1861*

Opposite: the Chicago home of the Potter Palmers, designed in 1882 by the Boston architect Henry Ives Cobb

The huge pile that James Flood had erected at Menlo Park was characterized by *Harper's Weekly* as being stylistically "a modification of the Louis Quatorze." Elsewhere it was reported, less reverently, that it "looked more like a house on a wedding cake than something to live in." The house was demolished in 1934 and all its elaborate trappings auctioned off. So, too, the Potter Palmer house has vanished from the Chicago scene leaving only legends of its former splendor. In deference to her remote Gallic origins Mrs. Palmer (known to her social friends as "the Queen") luxuriated with a Louis Quatorze salon and a gallery of French paintings. She also enjoyed a Japanese room and a Moorish-style music room. However, the French dandy Boni de Castellane concluded quite flatly that the Palmer palace was "sumptuous and abominable." More exotic than either of those architectural fantasies was the design proposed in 1861 by the Philadelphia architect Samuel Sloan for an Oriental villa "particularly suitable for the home of the retired Southern planter" which was almost completely realized.

Longwood, Haller Nutt's Oriental folly designed by architect Samuel Sloan
Floor plan of an octagonal house from Orson Fowler's A Home For All

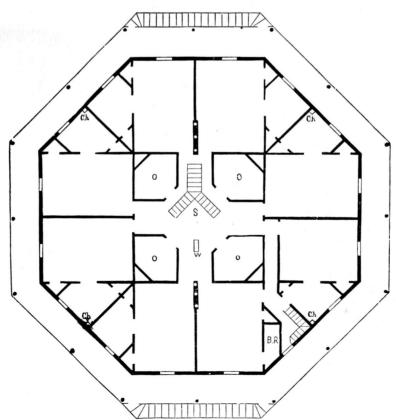

"The choice of style in this example," Samuel Sloan wrote in describing his Oriental villa, "was less a matter of caprice than the natural growth of the ground-plan adopted." That plan, basically, was octagonal. ("Fancy dictated that the dome should be bulbiform . . .," he conceded.) Sloan modified and refined his published scheme when he designed Longwood, otherwise known as "Nutt's Folly," for Haller Nutt. Large mirrors were to be placed in the dome, among other details, to provide indirect lighting by playing reflections of the sun against smaller mirrors downstairs. Slaves started the actual construction, and in 1861 Sloan brought a contingent of Pennsylvania craftsmen to the site to complete it. But when the Civil War erupted the workmen left the job. Nutt himself died during the war and his dream house was never finished. A fad for octagonal houses had been spurred by an eccentric phrenologist named Orson Squire Fowler, who published *A Home For All, or the . . . Octagon Mode of Building* as early as 1849. (He had also written a book on "sexual science"—and he sired three children after he was seventy years old.) "Why continue to build in the same SQUARE form of all past ages," he asked; especially since an octagonal house "contains one fifth more room for its wall."

LEFT: BULLOCK, JOHN, *THE AMERICAN COTTAGE BUILDER*, 1854. RIGHT: RICHARD WATHERWAX

Above: an octagonal house with a domed roof replacing an earlier mansard roof
Top left: profile of octagonal house, from American Cottage Builder, *1868*

Above: a contemporary illustration of Armsmere, the home of Samuel Colt at Hartford, Conn.

Opposite: the Gresham House, Galveston, Tex.; later, residence of bishops of the local diocese

Armsmere, the Hartford home of Samuel Colt, inventor of the revolver, was indeed the "long, grand, impressive, contradicting, beautiful, strange thing" that *The Art Journal* called it; at least it had a number of those characteristics. It was, further, a remote descendant of an Italian villa with "an Oriental, capricious, glass dome in the rear contrasting strangely with the lofty solid tower at the front, as if the owner had begun by being an English lord, and had ended by being a Turkish magnate, looking out on the Bosphorus." German musicians from Colt's factory played at his garden parties as guests savored exotic fruits from the vast greenhouses. There were ponds and fountains and swans, and thirty men to roll and trim the lawns daily. Far away in Galveston, Texas, in 1886, Colonel Walter Gresham, a local attorney, commissioned a massive palace to be built of stone by Nicholas J. Clayton. The architect approached his assignment with unflinching confidence, combining motifs of rich variety in a conglomerate of unusual authority. With its combination of turrets and gables, roof lines of constantly changing character, and chimneys of assorted designs, the profile of the house reveals a thoroughly restless imagination. Within, fireplaces from around the world were installed, including one of Mexican silver, onyx, and satinwood (a prize winner at the New Orleans Exposition of 1886), and one of marble from Italy. Interiors were embellished with rosewood, satinwood, white mahogany, and native woods of several kinds. There were stained-glass windows, a handsomely carved great staircase, and a domed ceiling with painted decorations. The house cost Colonel Gresham around one quarter of a million dollars.

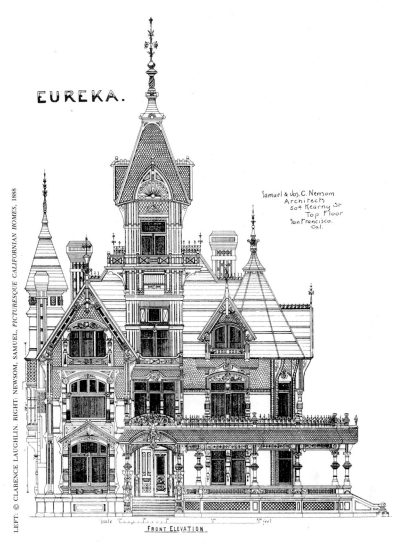

EUREKA.

Samuel & Jos. C. Newsom
Architects
504 Kearny St
Top Floor
San Francisco.
Cal.

FRONT ELEVATION

Above: the architects' rendering of the Carson House in Eureka, Calif.
Left: main staircase of the Warner House, St. Louis, Mo., about 1890

The exuberances that led toward folly were manifest throughout the land, from Maine to the West Coast. About 1888 William Carson, a successful lumber magnate, commissioned the architects Samuel and Joseph C. Newsom to build a wooden mansion at Eureka, California, next to his lumberyards. The finished house, which still stands, faithfully followed the architects' drawing reproduced above. A few years later another western lumberman, Erastus H. Warner, settled in St. Louis, Missouri, and built his permanent home in that city. By the time those two extravaganzas were raised, steam-powered woodworking machinery had long since taken over the production of much of the carved and turned ornamental detail that had for ages past been the province of hand craftsmen. The relative ease with which such machinery could manipulate the materials fed to it often encouraged architects, builders, and decorators to attempt a bewilderment of decorative woodwork of miscellaneous design.

A Woman's Guide to Living

In these passages from their 1869 guide to good housekeeping, Catharine E. Beecher and Harriet Beecher Stowe show unemancipated women of the day how to run economical, healthful, and moral homes.

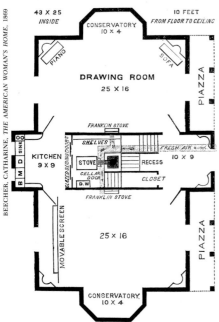

Top: Catharine E. Beecher, author and advocate of principles of domestic science

Above: floor plan of a "Christian house" with a functional arrangement of space

. . . a Christian house [is] a house contrived for the express purpose of enabling every member of a family to labor with the hands for the common good, and by modes at once healthful, economical, and tasteful.

. . . the ground-plan of the first floor . . . is forty-three feet long and twenty five wide, excluding conservatories and front and back projections. . . . The piazzas . . . have sliding-windows to the floor, and can, by glazed sashes, be made green-houses in winter.

. . . by the close packing of conveniences . . . small and economical houses can be made to secure more of the comforts and many of the refinements of large and expensive ones.

Between the [kitchen and stove-room] glazed sliding-doors, passing each other, serve to shut out heat and smells from the kitchen. The sides of the stove-room must be lined with shelves. . . . Boxes with lids, to receive stove utensils, must be placed near the stove. On these shelves, and in the closet and boxes, can be placed every material used for cooking, all the table and cooking utensils, and all the articles used in house work, and yet much spare room will be left. The cook's galley in a steamship has every article and utensil used in cooking for two hundred persons, in a space not larger than this stove-room, and so arranged that with one or two steps the cook can reach all he uses. In contrast to this, in most large houses, the table furniture, the cooking materials and utensils, the sink, and the eating-room, are at such distances apart, that half the time and strength is employed in walking back and forth to collect and return the articles used.

[As seen in] an enlarged plan of the sink and cooking-form . . . the flour-barrel just fills the closet. . . . Beside it, is the form for cooking, with a moulding-board laid on it; one side used for preparing vegetables and meat, and the other for moulding bread. The sink has two pumps for well and for rain water—one having a forcing power to throw water into the reservoir in the garret, which supplies the water-closet and bathroom. On the other side of the sink is the dish-drainer. . . . It has hinges, so that it can either rest on the cook-form or be turned over and cover the sink. Under the sink are shelf-boxes . . . for scouring-materials, dish-towels, and dish-cloths. . . . Under the cook-form are shelves and shelf-boxes for unbolted wheat, corn-meal, rye, etc. Beneath these, for white and brown sugar, are wooden can-pails.... Beside them is the tin molasses-can with a tight, movable cover, and a cork in the spout. . . . The articles used for setting tables are to be placed on the shelves at the front and side of the sink. . . . The sink should be three feet long and three inches deep, its width matching the cook-form.

In the bath-room must be the opening to the garret, and a step-ladder to reach it. A reservoir in the garret, supplied by a forcing-pump in the cellar or at the sink, must be well supported by timbers, and the plumbing must be well done, or much annoyance will ensue. . . . The water-closets must have the latest improvements for safe discharge, and there will be no trouble. They cost no more than an out-door building, and save from the most disagreeable house-labor. A great improvement, called earth-closets, will probably take the place of water-closets to some extent. . . . The general principle of construction is somewhat like that of a water-closet, except that in place of water is used dried earth. The resulting compost is without disagreeable odor, and is the richest species of manure. The expense of its construction and use is no greater than that of the common water-closet; indeed, when the outlays for plumber's work, the almost inevitable troubles and disorders of water-pipes in a house, and the constant stream of petty repairs . . . are considered, the earth-closet is in itself much cheaper, besides being an accumulator of valuable matter.

The grand art of ventilating houses is by some method that will empty rooms of the vitiated air and bring in a supply of pure air by *small and imperceptible currents.*

Unventilated parlors, with gas-burners, (each consuming as much oxygen as several men), made as tight as possible, and a party of ladies and gentlemen spending half the night in them! In 1861, I visited a legislative hall, the legislature being in session. I remained half an hour in the most impure air I ever breathed. . . . Theatres and concert-rooms are so foul that only reckless people continue to visit them. Twelve hours in a railway-car exhausts one, not by the journeying, but because of the devitalized air. While crossing the ocean in a Cunard steamer, I was amazed that men who knew enough to construct such ships did not know enough to furnish air to the passengers. The distress of sea-sickness is greatly intensified by the sickening air of the ship. Were carbonic acid *only black,* what a contrast there would be between our hotels in their elaborate ornament!

. . . the customs of society that bring sleeping hours into daylight, and working and study hours into the night, are direct violations of the laws of health. . . . To this we must add the great neglect of economy as well as health in substituting unhealthful gaslight, poisonous, anthracite warmth, for the life-giving light and warmth of the sun. Millions and

ALL BEECHER, CATHARINE, THE AMERICAN WOMAN'S HOME, 1869

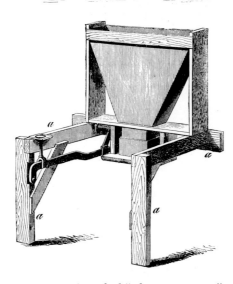

Top: view of an ideal "Christian cottage"
Center: a sink and work space containing storage bins for food and utensils
Above: a scale model of an earth-closet

millions would be saved to this nation in fuel and light, as well as in health, by returning to the good old ways of our forefathers, to rise with the sun, and retire to rest "when the bell rings for nine o'clock."

In this country there are three forms in which the use of . . . stimulants is common; namely, *alcoholic drinks, opium mixtures,* and *tobacco.* These are all alike in the main peculiarity of imparting that extra stimulus to the system which tends to exhaust its powers.

. . . if a person should bathe in warm water every day, debility would inevitably follow; for the frequent application of the stimulus of heat, like all other stimulants, eventually causes relaxation and weakness.

It has been supposed that large bath-tubs for immersing the whole person are indispensable to the proper cleaning of the skin. This is not so. A wet towel, applied every morning to the skin, followed by friction in pure air, is all that is absolutely needed; although a full bath is a great luxury.

The authors of this volume, while they sympathize with every honest effort to relieve the disabilities and sufferings of their sex, are confident that the chief cause of these evils is the fact that the honor and duties of the family state are not duly appreciated, that women are not trained for these duties as men are trained for their trades . . . and that, as the consequence, family labor is poorly done, poorly paid, and regarded as menial and disgraceful.

Cultivated, intelligent women, who are brought up to do the work of their own families, are labor-saving institutions. They make the head save the wear of the muscles. By forethought, contrivance, system, and arrangement they lessen the amount to be done, and do it with less expense of time and strength than others. The old New-England motto, *Get your work done up in the forenoon,* applied to an amount of work which would keep a common Irish servant toiling from daylight to sunset.

. . . let any man of sense and discernment become the member of a large household, in which a well-educated and pious woman is endeavoring systematically to discharge her multiform duties; let him fully comprehend all her cares, difficulties, and perplexities; and it is probable he would coincide in the opinion that no statesman, at the head of a nation's affairs, had more frequent calls for wisdom, firmness, tact, discrimination, prudence, and versatility of talent, than such a woman.

The writer would here urge every mistress of a family, who keeps more than one domestic servant, to provide them with single beds, that they might not be obliged to sleep with all the changing domestics, who come and go so often.

There is at the present time an increasing agitation of the public mind . . . as to woman's rights and duties. That there is a great social and moral power in her keeping, which is now seeking expression by organization, is manifest, and that resulting plans and efforts will involve some collisions . . . all must expect.

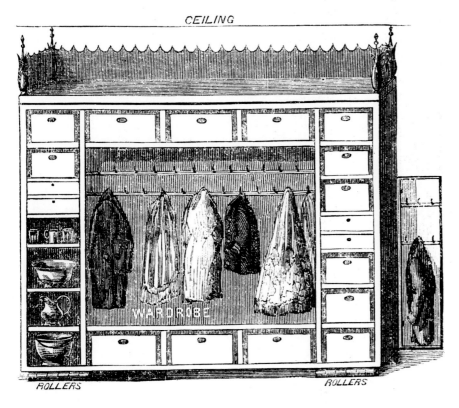

A wardrobe with drawers and hooks enhances the usefulness of a movable room divider.

264

Stick and Shingle Styles

The Wooden Tradition

Like all countries with an abundance of timber, America has throughout its history turned to wood as a favored building material for domestic structures. Even houses whose style, or styles, derived from the stone, brick, and stucco forms of baroque and classical European tradition were customarily of frame construction in this country. This translation of other materials into wood, however derivative the factors of style may have been, in itself accounted for the growth of an American idiom in domestic architecture. From the pattern books of earlier years a host of anonymous builders had learned and practiced that idiom throughout the nation. During the 1870s and 1880s a whole new generation of architects came to maturity. For the first time such professionally trained men exerted a dominant influence on the main trends of house design and construction, and they developed that native idiom into a highly eloquent vernacular. Memorable names in the history of the profession in this country became prominently associated with the design and building of such houses; notably, Henry Hobson Richardson, Charles Follen McKim, William Rutherford Mead, Stanford White, William Ralph Emerson, Bruce Price, and many others. Their synthesis of current trends or ideas, achieved in a relatively brief span of years, was not only highly successful in itself, but it laid a firm foundation for later, more advanced accomplishments. In 1876 even a hostile critic was obliged to admit that the new vernacular was "enterprising, inventive . . . , full of vivacity . . . and . . . it has life

A shingled house, roof detail

in it." Some years earlier an immigrant English architect had advised that a builder should "Let timber, and timber only, be evident in every part of your design" —which, in fact, was what seventeenth-century builders had done quite unself-consciously. In the later houses wooden framing techniques were in themselves an expressive factor in the shapes and articulation of houses. "Style" became an almost irrelevant consideration as the plans of such houses opened up and the buildings themselves assumed an organic character that frankly proclaimed the purpose and nature of the structure and owed no debts to precedent. As mechanical household operations became more commonplace they too affected the actual structure of living arrangements. With central heating, for example, the interior of a house, even in regions where the winters were cold, could be opened up to provide a new sense of space. Indeed, one of the significant developments in the houses here discussed was the expansion of the hall into a large and informal main living area. With this new freedom of interior planning the traditional parlors—those decorously furnished, lugubrious chambers that for decades had generally been reserved for such formal occasions as the last rites of the deceased, visits from the clergyman, and proposals of marriage—those "ceremonial deserts," as one critic called them, began to seem useless and out of place in modern life. The best room in the house became the "living room," where general domestic activities could be enjoyed by all members of a household.

BOTH: WAYNE ANDREWS

Left: the W. Watts Sherman House, built of stone and wood by Richardson at Newport, R.I.

Below: frame house designed by Richardson in 1868 as his own residence on Staten Island, N.Y.

Opposite: the Cram House, built in the "stick style" at Middletown, R.I., by Dudley Newton

"Stick style" is a term that has been applied to early examples of our indigenous wooden architecture in which the frame construction frankly expresses the essential character of the building, without particular reference to historic precedents. That freedom from bondage to past styles opened the way to a wide variety of experiment. The house built in the early 1870s for Jacob Cram at Middletown, Rhode Island, clearly demonstrates the case. The picturesque but functional arrangement of its framework and the irregular massing of separate elements of the house bespeak the high rooms and varied accommodations within. In 1868 Richardson, who was to be the leading spirit of the period, built a frame house for himself in Arrochar on Staten Island, which shows lingering traces of conventional design of the time in its mansard roof crowned by the inevitable iron casting. The Watts Sherman House he built at Newport in 1874 marks another phase of Richardson's development. Here he Americanized the so-called Queen Anne type of house based on the concept of the large living hall, so handsomely refined by the progressive architect Richard Norman Shaw in England, and brought it prominently to the attention of other American architects.

PRESERVATION SOCIETY OF NEWPORT COUNTY

AMERICAN ARCHITECT AND BUILDING NEWS, NOVEMBER 11, 1884

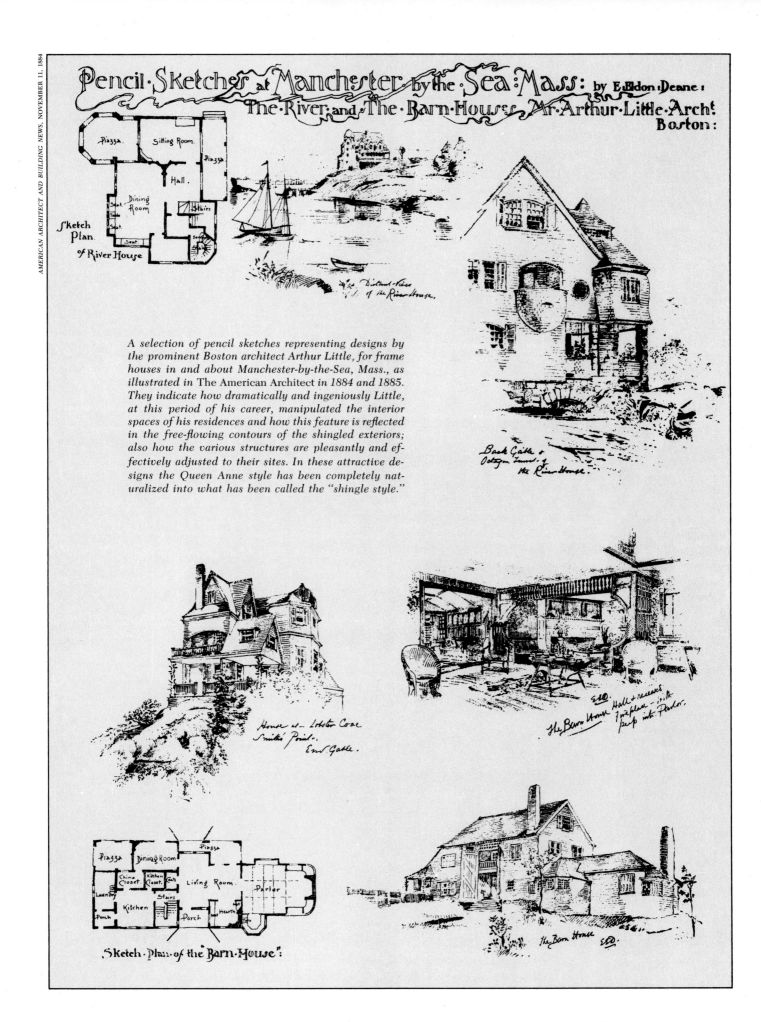

Pencil·Sketches at Manchester·by·the·Sea·Mass: by E·Eldon·Deane:
The·River·and·The·Barn·Houses, Mr·Arthur·Little·Archt·Boston:

Piazza. Sitting Room.

Piazza

Hall.

Dining Room

Stairs

Seat.

Seat.

Seat

Sketch Plan of River House

The Distant·View of the River House.

Back Gable & Octagon Tower of the River House.

A selection of pencil sketches representing designs by the prominent Boston architect Arthur Little, for frame houses in and about Manchester-by-the-Sea, Mass., as illustrated in The American Architect *in 1884 and 1885. They indicate how dramatically and ingeniously Little, at this period of his career, manipulated the interior spaces of his residences and how this feature is reflected in the free-flowing contours of the shingled exteriors; also how the various structures are pleasantly and effectively adjusted to their sites. In these attractive designs the Queen Anne style has been completely naturalized into what has been called the "shingle style."*

House at Lobster Cove Smith's Point. End Gable.

The Barn House Hall & recess, fireplace – with peep into Parlor.

Piazza Dining Room

Piazza

China Closet

Kitchen Closet

Closet

Living Room.

Parlor

Laundry

Kitchen

Stairs

Porch

Porch

Hearth

Sketch·Plan·of the "Barn·House".

The Barn House

First·Floor·Plan

Basement·Plan

of·the·Fort·House.

House at Lobster Cove
Smiths Point. Manchester.
Mr. Arthur L. Little. Architect

House of Mr. Prim
Beverley Farms

The Fort House.

Pencil
Sketches
in·and·around
Manchester-
-by·the·sea:
Mass: by E. Eldon Deane.

Stables to the River Fort & Barn Houses
Mr. Arthur Little. Archt.

Hall & Fireplace
The Fort House

Distant Sketch
of the Fort House.

The Isaac Bell House, built in 1882–83 by the McKim, Mead, and White firm at Newport, R.I.

Numerous architects and architectural firms worked in the shingle style in the 1880s, freely experimenting with problems of interior arrangements and exterior appearance. Among Richardson's pupils were Charles McKim and Stanford White who, with Rutherford Mead, in 1882–83 undertook to build a house in Newport for Isaac Bell. With its wide porches, irregular but harmonious masses, and great living hall, the Bell House was characteristic of houses in this style. Another and an extreme example of the shingle style house was also built by McKim, Mead, and White in 1887 as a summer residence for W. G. Low at Bristol, Rhode Island. The great sloping roof that overhangs the spacious porch unifies the mass of the structure with serene dignity and strongly emphasizes the horizontal planes of the house, which seems to settle on its site with natural ease and grace. Windows clustered in bays of generous size are overhung with horizontal eaves of their own.

A view of the fireplace nook in the living hall of the Bell House, showing the great staircase that rises from the open room
The shingle style house built at Bristol, R.I., in 1887, also by McKim, Mead, and White, as a summer residence for W. G. Low

The Low House, just mentioned, marks a culmination of the shingle style. It is classic in its clean-lined, unified design, although it has no references whatsoever to classical architecture — or, indeed, to any traditional academic formulas. Virtually all applied decoration, of any nature, was omitted from the shingled exterior surfaces, broad expanses that became an attractive silver gray with exposure to the sea air. Here the best characteristics of Richardson's later frame houses were clearly and cleanly expressed. It might be said that the Low House is a very successful demonstration of freedom of design completely disciplined. In spirit it heralds the simplicity and functionalism that was so remarkably developed in the houses of Frank Lloyd Wright about fifteen years later. The architects — the firm of McKim, Mead, and White — did not themselves progress further in that direction. Ten years before, McKim, Mead, and White had taken a celebrated trip to New England, in the course of which they made sketches and measured drawings of colonial houses for future reference. Newport, Rhode Island, with its abundance of such structures, was one of the towns important for their purpose that they visited. Those attractive reminders of eighteenth-century design had an inevitable attraction for architects concerned with frame construction. Actually, the development of the shingle style coincided with an awakening interest in American colonial architecture in general, an interest that had been stimulated by displays at the Philadelphia Centennial Exhibition in 1876 and that spread in epidemic fashion in years to come. With the completion of the Low House, McKim, Mead, and White virtually abandoned the shingle style in favor of more conventional formulas involving the full apparatus of academic design and including houses in the colonial revival style.

STEVENS, JOHN C. EXAMPLES OF AMERICAN DOMESTIC ARCHITECTURE, 1889

Project for a "House by the Sea" in the shingle style, designed in 1885 by John C. Stevens

The Return of Past Glories

Beaux-Arts Revivals

Although since Appomattox architects had sought the ideal formula for creating suitable residences for the very rich, throughout the 1870s they generally concocted overblown confections in such a variety of styles that American architecture was left on the brink of chaos. It was only in the 1880s, when Richard Morris Hunt launched the American Renaissance, that a new sense of formal

Portrait of G. W. Vanderbilt

order and more exacting standards of design and technical competence emerged. The first American to attend the École des Beaux-Arts in Paris, Hunt returned to the United States thoroughly steeped in French classical traditions, and he began his practice determined to rival the best of the past.

In an age when, as Ward McAllister described it, "New York's ideas as to values, when fortune was concerned, leaped boldly up to ten millions, fifty millions, one hundred millions," Hunt had little difficulty securing wealthy patrons. In 1881, he completed a private palace for William Kissam Vanderbilt on Fifth Avenue, designed in the manner of a French Renaissance château from the Loire Valley. Following this revolutionary feat, other architects took up the banner of eclecticism, and produced their own adaptations of Renaissance palaces, derived not only from French, but from Italian and other European sources as well. Around the turn of the century, Fifth Avenue from Forty-Sixth to Seventy-Second Streets was an almost uninterrupted mile and a half of châteaux, palazzi, and fortresses, and a foreign visitor aptly observed that "the absence of gardens and trees around these sumptuous residences proves the newness of all this wealth. . . . This avenue has been willed and created by the sheer force of millions."

From New York, the American Renaissance spread to other affluent areas. Newport's miles of sandy beaches, available farmland for building, genial summer climate, and aura of remoteness attracted vacationers of wealth and station, who transformed the former shipping center into a bastion of exclusiveness. These "summer people" proceeded to erect luxurious habitations, fitted with extravagant furnishings and valuable art collections, the sheer ostentation of which must have seemed an insult to the staid and frugal New England townsfolk.

To some viewers of the American scene, the eclectics seemed to create one architectural triumph after another, and several masterpieces were erected as late as the 1920s. However, as early as 1907, Henry James noticed that some of the Newport palaces built in the previous generation had already become "white elephants . . . queer . . . and lumpish." And, even such noted eclectic architects as Thomas Hastings began to question the validity of the historical approach in view of the pressing demands of the twentieth century. "Copying," he admitted, "destroys progress in art and all spontaneity. The problem solved makes style. . . . our Renaissance must not be merely archaeological, the literal following of certain periods of the style. To build a French Louis XII or Francis I or Louis XIV house, or to make an Italian *cinquecento* design, is indisputably not modern architecture."

Above: raised in 1891, the Fifth Avenue mansion of Mrs. William Astor was created in the manner of a French Renaissance château by R. M. Hunt.

Right: the formal sunken French gardens and sprawling lawns of The Elms, erected on a terraced slope in 1901, are surrounded by high stone walls.

Opposite: the spacious staircase, highlighted by bronze lamp standards at the landings, was designed when Château-sur-Mer was modernized.

274

In order to live flamboyantly and entertain expensively, the new millionaires of the Gilded Age erected enormous houses that were elaborately decorated inside and out, with more rooms and services than American homes had ever before required. Between 1850 and 1900, the fashionable resort of Newport became a place of many mansions, the stylistic gamut of which ran from Tudor castles and Renaissance palazzi, to French châteaux like The Elms, a residence romantically situated on grounds laid out by the noted landscape architect Jacques Gréber, whose *pièce de résistance* was a formal sunken garden reminiscent of ones in the era of Louis XIV. Although Château-sur-Mer had been rated Newport's finest dwelling at the time it was built for the China Trader William Wetmore, in 1852, twenty years later it was eclipsed by more pretentious palaces, and the society architect Richard Morris Hunt was hired to give the house a face lifting. Among Hunt's renovations was a massive oak staircase that cascaded down three stories through the center of the mansion, unifying it and imparting it with a lofty new grandeur. During Newport's summer social season of 1891, Hunt was commissioned by Mrs. Willian B. Astor, the acknowledged leader of the Four Hundred, to build a double town house for herself and her son, John Jacob, at the corner of Sixty-Fifth Street and Fifth Avenue in New York. Borrowing various aspects of its design from such Loire Valley châteaux as Blois, Chambord, and the Château de Maisons, the twin residence not only inspired awe and envy by the sheer massiveness of its facade, but, on a symbolic level, seemed to serve as a visual summation of the system of free enterprise.

Above: built between 1893 and 1895 of Indiana limestone, The Breakers is situated on a broad promontory overlooking the Atlantic.
Opposite: the elaborately enriched main hall of The Elms, designed in 1901 by the noted Philadelphia architect Horace Trumbauer

With their intention to re-create the magnificence of earlier eras in their elaborate mansions, tycoons of the late 1800s looked for assurance that their wealth would be tastefully and conspicuously displayed. At exclusive Newport, the rich and well-born passed the summer season in palatial "country cottages" like The Breakers, created for the waterfront estate of Cornelius Vanderbilt II by Richard Morris Hunt. Despite its apparent magnitude, this seventy-room rendition of a sixteenth-century Genoa palazzo was considered confining by its owners, and an extra story was added to accommodate the domestic help. Similarly, the coal magnate Edward J. Berwind spared no expense decorating his seashore retreat, The Elms. Recalling the rococo richness of Louis XV's France, the main hall featured twin columns of *brèche violette* marble and lanterns of gilded bronze. Among the last monuments of the age of elegance was the Manhattan residence of Henry Clay Frick, a man who devoted much of his life and steel fortune to his art collection. Erected in 1913 on Fifth Avenue, this block-long adaptation of an eighteenth-century French town house cost about ten million dollars and required nearly one thousand dollars a day maintenance. The adoption of the Sixteenth Amendment that year seriously curtailed the palace-building penchant of millionaires, who now had to share their wealth with the government.

Detail of the Frick Mansion, a masterpiece by Thomas Hastings

The 780-foot-long facade of Biltmore, built from 1890 to 1895 near Asheville, N.C.

Armorial bearings, Flemish tapestries, and hunting trophies decorate the banquet hall.

When George Washington Vanderbilt II, in 1885, inherited one eighteenth of his father's one hundred and eighty million dollar estate, he put his meager millions into the construction of what he hoped would be the finest country house in America. A decade later, and nearly five million dollars poorer, Vanderbilt gave a formal housewarming at an immense château that took its name of Biltmore from the Dutch town of Bildt, whence came the family forebears, and that by all appearances seemed to have been lifted from the Loire Valley to an equally noble setting in the foothills of the Great Smoky Mountains in North Carolina. While the mansion was being raised, its owner had a special spur of railway constructed to carry materials from Asheville to the site, and employed about one

278

In the library, a spiral staircase of gilded bronze winds to upper-level shelves.

thousand highly trained artisans and workers. Although the architect, Richard Morris Hunt, borrowed ideas for Biltmore from famous French châteaux, he also gave the structure a personality of its own, as seen in its asymmetrical facade, dominated by an entrance pavilion with a pierced stone parapet, clustered pinnacles, and tiny flying buttresses. However aloof and austere the building might appear on the outside, its two hundred and fifty room interior was brought to life with a colorful array of paintings, tapestries, statuary, porcelain, and rare books. Of particular architectural interest was the massive medieval banquet hall, which had such perfect acoustics that people at opposite ends of the huge oak table could hear one another without shouting, and the library, paneled in Circassian walnut.

D.P.I.: MARY ELEANOR BROWNING

Richard Morris Hunt

Richard M. Hunt, the society architect

In the years following the Centennial, Richard Morris Hunt, more than any other American architect, personified the artistic taste of the very rich. His career coincided with the emergence of a moneyed leisure class made up of second, third, and even forth generation scions of men who had founded great fortunes, but had neither the time, nor the ingenuity to spend them. Spared the onus of the income tax, these millionaires tried to surpass one another in the size and magnificence of their homes, the costliness of their furnishings and art collections, and the lavishness of their entertainments. From New York to Newport, and south to Asheville, North Carolina, Hunt created elegantly eclectic châteaux for railway kings like the Vanderbilts and clients of similar station. Although the architect maintained rigid standards of scholarship in the belief that his achievement rested not on originality, but in intelligently adapting the great styles of the past to the needs of the present, he also tried to get along amicably with his wealthy patrons. As he once wrote his son, "The first thing you've got to remember is that it's your clients' money you're spending.

Your business is to get the best result you can, following their wishes. If they want you to build a house upside down, standing on its chimney, it's up to you to do it."

Born in 1827 at Brattleboro, Vermont, the son of Congressman Jonathan Hunt and the former Maria Jane Leavitt spent his childhood in the socially prominent circles of New Haven and Boston. At the age of sixteen, he accompanied his widowed mother and brother, William Morris Hunt—who later became a distinguished painter—to Europe, where he prepared for the École des Beaux-Arts at the Paris atelier of the architect Hector-Martin Lefuel. In 1846 Richard became the first United States citizen to be admitted to the École and receive the instruction that later in the century was *de rigueur* for aspiring American architects. Here, Hunt studied painting and sculpture, as well as architecture, and interspersed his formal schooling with the *gaietés* of Parisian life, and travel through Egypt, Turkey, Italy, and the Loire Valley. Upon receiving his diploma, Hunt, in 1854, assisted Lefuel, who had been appointed architect to Napoleon III, with the design and construction of an addition to the Louvre known as the Pavillon de la Bibliothèque, a building which gives some idea of the fussy elegance of the Second Empire. This Yankee lad might have remained in France had he not been attracted by the challenge of his native country. He wrote his mother: "It has been represented to me, that America was not ready for the fine arts, but I think they are mistaken. There is no place in the world where they are more needed, or where they should be more encouraged. Why, there are more luxurious houses put up in New York than in Paris! At any rate the desire is evinced and the money spent and if the object is

not attained it is the fault of the architects. Why should not our public hotels . . . rival or even surpass the palaces of Europe? . . . There are no greater fools in America than in any other part of the world: the only thing is that the professional man with us has got to make his own standing." Thus, after the most extensive training that any native architect had ever received, the "handsomest American in Paris" returned to the United States in 1856.

Hunt, at first, worked for Thomas U. Walter, who was in charge of designing the dome for the Capitol in Washington, D. C. No sooner did Hunt establish his own practice in New York in 1857 than he involved himself in a lawsuit that became a *cause célèbre* of the architectural profession. Having designed a costly house for the wealthy and eccentric dentist Dr. Eleazer Parmly, Hunt presented his bill. Parmly, "outraged at the charge of five per cent which also covered the cost of the interior decoration," refused to honor it, and Hunt sued. A jury of the New York Supreme Court awarded the architect two and one half per cent, the minimum commission in those days, but the case made it clear to the public that architects could properly command adequate compensation for their services.

During the late 1860s and the 1870s, Hunt experimented with various styles, offering one solution, then another, to the problems that beset American life. At the Studio Building on West Tenth Street, a structure of his own design, Hunt surrounded himself with talented young apprentices, including Henry Van Brunt, George B. Post, Charles D. Gambrill, and later Frank Furness. He fired his students' imaginations with the glories of Beaux-Arts classicism and continually exhorted them to "draw, draw, draw, sketch, sketch,

sketch! If you can't draw anything else, draw your boots . . . it will ultimately give you control of your pencil so that you can more readily express on paper your thoughts on designing." During this period, Hunt planned the Stuyvesant Apartment House, a building said to contain the first "French flats" in New York. It caused something of a scandal, because, heretofore, such a domestic arrangement was limited to squalid tenements. And, a few years later, he created the nine-story Tribune Building, the first elevator office building in the country.

Hunt's fame as an architect dates from 1879, when he was commissioned to build a town house at Fifth Avenue and Fifty-Second Street for William Kissam Vanderbilt and his socially ambitious wife, Alva. The spectacle of a sixteenth-century French château of gray limestone, blossoming forth in pinnacles and turrets, was nothing short of revolutionary in a city where millionaires had customarily concealed their worldly success behind seemingly identical brownstone facades. The unparalleled elegance of the mansion indirectly caused Mrs. William Astor, the lofty grande dame of New York society, to accept the upstart Vanderbilts into her fold. She attended a ball held at the Vanderbilt Château on March 26, 1883, that was generally acknowledged to be the most brilliant in the annals of Manhattan. The house received all but universal praise from Hunt's architectural colleagues. Charles Follen McKim asserted that he had to stroll past the house every night before he could fall asleep. The lone voice of dissent came from a young midwestern architect, Louis Sullivan, who asked disdainfully, "Must I show you . . . this little Château de Blois on this street corner, here in New York, and still you do not laugh?

Above: a Louvre wing, designed by Hunt
Below: Vanderbilt family mausoleum
Bottom: E. K. Rossiter home, 38th Street

WAYNE ANDREWS

AMERICAN ARCHITECT AND BUILDING NEWS, JUNE 2, 1878

Must you wait until you see a *gentleman* in a silk hat come out of it before you laugh? . . . Must I tell you that while the man may live in the house physically . . . that he cannot possibly live in it morally, mentally, or spiritually, that he and his home are a paradox . . . an absurdity; that he is no part of the house, and his house is no part of him."

Although Hunt was subsequently besieged with requests for Fifth Avenue châteaux from other members of the Four Hundred, he became an unofficial architect in residence to the Vanderbilts. In 1886 Hunt completed the Vanderbilt mausoleum on Staten Island. In this replica of a Romanesque stone chapel, the bodies of the Commodore and his son, William H. Vanderbilt, were interred. And, for fear of body snatchers, the family hired watchmen, who were required to punch a time clock every fifteen minutes, to guard the hallowed remains. Beginning in 1888, Hunt designed a spectacular cluster of palaces at Newport, the fashionable resort of wealthy New Yorkers. Besides building The Breakers and Marble House for various Vanderbilts, Hunt erected imposing residences for the Astors and for the Oliver Hazard Perry Belmonts. Ochre Court, owned by the Ogden Goelets, the New York real estate dynasty, with its dramatic cliffside location and gigantic iron gates, was, perhaps, the most architecturally successful of all Hunt's Gothic châteaux. These ostentatious summer houses bedazzled visitors by the sumptuousness of their interiors, which typically contained entrance halls of two or three stories, encrusted with balconies, balustrades, carving, wrought iron, chandeliers, sculpture, nymphs, and allegorical ceiling paintings. There also might be Moorish or Byzantine rooms, palm courts, Jacobean suites,

281

solariums, and grand staircases fit for princesses in train to descend.

Toward the end of his career, in the early 1890s, Hunt's commissions ranged from New York town houses, to the central portion of the facade of the Metropolitan Museum, to the base of the Statue of Liberty, to the Administration Hall of the World's Columbian Exposition in Chicago. When George Washington Vanderbilt, the younger brother of William Kissam, decided to build a castle on a tract of North Carolina woodland and devote his fortune to experimental forestry, it was not surprising that he selected Hunt as his architect. Of all Hunt's creations, Biltmore, with its steep roof covering a larger area than any other private or public building in the country, neared the ultimate in magnificence, although Henry James, a master of understatement, described it merely as "a thing of the high Rothschild manner."

Hunt died in 1895 in Newport of nothing less fashionable than the gout, complicated by a cold caught while attending one of the Vander-bilt weddings. Hunt's malady had caused "cruel bodily distress" for years, but he bravely practiced his profession until two weeks before his demise. Eulogies to this "vigorous, virile, energetic, tempestuous character" poured in from members of the press and Hunt's fellow architects. None, however, was as sincere in its sentiment as the "resolutions" sent to Mrs. Hunt by the carpenters, bricklayers, stonecutters, plumbers, electricians, and others who had worked on Biltmore. They wrote, "we who have worked under him, deeming it fitting that we record our love and appreciation of him, have *Resolved* that in his death our country has lost its greatest architect . . . and a kind, considerate and constant friend, for neither his great fame nor his great wealth ever caused him to be forgetful, indifferent, or careless of the rights and feelings of his fellow men and laborers who were aiding in an humbler way in erecting these beautiful buildings, which only marvelous genius could have imagined and planned."

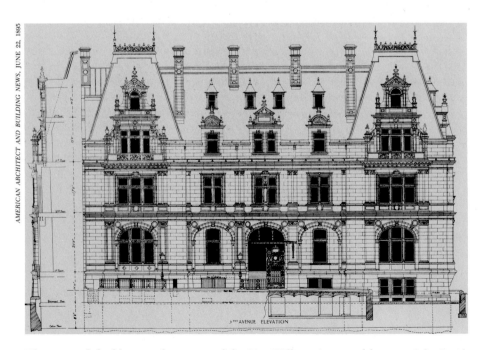

AMERICAN ARCHITECT AND BUILDING NEWS, JUNE 22, 1895

Elevation of double town house raised for Mrs. William Astor and her son, John Jacob

The Growing Needs of Cities

Urban Building

As the new industrialism swept over the land of the dollar in the wake of the Civil War, people flocked to the nation's cities in unprecedented numbers from rural regions, villages, and foreign countries. Nowhere did opportunity seem to knock louder than in New York, at the very threshold of America, with its vast concentrations of capital, business and financial institutions, railroad yards, and recreational facilities. Sightseers to the nation's largest metropolis marveled at its imposing buildings; this tourist's response was typical: "The streets are narrow, and overshadowed as they are by edifices six or more stories in height, seem to be dwarfed into mere alley-ways." By the 1880s, the city's architecture also appeared to have "a universal chocolate-covered coating," as Edith Wharton put it, of brownstone, a somber-colored sandstone popularized by the Vanderbilts.

Manhattan's large population, poor transportation, and spiraling cost of real estate inevitably led to the proliferation of apartment houses, which had evolved from high-class tenements known as French flats. Despite protests from a few diehard traditionalists like William Dean Howells, who warned, "The flat abolishes the family consciousness. It's confinement without coziness; it's cluttered without being snug. You couldn't keep a self-respecting cat in a flat; you couldn't go down cellar to get cider," these conveniently located buildings gradually replaced boardinghouses as acceptable rental accommodations for well-to-do urbanites. Others, reluctant to part with their own personal front door to

Detail of Dakota Apartments

RICHARD WATHERWAX

the street, or bit of back yard, found a practical alternative in the row house, which became popular from New York to San Francisco.

Fifth Avenue, America's most splendid thoroughfare, bedazzled its visitors with a continuous pageant of "palatial hotels, gorgeous club-houses, brownstone mansions and magnificent churches." Along Fifth and neighboring Madison Avenues arose one sumptuous residence after another in a steady uptown progression. These adaptations of French châteaux or Italian Renaissance palaces were designed by such distinguished architects as Richard Morris Hunt and by the firm of McKim, Mead, and White for their millionaire clients.

New York, however, remained a city of contrasts. Often within walking distance of the citadels of wealth were festering clots of poverty where the less prosperous classes, and particularly immigrants, were forced to reside. Their dwellings were dark, insanitary tenements, usually referred to as "dumbbells" because of the outline of their floor plans. By 1888 there were over thirty-two thousand such buildings, containing a human population of more than one million, not to mention rats, vermin, and other parasites. Although a few philanthropic citizens tried to erect decent model lodgings for the poor, the Danish reporter Jacob Riis aptly observed that while many New York tenements had less of the slum look than those in other cities, and some even had brownstone facades, "To get at the pregnant facts of tenement-house life, one must look beneath the surface."

Above: clock in sculptured setting by Saint-Gaudens on the Villard staircase
Left: characteristic "dumbbell" floor plan of an Old Law tenement in New York

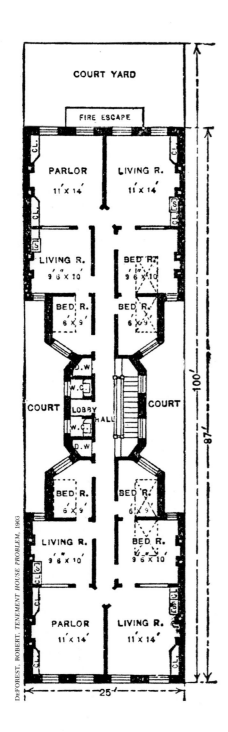

COURT YARD

FIRE ESCAPE

PARLOR
11' x 14'

LIVING R.
11' x 14'

LIVING R.
9' 6" x 10'

BED R.
9' 6" x 10'

BED R.
6' x 9'

BED R.
6' x 9'

D.W

W.C

COURT LOBBY HALL COURT

W.C

D.W

BED R.
6' x 9'

BED R.
6' x 9'

LIVING R.
9' 6" x 10'

BED R.
9' 6" x 10'

PARLOR
11' x 14'

LIVING R.
11' x 14'

100'

87'

25'

Of all the palatial residences to arise in Manhattan during the Gilded Age, the most distinguished was the complex of town houses planned by the railroad financier Henry Villard, for himself and four of his friends. Despite its midtown location on Madison Avenue between Fiftieth and Fifty-First Streets, this superb evocation of an Italian Renaissance palazzo, with its U-shaped plan, uniform facade, and court of honor, would have made even the Medicis feel at home. Stanford White of McKim, Mead, and White not only designed the block-long brownstone edifice, but persuaded artists of the day like Augustus Saint-Gaudens, who sculpted a magnificent clock for the Villard staircase, to contribute to its interior decoration. The structure's surpassing elegance may, however, have inconvenienced its owner. When Villard moved into the house in 1885, he was suspected of mismanaging the Northern Pacific and cheating its stockholders. Angry crowds gathered outside, wrongly imagining that Villard was to occupy the entire building, although he actually resided in its southernmost wing and had moved in prematurely to save the expense of other accommodations. On the other side of the tracks, meanwhile, the poor were crowded into tenements as spectacular in their squalor as the Villard Mansion was in its splendor. The passage of a Tenement House Law of 1879 did little to deprive slumlords of their profits. They continued to build narrow, deep buildings, with two to four flats on a floor, run out from front to back "railroad" style, with public toilets on the landings. Inner rooms received light and air only from the stairwell and a walled-in court. Although such well-meaning but misguided philanthropies as the Improved Dwelling Association erected model tenements, like the one illustrated, these airless, sunless, bathless buildings soon became vile slums themselves, and set a general pattern of blight for future attempts to house the lower classes.

Top: the mansion on Madison Avenue, completed in 1885 for Villard by McKim, Mead, and White, now houses the Archdiocese of New York.
Above: Vaux' and Radford's drawing of a model New York tenement, built in 1880 on First Avenue between 71st and 72nd Streets

This block of row houses, completed in 1891, was designed by William H. Lillie for the Rountree brothers, San Francisco builders. A row of narrow brownstones, with repetitive masonry trim in their cornices, windows, and doorways, lines a New York City street.

During the period of urban expansion following the Civil War, speculative builders discovered a bonanza in the form of the row house. Designed for single family occupancy, these dwellings cost relatively little to construct, because they shared common walls with their neighbors, and because many could be erected side by side on a narrow street frontage. Along New York's gridiron of streets and avenues rose block after block of row houses, which, by the 1880s, were almost invariably faced with brownstone. In contrast, wooden row houses on the West Coast appeared light and airy with their coats of bright paint. San Francisco developed a particularly successful row vernacular, suitable for rich and poor alike, as typified by clusters of homes like the Rountree group, which featured Queen Anne elements in their pitched roofs and heavily decorated exteriors. Although critics likened the facades of such structures to the "puffing, paint and powder of our female friends," the houses were efficiently planned, sanitary, and well-lighted. Virtually every dwelling boasted one or more bay windows, which were as important to sun-loving San Franciscans as brownstone fronts were to New Yorkers. As an English traveler observed, California architecture, "with all the windows gracefully leaping out at themselves," should rightly be called the "bay-window order."

288

The sculpture on these pages exemplifies the ornamental brownstone trim that was applied to single family dwellings in New York during the late 1800s. Using brownstone imported from quarries in New Jersey, journeyman craftsmen produced moldings, entablatures, and brackets by the gross for speculative builders. Copied from available sources, designs included such wholesale borrowings from the past as acanthus leaves, garlands, masks, and mythological figures.

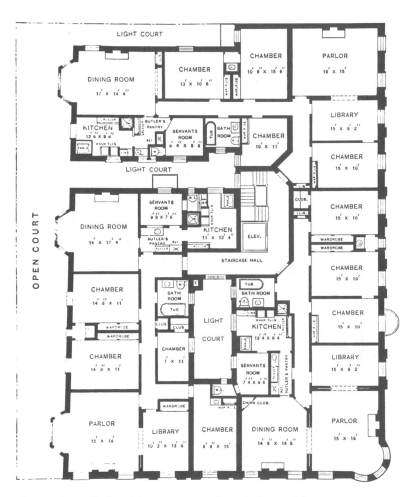

Above: the well-thought-out interior plan of three adjoining apartments
Left: Dakota Apartments, completed 1884 on New York's Central Park West

In the 1880s increasing numbers of New Yorkers discovered that apartment houses, with elevators, central heating, efficient plumbing, and electricity, eased many of the difficulties of urban life. Even the very rich, who could afford to own mansions, overcame their fashionable prejudices and began to find rental accommodations acceptable. The New York paradigm for people at the top of the social and economic totem pole was typified by the Dakota Apartments, so named because the neighborhood in which the structure was raised—at Central Park West, between Seventy-Second and Seventy-Third Streets—was thought to be as remote from the heart of Manhattan as the Dakota Territory. Designed in the manner of the German Renaissance by Henry Janeway Hardenbergh, this communal palace, with its profusion of peaked roofs, chimneys, dormers, and sculptured ornament, was the first of the great super-block buildings with a central drive-in courtyard. Here, the conveniences of a private residence were combined, in multiple, with the services of a luxury hotel. Individual suites were carefully laid out to provide a maximum of privacy and light, and, as the above plan indicates, the latest of modern facilities for everyone but the servants, whose own comparatively cramped quarters lacked bathtubs.

For New York's toiling masses and leisured classes, Central Park was a fundamental feature of the cityscape. Extending from Fifty-Ninth to One Hundred Tenth Streets, and from Fifth to Eighth Avenues, this eight-hundred-acre oasis of greenery, with its woods, hills, ponds, and fields, gave urbanites in search of relaxation and recreation a brief respite from the frantic pace, pressing crowds, and noisome congestion of the metropolis. Completed in 1876, Central Park was largely the inspired creation of Frederick Law Olmsted, who, nineteen years earlier, along with Calvert Vaux, began developing a barren stretch of land in the middle of Manhattan that was dotted with squatters' shanties, scrubland, farms, and reservoirs for Croton aqueduct water. Despite the site's dearth of natural riches, Olmsted and Vaux, aided by relief workers who were left jobless in the depression of 1857, and underwritten with the considerable sum of $16,500,000, succeeded in transforming the wasteland into a miniature Eden, in which nature was presented in a delicate balance of wilds with tamed parts, open vistas with densely planted sections. Here, free-flowing paths and walks wound around such "natural" features as a sheep meadow, which was actually artificially created to enhance the impression of a remote rural setting. In a day before the motor vehicle, Olmsted's scheme also included the far-sighted novelty of having transverse roads dropped below the level of the park so that carriages and equestrians would not interfere with pedestrians. Over the years, Central Park was given a backdrop of luxury buildings, like the Dakota Apartments, which arose on the streets along its perimeters, and accumulated a wide variety of structures, including zoos, skating rinks, and outdoor theaters. However, as late as 1899, a writer still could rhapsodize about "the craft of the illusion and the perfection of the art that can produce such a panorama of Nature in so little space."

An 1890's skating scene in Central Park, with the Dakota Apartments in the distance

In the Last Resorts

Vacation Architecture

Among the nomadic peoples of the world, none has raised such a variety of interesting and curious monuments to mark its seasonal treks as the Americans. From the gingerbread fairylands of Saratoga Springs to the Spanish baroque splendors of St. Augustine, resort hotels stand as monuments to the democratic longing for a life of princely luxury. As architecture, those pleasure domes that were built in the late years of the nineteenth century tended to be large-scale parodies of the homes of the period, ranging from masterpieces to absurdities. It was the magic touch of the railroads as they fingered their way through the land that brought most of the first great resorts to life. Some of those early landmarks, bearing traces of the Pullman-car eclecticism of their heyday, still survive in the web of thruways and air lanes of the present, and some are gone forever. When the Hotel del Coronado was opened in 1888 near San Diego, California, a stop on the Santa Fe, its architecture was described as of "a mixed character, partaking largely of the Queen Anne style, and having much that is also characteristic of the Elizabethan era" along with "many of the excellences of other schools, both ancient and modern." Also in 1888, the financier Henry Morrison Flagler opened "the world's finest hotel," the Ponce de Leon, in St. Augustine, Florida, by the well-known architects Carrère and Hastings "in the style of the Spanish Renaissance." To provide access for its guests Flagler purchased and rehabilitated a parcel of small railroads. The ornate pile, it was claimed, set a new standard in American architecture.

Taking the waters at Saratoga

Flagler continued to promote Florida as a winter playground for the rich, building such other resplendent hostelries as The Breakers and the Royal Poinciana at Palm Beach; the latter was the largest wooden structure in history. By lakesides and on mountaintops, as well as along the seashore, other great resorts were built as temporary retreats for vacationers, not always wealthy. Some years earlier Cornelius Vanderbilt, another sound-thinking railroad man, had opened the Grand Hotel on Mackinac Island in northern Michigan, with its 885-foot-long colonnaded porch. The railroads never actually reached the island, and automobiles are banned. Here one can step back, after a fashion, into the Victorian past; and among Midwesterners it is still a fashionable step to take. The Mountain House, built as a "Temperance House" high in the Shawangunk Mountains not far from New York City, boasted more than four hundred feet of broad piazzas for public use. Baedeker's guide to the United States referred to Ocean Grove, New Jersey, established in 1870 by the Methodist Episcopal Church, as an "extraordinary settlement, possible only in America, in which many thousands of persons, young and old, voluntarily elect to spend their summer vacations under a religious autocracy, which is severe both in its positive and negative regulations." No drinking, no tobacco, no theater, and, on Sundays, no bathing, riding, or driving; a place, Baedeker concluded, "curious enough to repay a short visit." It was "God's Square Mile of Health & Happiness," where austerity could be enjoyed.

Above: a view of the Columbian Spring from Congress Park, Saratoga Springs, N.Y.
Opposite: the facade of the Grand Union Hotel, with its long, three-story veranda

The reputation of Saratoga Springs as a salubrious watering place goes back beyond the memory of man. Wild animals as well as redmen were attracted to *Saraghoga* ("place of swift water"), as the Indians called it, when the area was a complete wilderness. In 1783 George Washington tried to buy property there where springs were located. The place was already famed as a resort by the early years of the last century (pages 206–7) when Philip Hone described its wealthy and fashionable visitors. But it was during the latter decades of that century that Saratoga, to be called the Queen of the Spas, reached full blossom as a summer retreat for high society and its attendants. Of the great hotels that sprouted there, the Grand Union, as rebuilt in 1864, enjoyed singular distinction. Its three-story piazza, "the longest single porch in the world," was just over a quarter of a mile, its dining room 306 feet long. The marble used in the construction would have covered a solid acre, the carpeting more than twelve acres. And it was otherwise furbished with unrestrained elegance. Shortly before this remarkable landmark was demolished some years ago, a sign on its walls advertised for sale "period furniture used at the time of Lillian Russell, Diamond Jim Brady, Otis Skinner, Victor Herbert, John Drew, A. T. Stewart," listing a mere handful of the celebrated names associated with the hotel. Gambling, horse racing, and dalliance were prominent activities on the summer's schedule. One observer referred to Saratoga at its prime as the "seraglio of the prurient aristocracy." Here, it was later reported, the visitor would find both "elegant hells" and "elegant belles." It was the resort that had everything but salt-water bathing.

The Hotel del Coronado in California, an immense, rambling, towered resort designed by Stanford White; noted for the beauty of its patio with a huge flame-colored bougainvillea vine

The Grand Hotel on Mackinac Island, Mich., with its unprecedentedly long, colonnaded porch; energetic strolling guests could cover approximately a mile by walking about six lengths.

In the fourth edition of his guide book to the United States Baedeker referred to the Hotel del Coronado in California as "one of the largest, finest, and most comfortable hotels in California . . . delightfully situated close to the ocean. . . . Adjacent are bathing-tanks of salt water, for summer and winter use, while steam-yachts, launches, and boats afford opportunity for excursions by water." From the hotel tower, Baedeker wrote, one commanded "a splendid View," overlooking among other things "flower-beds . . . of astonishing brilliancy." To its variegated splendors, he noted, had come four presidents of the United States, the king of Hawaii, and assorted merchant princes of the highest rank. It has been claimed that the porch is an American institution, one hallowed by the example at Mount Vernon. In any case, it is a recurrent feature of our "classical" resort architecture. Nowhere was it carried to such lengths as at the Grand Hotel on Mackinac Island, Michigan, built in 1887 to accommodate wealthy visitors to that picturesque site.

OVERLEAF: *the Mountain House on Lake Mohonk, Shawangunk Mountains, N.Y.*
HANNAU ROBINSON, INC., ORLANDO

The Ponce de Leon, first of the great hotels designed to lure vacationers to Florida

The formal opening of "the world's finest hotel," the Ponce de Leon, built for Henry Morrison Flagler at St. Augustine, Florida, was an important event not only for the first guests but for the entire state of Florida, which was now on its way to becoming a winter playground for half a continent. The hotel itself was one of the first large structures in this country to be made of poured concrete, which was mixed with tons of coquina (a local shell rock) brought over from a neighboring island and trampled into the forms by a small army of twelve hundred workmen. There were 540 rooms, each with electric lights — something of a novelty at the time — and each with a complement of furnishings reported to have cost one thousand dollars. Most of the rich and varied ornament of the hotel was conceived by Bernard Maybeck, an associate whose fertile imagination practically forced the architects to take unexpected liberties with their theme. By January 10, 1888, more than a million dollars after the project was started, a great omnibus drawn by six white horses brought the first customers from the railroad station; as the gates of the resplendent palace rose, a cannon boomed, an orchestra played "The Star-Spangled Banner," and Floridians rejoiced. With its elaborately sculptured woodwork, its stair walls of solid polished marble, its stained-glass windows, and its dazzling lights, all enclosed by three-foot-thick walls, it added an entirely new dimension to the Florida scene. The Royal Poinciana, opened by Flagler in Palm Beach in 1894, was designed to accommodate as many as 1,750 people. The first guests to reach that great wooden hostelry by rail, however, comprised a private trainful of just seventeen selected socialites, including four Vanderbilts, who were brought there over the new Flagler Bridge completed in 1896. It soon became the nation's most fashionable gathering place. Flagler built or purchased several other palatial Florida hotels to entice vacationers to the state — via a network of judiciously and profitably planned Flagler railroads.

The lobby of the Ponce de Leon, with carved woodwork and polished marble
The palatial dining room; the old resort building is now Flagler College

*T*he turn of a century always serves as a dividing line in history, a time to discard the old and look to the new. Nothing changes overnight, to be sure; the main currents of history flow along at their wonted pace without regard for the calendar. The past lingers into the present and dies only slowly in time to come; the future is born of the present out of the past. No historical period, however sharply defined for the convenience of chroniclers, is ever uniform in its character or in its style. At any given moment the scene is a blend of gradually changing elements. Yet, to celebrate one century's end and another's beginning has a symbolic importance. It invokes a certain amount of stock-taking and reckoning; some effort to comprehend what the preceeding hundred years have led to, and what the next hundred might hold in store.

America acted as though it could not wait for the twentieth century to arrive. In 1893, to take the measure of its achievements in the fading century that had already seen such extraordinary changes and such remarkable progress, and to catch an early glimpse of its even brighter tomorrow, the nation mounted the World's Columbian Exposition at Chicago, the largest and most influential fair ever held in this country.

When America held its first international exhibition in 1853 at the Crystal Palace in New York, it had already become apparent that the industrial nations would inherit the earth, and that America was on its way to taking a high place among such countries. Forty years later, as demonstrated at Chicago, America had become a leader, and the world was impressed by this fact. As one token of such leadership, the giant Allis-Corliss reciprocating steam engine that provided the power that turned the dynamos that generated the electricity was probably the greatest stationary engine in the world. When Henry Adams visited the fair he "lingered among the dynamos," for, as he later wrote, "they . . . gave to history a new phase"; they became for Adams symbols of infinity and ultimate energy.

That the coming years would, indeed, and quite literally, be brighter was impressively demonstrated by the electrical displays. Here for the first time the general public got some notion of what untold services electricity might provide. Among other wonders, the fair grounds were bathed in electric light that turned night into day. To the many who were unfamiliar with anything brighter than a kerosene lamp or gaslight that spectacle was

Opposite: entry door and hall of the David B. Gamble House, Pasadena, Calif., built in 1907

Top: *the great Allis-Corliss engine*
Above: *Chicago fair at night, 1893*
Opposite: *the Woolworth Building*

illuminating in every sense of the word. The fact that power could be converted into light and heat and motion, and could be dispatched through a thin copper wire wherever it was needed, seemed almost like a supernatural revelation.

If the industrial and scientific demonstrations at Chicago foretold a future of progressive advances, the buildings that housed them gave no indication of such an outlook. With a few exceptions those structures were strongly influenced by the canons of the classical past—as far back in time as the architects could safely go for their inspiration. Richard Morris Hunt, steeped in the traditions of the École des Beaux-Arts in Paris, was summoned from the East to help plan the exposition complex, with Stanford White, Daniel Burnham, Louis Sullivan, and others as colleagues. Among the artists called upon to grace the scene with examples of their work were the sculptors Augustus Saint-Gaudens, Daniel Chester French, and Frederick Mac-Monnies—all classicists of sorts. At one of the planning sessions held by the group Saint-Gaudens turned to Burnham and remarked, "Look here, old fellow, do you realize that this is the greatest meeting of artists since the fifteenth century?"

Allowing for some hyperbole the question was not altogether rhetorical. The resulting city of "snowy palaces, vast and beautiful," with their glittering facades of plaster of Paris rising with fluttering flags on the shores of Lake Michigan, dazzled most of the visitors. To Theodore Dreiser it was a "fairyland," created "as though some brooding spirit of beauty, inherent possibly in some directing over-soul, had waved a magic wand" and transformed the bleak lakeshore into a "vast and harmonious collection of perfectly constructed . . . buildings." Burnham, one of the architects, concluded that this was "what the Romans would have wished to create in permanent form." He also predicted that all America would soon be constructed in the "noble, dignified classic style," and in this he came close to the truth. In the years that followed that style did become all but a standard brand for state capitols and official buildings in general, banks, libraries, railroad stations, and other types of public edifices. Domestic architecture was also affected. The wave of colonial revivalism that had risen from the Philadelphia Centennial celebrations now surged over the nation, leaving a wake of houses designed more or less faithfully after neoclassical structures of the late eighteenth and early nineteenth centuries.

But there were critics of the veneer of classical order, so redolent of the long dead past, that had been spread over the Chicago fairgrounds. Louis Sullivan, the young Chicago architect, whose steel-frame skyscrapers had already won acclaim and whose Transportation Building at the Exposition was a brilliant exception to the work of his older colleagues, thought that the influence of those flimsy "masterpieces" was all but disastrous. The epidemic of classicism that had germinated in the East, he wrote, had spread westward contaminating everything it touched. "Thus did the virus of a culture, snobbish and alien" to the land of the free and the home of the brave, he declared, subvert progress in the arts and sciences of building.

In his own work Sullivan turned his back on the "fraudulent and surreptitious use of historical documents" and set himself to the task of creating an entirely new architecture at a time when America sorely needed the spur of a fresh vision. Most of his significant work was with multistoried commercial structures, such as the Schlesinger and Mayer department store in Chicago, where the audacity and the poetry of his creative spirit were conspicuously displayed. Sullivan left a rich heritage, not only in the actual buildings he designed but in the profound thought he devoted to the nature of his profession and the eloquent expression he gave to the principles he applied to his work.

Years before Sullivan's time, in America as in England, earnest efforts had been made to deliver art and architecture from thralldom to the past, to create designs that would speak importantly and uniquely for the present. At mid-century, during the days of the Greek Revival, the American sculptor and essayist Horatio Greenough had pleaded for a fresh approach to these matters, in terms that anticipated Sullivan's oft-quoted and much-abused dictum, "form follows function." "What imitation of the Greeks," Greenough asked, ever produced such a "marvel of construction" as a modern sailing ship? (The *America* had recently beaten the English contender in the first of the challenge races.) The men who have reduced locomotion to its simplest elements, in the trotting wagon and the yacht *America*," he continued, "are nearer to Athens at this moment than they who would bend the Greek temple to every use. I contend for Greek principles, not Greek things." Greenough was an outspoken functionalist before that word was coined. "By beauty," he wrote elsewhere, "I mean the promise of function. By character I mean the record of function."

At the time Greenough wrote, the industrial revolution had as yet made no profound impact on American life, at least compared to the changed conditions that would result from the explosive growth of technology in the decades immediately following. Greenough could not have visualized the new possibilities that would open up to engineers and architects of the next generation or two—technical developments that were far advanced when Sullivan voiced his protest at Chicago forty years later. In England, where the industrial revolution had had an earlier start, the implications of the developing new order were more quickly apparent, and aroused the notable English art critic John Ruskin to outbursts of fervent diatribe.

He viewed with horror the appalling discrepancy between the promise of the machine and the actual squalor, suffering, and ugliness of Victorian capitalism. He urged a return to handcraftsmanship as an antidote to the corroding effect of the machine. "No machine yet contrived, or hereafter contrivable," he wrote, "will ever equal the fine machinery of the human fingers." And he saw in the "honest" intentions and practices of medieval craftsmen a model to emulate.

Although he heartily disliked most Americans, Ruskin won a phenomenally wide hearing for his pronouncements in this country. By 1855, he observed, his audience in the United States was more significant than that in England; and by 1887 it was "numbered by tens of thousands." As one consequence of his persuasion, in the late nineteenth century more than

WAYNE ANDREWS

thirty organizations devoted to the revival of the arts and crafts sprang up in towns and cities of the United States, from one end of the continent to the other. However, whether or not Ruskin liked it, man's welfare was increasingly bound to the machine, and nowhere more inexorably than in America. The crafts continued to be practiced, but only along the margins of the nation's economy. Nevertheless, by the nature of their revolt against the plundering advances of industrialism the reformers called critical attention to the shoddy performances of which the machine was all too capable.

A contemporary working model of handcraftsmanship as it applied to architecture had been somewhat unexpectedly discovered at the Philadelphia Centennial Exhibition. On that occasion America had its first real introduction to Japanese culture. James McNeil Whistler, the expatriate American painter working in England, had some years earlier fallen under the spell of Japanese art, and more than a decade before the Exhibition, another American artist, John LaFarge, had imported the first Japanese prints into this country. But it was at the Philadelphia fair that the public at large could see with their own eyes native Japanese carpenters at work converting carloads of building materials by "peculiar construction" methods and with building tools "of eccentric uses" into structures of astonishing charm and perfection. Those who came to gawk at the exotic customs and outlandish costumes of the Oriental workmen remained to admire what they contrived with their nimble hands and traditional equipment. The straightforward, organic design, the "honest" woodwork construction, the open planning, and the discreet decoration of Japanese architecture were all features that appealed to those looking for an escape from the staid formalities of Victorian fashion, features that found a purely domestic equivalent in the shingle style houses built in the decades following the Philadelphia fair, as remarked in the previous chapter.

In his autobiography, published in 1943, the architect Frank Lloyd Wright recalled that he had begun collecting Japanese prints fairly early in his remarkable career. "Japanese prints . . . taught me much . . . ," he wrote. "Japanese art and architecture . . . have organic character. Their art . . . [is] more nearly modern . . . than [that of] any European civilization alive or dead." By coincidence Wright was born (at Richland Center, Wisconsin) in the year that the Beecher sisters published *The American Woman's Home*, in which they formulated plans and procedures that foreshadowed the urban house that Wright would later raise to the level of a work of art. At eighteen he quit the School of Engineering at the University of Wisconsin and went to work as an apprentice in the architectural firm of Louis Sullivan—his *lieber Meister*, as Wright long referred to Sullivan.

Sullivan, in his turn, had been deeply impressed by the work of H. H. Richardson, after the latter came to Chicago in 1885 to build the famous wholesale warehouse for Marshall Field. Here, as he wrote admiringly, Sullivan saw a "direct, large, and simple" mind at work, and he quickly assimilated what he found valuable in the older man's concepts of form and function. Without stretching a point too far it could be said that Richardson, in his own turn, had been an early spiritual heir of Horatio Greenough.

Japanese building and garden at the Philadelphia Centennial fair, 1876

In 1851 (when Richardson was a lad and eighteen years before Wright was born) the Yankee sculptor wrote to Ralph Waldo Emerson offering his theory of structure. "Here is my theory . . . ," he explained. "A scientific arrangement of spaces and forms to functions and to site—An emphasis of features proportioned to their *gradated* importance in function—Color and ornament to be decided and arranged and varied by strictly organic laws—having a distinct reason for each decision—The entire and immediate banishment of all makeshift and make believe." In their separate ways Richardson, Sullivan, and Wright all said much the same thing in later years.

Wright left Sullivan to start his own practice the year of the Chicago fair. He took with him a precious legacy that came from six years of close association with his *lieber Meister.* By 1900 Sullivan's career was in effect over. The reactionary forces that dominated the architecture of the fair, and that he so heartily deplored, put harsh limits on the market for his brilliant but particular and contrary proposals. Referring to those circumstances Wright later remarked that "they killed Sullivan and they nearly killed me!" Sullivan lived until 1924, but when he died that year in a wretched hotel on Chicago's South Side he had been all but forgotten. Wright survived a number of misadventures and tragedies, periods of failures and frustrations, to die at the age of ninety, widely recognized, even by some of his many enemies, as the greatest American architect of the century.

In principle Wright resolutely turned his back on everything the classical buildings at the Chicago fair stood for; he eschewed all references to traditional form and ornament. He never violated the natural color and texture of wood and stone with uncalled-for embellishment. "Democracy needed something basically better than the box to live and work in," he claimed. "So I started to destroy the box as a building." In his autobiography he wrote that he saw a house "primarily as livable interior space under ample shelter. . . . So I declared the whole lower floor as one room, cutting off the kitchen as a laboratory. . . . Scores of unnecessary doors disappeared and no end of partition. . . . The house became more free as space and more livable too. Interior spaciousness began to dawn." Like the medieval cathedral builders, Wright used light and space as the equivalent of natural building materials.

Such freedom of planning had long before been encouraged by Alexander Jackson Davis and furthered by architects who worked in the Queen Anne and shingle styles. But with Wright these concepts reached a unique and culminating expression. For all the credit due his precursors, in Wright's work it became clearly apparent for the first time that, after centuries of reliance on European precedent, America had established independent standards of style and quality in building that the rest of the Western world could turn to as a model. His accomplishment won quicker and greater critical acclaim abroad than in this country. As early as 1910 and 1911 two studies of his work that were published in Germany spread Wright's fame across the Continent. One Dutch architect who came to America early in the century to see Wright's buildings and to talk with him went away "with

Presentation drawing by Frank Lloyd Wright inspired by Japanese screens

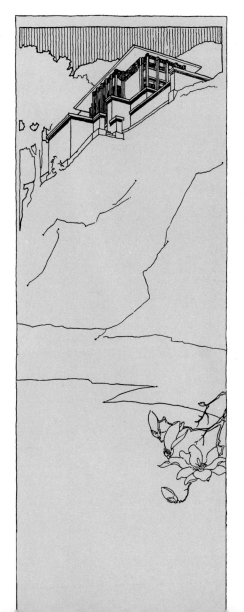

Frank Lloyd Wright at the Solomon R. Guggenheim Museum in 1959

the conviction of having seen a genuinely modern work, and with respect for the master able to create things which had no equal in Europe."

Few if any of his American colleagues at the time were prepared to give him such recognition, and the public at large was very far from understanding his aims. As late as the 1920s one eminent architectural critic in this country spoke of Wright's work with only the most guarded, faint praise. "It is a style of undeniable virility," he concluded, "bought at the price, some will maintain, of brutality. . . ." For all his gifts Wright had small chance of launching an immediate popular revolution in the art of housebuilding in America. He remained an uncompromising individualist. His patrons, wealthy beyond the common level, were themselves nonconformists in a society of generally orthodox tastes. Wright was a thoroughly trained, an immensely skilled, and a highly imaginative and daring professional architect. But he had to struggle against conservative opposition, general indifference, and perverse fortune to win his ultimate place in the estimation of his countrymen.

Ironically, the man who exercised a far wider and stronger influence than Wright on housebuilding and homemaking in America in the early years of the century was a Dutch immigrant named Edward Bok, who knew practically nothing about art, architecture, or decoration, but who had a profound faith in his mission to "make the world a better or more beautiful place to live in." Bok had arrived in this country as a child the year Wright was born. Twenty years later he became editor of a relatively new magazine, *The Ladies' Home Journal,* and it was from that platform that he led his crusade to improve the living accommodations of Americans at large, and of public taste in domestic matters. This he proposed to do by commissioning leading architects to prepare plans and elevations of small model houses that could be built at relatively modest cost, and publishing those in his magazine. Readers could obtain working drawings from *The Ladies' Home Journal* for five dollars a set. Bok had traveled about the country and was appalled by the "wretched" character of the average American home, and by the waste of money that went into "useless turrets, filigree work, or machine-made ornamentation." He also realized that most Americans had no access to or the means to buy the services of a professional architect, and perforce relied upon local builders and contractors to design their homes.

His program was a major success; that is to say, public response to it was enthusiastic. Unfortunately, most architects who were approached at first considered Bok's proposal either as beneath their dignity or as a scheme to bypass their personal and lucrative supervision of the work to be done. However, their resistance waned as Bok's campaign waxed and the circulation of the *Journal* soared to one million a month. "I firmly believe," wrote Stanford White, one of the most fashionable architects of the time, shortly before he was murdered in 1906, "that Edward Bok has more completely influenced American domestic architecture for the better than any man in this generation. When he began, I was short-sighted enough to discourage him, and refused to cooperate with him. If Bok came to me now, I would not only make plans for him, but I would waive any fee for them in retribution for my early mistake."

As a result of those periodical features, Theodore Roosevelt expansively remarked, the architecture of the whole nation had been changed for the better—"so quickly and yet so effectively that we didn't know it was begun before it was finished." Meanwhile, Wright had not demurred when he was solicited by Bok. In 1901 two of his designs were published. But as a footnote to that episode, the national publicity he thereby gained apparently brought him no business whatsoever.

By the time Bok ran those articles, mechanical household equipment that a generation earlier had been rare and primitive had become commonplace and highly developed; and these affected the actual structure of living arrangements. Central heating had by now become a standard convenience and this, as already noted, made it possible to open the interior of a house, even in regions where winters were cold, to provide a new sense of space—as Wright so emphatically demonstrated in his prairie houses. (Part of Bok's plan was to eliminate the old-fashioned parlor once and for all in favor of a living room.) Electrical services, more complicated and efficient plumbing, the telephone, gas kitchen ranges, and other facilities were changing the nature of domestic routine. With the elevator they also made apartment house living a more practical scheme for urbanites, and such tall structures rose in growing numbers in all the major cities of the country. Meanwhile, industrial architecture had taken full advantage of the new technology, and the skyscraper was fast becoming virtually a symbol of American enterprise.

In the first three decades of the twentieth century America experienced an enormous building boom. More structures of every kind—houses, apartments, schools, factories, churches, skyscrapers—were built during those years, by far, than ever before in so short a time. As one reporter of that changing scene has written, "a century of slow handicraft accretion gave way suddenly, like a log jam, to the full flood of industrialized mass production." Never before in history had so many people enjoyed so many and so much varied household conveniences and comforts. But for those who looked for progressive developments in domestic architecture as such, the contemporary scene resembled a wasteland. In spite of Bok's earnest proselytizing and the creative inventions of men like Wright, and whatever bland optimism President Roosevelt revealed in his pronouncements, the general level of design remained mediocre at the very best. As one critic wrote, reviewing the scene in 1926, "it remained for the bungalow books, the stock ready-built houses, and the great mail-order stores of to-day to complete the architectural ruin."

The author was referring principally to the average, modest, nonurban houses of the time. In and about large cities, as he pointed out, the picture was different. "The country's loss has been the city's gain," he explained. "The great development of American domestic architecture is essentially a result of city life; it is essentially a suburban development." The suburban house was, typically, "an adjunct to a successful man's city-office" and in

An issue of the Journal, *edited by Bok*

the suburbs were to be found modern houses that were "the most highly developed results of sophistication." From today's vantage those structures were anything but "modern." People of substance with "good" taste were commissioning residences that in terms of style pointed everywhere but to the present, not to mention the future. A rash of elaborate establishments spread across the country, carrying with it the germs of a new eclecticism that found its more or less remote inspiration in Tudor or Georgian England, Renaissance Italy, sixteenth-century France and Spain, colonial and Federal America, and elsewhere. Even the world's tallest skyscraper at the time it was built, the Woolworth Building, was dressed in "Gothic" elaborations. As the eminent decorator Elsie de Wolfe, sometimes known as "The Chintz Lady," despairingly wrote, "We have not succeeded in creating a style adapted to our modern life. It is just as well!" The haste, nervousness, and preoccupation of contemporary life, she concluded, provided no true inspirations to designers.

The Great Depression and then World War II all but shattered that romantic complacency. Even while it lasted undercurrents of progressive design in building had continued to flow beneath the surface of eclecticism. It was in the early 1930s that Americans, architects and public alike, were shocked by a realization of what *avant-garde* European architects had accomplished over decades of the recent past (influenced to a degree by Wright's own pioneering work). It was after the war that the new architectural language, proposed by what was known as the international style, won wide currency in this country. Once again the provocative but half-forgotten issues so much earlier raised by Sullivan and Wright were brought out into open controversy. Wright himself was rediscovered by a younger generation. By the war's end, as well, many of Europe's most advanced architects, including Marcel Breuer, Ludwig Mies van der Rohe, Walter Gropius, and others, were living in the United States, and by their commanding presence and teachings added new dimensions to the whole range of building in this country. Notable houses are still constantly rising about us, bearing witness to the ever-changing aspects of life in America.

A portion of the Chicago skyline dominated by the 100-story John Hancock Center, built 1969
EZRA STOLLER

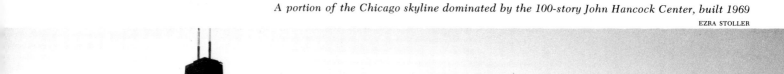

A Return to America's Past

The Colonial Revival

The riot of historical revivals that raged through the last three quarters of the nineteenth century ransacked virtually every period of the past and all corners of the globe for precedents and models. In that "battle of styles" only one principal source of inspiration remained untouched — America's own colonial past. By the time of the centennial celebrations of 1776, however, that phase of the nation's history had become sufficiently remote to attract romantic associations such as had up until then clustered about the historical experience of other and older lands. "As the one hundredth anniversary of our national independence draws near," reported *Harper's New Monthly Magazine* in 1874, "the thoughts of our people are eagerly turned . . . to a more familiar observation of the men and women who were actors in that great event . . . to cross their thresholds and see . . . what entered into their domestic appointments and belongings." At the Philadelphia Exhibition two years later a "New England Kitchen of 1776" was exhibited complete with beamed ceiling, leaded casement windows, and early furnishings to match, including "a few wrinkled pictures and relics." A trilingual sign posted over the entrance identified the building housing the exhibit as "Ye Olden Time; *Die Alten Zeiten; Les Vieux Temps;* Welcome to All." The crowds were enchanted and the colonial revival was off to a start. (A year later McKim, Mead, and White made their sketches and measured drawings of early New England houses for future reference in their architectural practice.) The interest that was

Lamp at Colonial Williamsburg

awakened in those years sprang partly from nostalgia, partly from a quest for a new and indigenous style of American architecture, and partly from a form of ancestor worship. The fact that before the end of the century a substantial number of Americans had come to this country in cramped steamships, centuries after the *Mayflower,* and owned ancestors who probably never heard of Bunker Hill or Saratoga, was not important in all this. Immigrants from the most outlandish places, with a touching desire to identify with American traditions, soon learned to venerate the deeds of adopted ancestors and to sing of this "land where my fathers died, land of the Pilgrim's pride." It seemed increasingly apparent that in matters of taste "our" colonial forefathers could not err. For all its spareness and formality, reported the *American Architect and Building News,* colonial architecture was "on the whole, decidedly superior in style and good breeding, if we may say so, to most that has followed it." And one somewhat more objective but sympathetic Englishman observed in 1877 that "if ever America is to become possessed of an historical style, it must spring from the work of the old colonialists." In any case, the colonial revival gathered force as the decades passed, and it has not yet abated. That fresh interest in our early architecture — and artifacts to be sure — led in various directions: to whimsical inventions labeled "colonial" but bearing slight resemblance to any actual models; on the other hand, to such scholarly restorations of the past as Colonial Williamsburg.

Above: house designed in the colonial revival style by McKim, Mead, and White for James L. Breese at Southampton, L.I.
Below: facade of the John Jay Chapman House, built in 1914 at Barrytown, N.Y., by the architect Charles Adams Platt
Opposite: "Dutch colonial" style house built in the 1920s at Sparkill, N.Y., with bell-cast eaves and dormer windows

The vogue for modern architecture in the "colonial" style that grew with mounting enthusiasm as the nineteenth century waned and that continued without recess in the decades to come, was part of a much wider revival of interest in all aspects of the early American scene. Historians and antiquarians, as well as architects, plumbed the country's past and the countryside itself for evidence that would increase their understanding of colonial days and ways. As early as 1878 *Godey's Lady's Book* observed that the "latest mania among fashionable people" was collecting old furniture. "A curious feature of this fashion," the editors observed, "is the aid it affords people desiring to lay claim to a respectable ancestry." Apparently the demand for such artifacts soon surpassed the available supply, for it was noted just a few years later in another periodical that "the manufacture of antiques has become a modern industry." McKim, Mead, and White were among the earliest and most prominent advocates of the colonial revival style. In 1906 they designed a handsome residence more or less in that style at Southampton, Long Island, for James L. Breese. The studied formality of the design (with overtones of Mount Vernon in its columned porch) was a very far cry from the rambling, free-flowing arrangements in the almost exactly contemporary work of Frank Lloyd Wright and other practitioners of modern architecture, but convenient enough in a day when servants were plentiful. Somewhat later, in 1914, Charles Adams Platt designed a house at Barrytown, New York, for the critic John Jay Chapman, that with its monumental portico bore more than a passing resemblance to the most formal of William Buckland's eighteenth-century buildings. Not all revival houses were of such pretention and elegance. The "Dutch colonial" house by Aymar Embury II for Mrs. W. H. Fallon at Sparkill, New York, was, according to one critic, "cosey." "Placed among the Dutch eighteenth-century buildings . . . this modern building could never be out of place."

Above: the New England kitchen at the Centennial, from Harper's Weekly *magazine*
Below right: design for a "Colonial House," from The Ladies' Home Journal, *1896*

The seventeenth-century New England kitchen installed at the Philadelphia Centennial, with its "quaint architecture" and "antiquated furniture," was hardly a model of scholarly reconstruction, but it evoked a nostalgia that led in all directions. As time passed the word *colonial* assumed an all-purpose meaning, whether the styles considered actually fell within the colonial period or not; and the relation between reconstructions and true models was often tenuous at best. "The closer the adaptation, up to a certain point," one informed reporter advised, "the greater the success"—although, it was elsewhere cautioned, too much concern for exact reproduction was to be avoided. "Much modern Colonial," it was written in the 1920s, "is still very archaeological, but this is no vice providing the archaeologising appears not as an aim in itself but as a means to obtain an aesthetic result." "That this Colonial revival was an excellent thing for American architecture," observed the same reporter, "few will deny.... The result was a purification of the work and an increase of simplicity and chastity in American taste." A half century before, *The American Architect* had commented on the "good breeding" of colonial design. The conviction grew that in matters of taste our early ancestors could do no wrong.

A 1923 version of a 17th-century New England clapboard house, with central chimney, overhang, pendants, and lean-to

Over the past fifty years, along with the continued prevalence of department-store and suburban-development "American," serious historical restoration and preservation of early American houses has steadily grown into an important nationwide movement. Colonial Williamsburg is the most dramatic demonstration of such recovery and re-creation of the country's past, but it is only one of many projects of similar nature that have been undertaken as both public and private enterprises. Shortly before the Revolution, Britain's royal governor William Tryon built a great palace at New Bern in North Carolina to serve as his official residence. With its forty-five rooms, twenty-seven fireplaces, lavish appointments, auxiliary buildings, and large gardens, it was one of the most extravagant and pretentious structures in the colonies. When George Washington visited New Bern in 1791 he recorded in his diary: "Dined with the Citizens . . . and went to a dancing assembly in the evening; both of which was at what they call the Pallace, formerly the Government House and a good brick building but," he added, "now hastening to Ruins." A few years later the main building was gutted by fire and the ruin was all but complete. Within the last thirty years, however, the entire complex has been carefully reconstructed following plans of the original architect and contemporary inventories of the furnishings. Almost everywhere in the country significant survivals from earlier days are now being jealously guarded by self-appointed and official guardians of the nation's heritage. As a curious sidelight to such adventures into the past, J. Walter Thompson, advertising agency, installed a simulated seventeenth-century interior as its executive dining room (opposite) in a New York skyscraper.

Below: the reconstructed colonial palace of Governor William Tryon, built at New Bern, N. C.
Opposite: a simulated 17th-century interior installed in a New York skyscraper in the 1920s

During the 1920s America became aware to an unprecedented degree of the need for more adequate housing to shelter its growing millions of people. Those years also—until 1929, that is—witnessed an extraordinary prosperity among a large part of the population. In the building trades it was a period of intense activity. Suburbia mushroomed with new houses; houses conceived in more different styles than even Alexander Jackson Davis had considered during the earlier boom of the 1830s and 1840s. "Interesting works of all types are appearing all over New England," wrote one contemporary observer. "The perfection of the motor-car, the attendant improvement in roads, and the ease of communications between the city and the country has encouraged people, even of fairly modest means, to go long distances into the country, drawn thither either by sentimental ties of ancestry or by individual predilection for the scenic charm of a given district, and there to erect homes which are in harmony with the older architecture to be found in the region." Of the myriad designs that were attempted to fill the needs, probably none were so ubiquitous as those derived from the early Cape Cod cottages (pages 165–67). "Twentieth century America's most popular house design, now scattered throughout the entire country," wrote one architectural historian, "is the Cape Cod Cottage, 280-year-old native of a narrow strip of seawashed sand, the folk product of a handful of colonial settlers"—the small, trim, story-and-a-half house, whose derivatives became known as "Capies" in the jargon of real estate developers. According to Alfred Levitt (of Levittown fame), "the Cape Cod was and still is the most efficient house ever developed in America." Elsewhere it has been judged as "a perfect mirror of a society most of whose members are desperately afraid of acting like independent individuals." The fact remains that what had been a logical solution to local site problems, primitive construction methods, and traditional craftsmanship has been over the years transplanted in totally different places and climates and adapted to a mass production culture for which the original was never planned.

Design for a Cape Cod cottage, from a popular building manual published in 1923

New Designs for Living

Futures Indicative

During the years about the turn of the century, as the enthusiasm for early American styles followed its various courses, a new type of architecture was developing, primarily in the Midwest where Louis Sullivan had broken such fertile prairie soil—and, changing metaphors, had broken so many lances against the entrenched champions of the classical past. Frank Lloyd Wright was Sul-

Hall light, the Gamble House

livan's great disciple; although he soon went his own, completely individualistic way, his debt to the older man was primary, and he acknowledged it. However, Wright's own influence upon American building has been profound. It is fair to say that the average level of domestic architecture in this country is much higher than it would have been had he not cleared the way for others with his bold, new approach to the timeless but ever-changing problems of human shelter. (His industrial and public buildings were, of course, no less pathbreaking in their radical solutions of different problems.) Wright had a long, dramatic career (he lived to be ninety) during which his restless imagination and enriched experience led to constant renewal of his vision. However, the work he completed before World War I had already set in motion trends that contributed directly and importantly to the modern movement in architecture. As remarked a few pages back, the significance of his accomplishment was clearly recognized abroad before it was apparent to most of his countrymen. By the 1920s that movement, so sharply spurred by Wright, was remaking the face of European architecture, a point registered with a shock of surprise in America in the following decade. Wright did not completely lack appreciation here, as Edward Bok's sponsorship of his designs partly indicates. But the nature of the skepticism that greeted his early work can be judged by a note in *The Western Architect*, about 1911, remarking that "none have gone so far into the realm of the picturesque, or failed so signally in the production of livable houses, as Frank Lloyd Wright." One sympathetic but not uncritical contemporary observer of Wright's early houses wrote that he was "a pioneer, and the utterance of a pioneer, as a poetical pioneer [Walt Whitman] has told us, is liable to fall upon unaccustomed ears as a 'barbaric yawp.'" In spite of all criticism, of personal difficulties and family tragedies, and other discouragements, Wright persevered and lived on to confound his critics.

There were other Americans, to be sure, working in the modern idiom, including sometime associates of Louis Sullivan and of Wright himself, as well as pioneering architects on the West Coast, who added individual and independent variations to the main theme Wright had so boldly stated. In almost all cases they turned their backs on traditional and European forms in favor of innovative designs for living that were native to this country. Although their accommodations were at times luxurious, such houses were planned primarily for comfort, convenience, and efficiency, and they deliberately avoided the pretension and restrictions of formal designs associated with the "fine" and "elegant" residences of past periods in history.

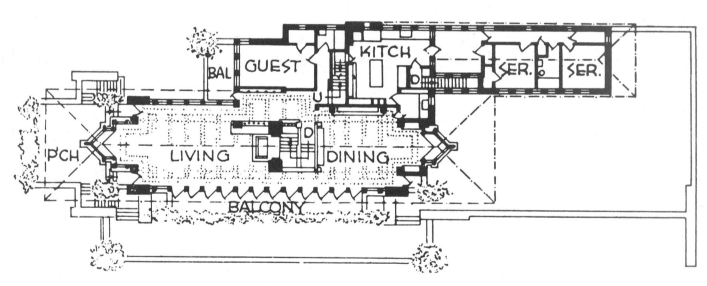

Top: an exterior view of the "prairie house" designed by Frank Lloyd Wright and built at Chicago, Ill., for Frederick Robie in 1908
Above: plan of the main floor of the Robie House, showing the interrelation of principal areas, with access to outside porches
Opposite: interior view of Taliesin, Wright's home and studio in Spring Green, Wis.; built in 1911, it burned, and was rebuilt, twice.

In 1908 Wright designed for Frederick Robie one of the most famous of his "prairie houses." It was built on Chicago's South Side, an area then still related to the outlying open prairie. To quote Henry James, it is a house "all beautified with omissions," and by that token as trim in its outline as a ship, to which it has been compared because of its long, horizontal "decks," its topmost "bridge," and its stacklike chimney. However, that external appearance, handsomely textured of brick with uninterrupted limestone cappings, was dictated by the arrangement of interior areas. The plan of the main floor is a remarkable design of fluid spaces separated but not divided by the pylon of the central chimney. Every major area of the house has access to a balcony or a porch, thus interrelating indoors with outdoors. Here, also, and perhaps for the first time in American architecture, a garage was incorporated in the design. In 1911 Wright built for himself a combined house and studio, called Taliesin after a Welsh poet, at Spring Green, Wisconsin. Twice Taliesin burned (the first time incinerating Wright's mistress and her two children) and twice it was rebuilt. Here the interiors are unsurpassed. Changes in ceiling levels, overhanging balconies, and upper clerestory windows provide those varieties of indoor spaces for which the architect was famous.

Above: garden facade of the Avery Coonley House, Riverside, Ill., designed by Frank Lloyd Wright, 1907

Right: an exterior view of the children's playhouse built by Wright in 1911 on the Coonley House grounds

About 1907 Mr. and Mrs. Avery Coonley commissioned Wright to design and build a house for them at Riverside, Illinois. Before approaching Wright the Coonleys had carefully viewed the work he had already done and had found in his houses "the countenance of principle" of which they approved. They left the project entirely in his hands, after making their requirements clear. "So," Wright later reflected, "I put my best into the Coonley house. Looking back upon it, I feel now that that building was the best I could do then in the way of a house." He placed all the principal rooms on the second level, looking out on the surrounding lawns and garden. To Wright all elements of a house were equally important and consequently it had neither front nor back. Here the back, or rather the garden front, with its terraces and reflecting pool, has a charm barely suggested by a photograph. The largest single area of the house is the living room, with its massive fireplace and series of casement windows, reached from the grade level by twin staircases. The sloping ceiling with its pattern of wooden beams, punctuated by leaded glass skylights, emphasizes the fact that one is directly beneath the great, low-pitched sheltering roof. Painted friezes over the bookcases on either side of the fireplace depict a forest of birch trees, further accenting the awareness of nature expressed in the design of the Coonley House.

Top: a view of the beamed, second-story living room of the Coonley House

Right: chair designed by Wright to complement his architectural interiors

Great as his peculiar genius was, Wright did not of course work in a vacuum. As a young man he had found his direction while working under the influence of Louis Sullivan, as has been told. Also, his early domestic architecture, including a house he built for himself in 1889 at Oak Park, Illinois, was based in good part on designs so successfully realized in shingle style dwellings of the time. There were others of the so-called Chicago School who learned under Sullivan and who subsequently proceeded along their own way. Two of Sullivan's protégés, William Gray Purcell and George Grant Elmslie, formed a partnership in 1910 and produced a number of distinguished designs. The firm's best work was accomplished in private houses and the greatest of their achievements in this form of expression was the shingled bungalow created as a summer residence at Woods Hole, Massachusetts, in 1912 for Harold C. Bradley, son-in-law of the benevolent Chicago millionaire Charles R. Crane. Like the Low House at Bristol, Rhode Island (pages 270–71), this low, horizontal structure, poised on a promontory overlooking the sea, seems to be an organic part of its site rather than something imposed upon it. As on the Low House, the unpainted shingled surface is left unadorned. At either end the second story with large rectangular windows facing the ocean is boldly cantilevered over the spaces beneath. On the ground floor the living room projects outward in a sweeping semicircular bay with a continuous range of large windows, facing the oncoming weather and the water in a manner that suggests naval architecture. The low-angled roof line with overhanging eaves is typical of the Chicago style of the time. (The plan of the house is T-shaped, the rear extension not being visible in the illustration.) The Bradley House is one of the few examples of the Chicago School on the East Coast—a happy marriage of regionalism and modernism.

The semicircular projecting bay of the living room of the Bradley House, built in 1912 at Woods Hole, Mass., by Purcell and Elmslie
The ocean-front facade of the Harold Bradley House with its lateral terraces and porches overhung by long cantilevered balconies

At almost precisely the same time that Wright was developing the "prairie house" in the Midwest, Charles Sumner Greene and his brother Henry Mather Greene were creating a distinctive style of modern domestic architecture in and about Pasadena, California. The brothers Greene were exact contemporaries of Wright, and like him, but more obviously, they were strongly influenced by Japanese building methods and designs. However, in their hands this exotic strain was domesticated into an architecture so well adapted to the American scene, so fresh in its interpretations, that its influence spread throughout Southern California and then over the entire country, in watered-down versions, as the "California bungalow style"—a forerunner of the modern ranch house. In 1906 the Greenes designed an elaborate residence in Pasadena for R. R. Blacker. Set in the midst of undulating lawns and handsome gardens with lotus pools and outlying pergolas, the Blacker House was one of their most remarkable achievements. The entry hall is a large, open area from which stairs rise to the floor above. On one side it opens into a spacious living room; on the other into a dining area that can be doubled by folding back a glass screen. Everywhere in the structure a variety of fine, carefully selected woods with exquisite textures were so meticulously joined that it is difficult to distinguish the doors from surrounding solid panels. Light switches are made of ebony set into mahogany plates. Doors concealed in the wall panels open electrically at the touch of hidden buttons. In 1907 the Greene brothers were commissioned by Mr. and Mrs. David Berry Gamble of Cincinnati to design for them another house, also in Pasadena. Here, as in the Blacker House, the spacious, open interior areas are largely paneled with fine woods. Fixtures and furniture were designed by the architects as part of the total scheme.

Top: the R. R. Blacker House in its landscaped setting. More than a hundred sheets of drawings were needed for the construction data.

Above: the porte-cochere of the Blacker House, built by the architects Greene and Greene at Pasadena, Calif., completed in 1907. The extensive bridgelike structure with its heavy timbers contributed to the Oriental character expressed throughout the house.

Opposite: the stairwell in the entry hall of the R. R. Blacker House exhibits the Greene brothers' extremely successful use of hand-rubbed, sculptured woods. The lighting fixture suspended by leather straps was also an integral part of their overall design.

The living room and tiled-fireplace alcove of the Gamble House. The architects designed the carpets and most other furnishings.

The Gamble House "will be somewhat Japanese in feeling," reported the local newspaper when plans were announced, "though it cannot be said to conform to the Japanese style. . . . The best of everything is to be used." The resulting structure remains today the most complete and best preserved of the architects' work. It was their intention to use the structural woodwork of the house, inside and out, as expressive elements of the composition and design. Thus the rounded and tapered beams that support the overhanging eaves and porches constitute a decorative pattern that adds immediate distinction to the exterior —a pattern that, as the day passes, casts changing shadows across the hand-split cedar shingles of the walls. Within, the rectangular pegs covering brass screws that clinch the joinery form a pattern of their own. Hand-finished teak, mahogany, quartered oak, cedar, and other attractive woods were used for the paneling and trim of the interior. The stained-glass panels of the front entrance (page 302) depict gnarled oak trees such as grow in the Pasadena area. Louis Comfort Tiffany provided some of the glass that, with other imported and locally made elements, was then assembled in a western studio by a method the Greenes developed especially for their work. As in the Blacker House, lanterns of Tiffany glass set in mahogany or plated metal frames and enclosing incandescent lights (a relatively novel utility) were hung from beams and ceilings by leather straps. Special carpets were woven following drawings by Charles Greene. The entire structure and its furnishings represent a rare and highly successful example of integrated design.

Above: detail of stained-glass panels of the Gamble House
Opposite: the projecting shaped beams of the Gamble House

Louis Henri Sullivan

With a vision that was, perhaps, too revolutionary for his generation, Louis Henri Sullivan strove to create an architecture that would necessarily evolve from and express the American environment. During the 1880s and 1890s, while his eclectic contemporaries were sheathing their buildings in historical mantles, this prophet of modern architecture turned instead to the living organism for inspiration, and eventually arrived at his often quoted and much abused principle, "The function of a building must . . . organize its form . . . as, for instance, the oak tree expressed the function oak, the pine tree the function pine." In his adopted city of Chicago, Sullivan enjoyed brief eminence as the unchallenged master of the skyscraper. By reconciling technology and utility with poetry and beauty, Sullivan transformed the steel-framed mass into "a proud and soaring thing." Although most architects have had a touch of the poet, they have also had to act as salesmen in order to succeed. Sullivan could not. For this dreamer and uncompromising champion of individualism, the clash with Chicago's industrial barons was inevitable, and he spent the last twenty-nine years of his career an architectural outcast. However, many of Sullivan's best ideas were adopted by his onetime disciple, Frank Lloyd Wright, and thus passed into the mainstream of modern architecture.

Born in Boston in 1856, the son of an Irish dancing master and Swiss pianist, Sullivan spent most of his childhood with his maternal grandparents in Reading, Massachusetts. According to his *Autobiography*, Louis at an early age felt a strong identification with nature. An elm tree on his grandfather's farm left a lasting impression, presenting ". . . such tall slender grace [as] he had never seen. Its broad slim fronds spreading so high and descending in

Sullivan, prophet of modern architecture

lovely curves . . . . he became infiltrated, suffused, inspired with the fateful sense of beauty." In contrast, the boy viewed the buildings of Boston with the utmost disdain, irreverently commenting, "Some said vile things, some said prudent things, some said pompous things, but none said noble things." After attending the Massachusetts Institute of Technology in 1872, he left school, worked in Philadelphia as a draftsman, and visited Chicago for the first time. He found the city in the aftermath of the Fire to be "magnificent and wild: A crude extravaganza, An intoxicating rawness," where "in spite of the panic, there was stir; an energy that made him tingle to be in the game." In 1874 the aspiring architect went to Paris and enrolled in the École des Beaux-Arts to receive the finest training then available.

Upon returning to Chicago in 1875, Sullivan pursued a generally undistinguished career until 1879 when he entered the architectural office of Dankmar Adler, a German-born Jew whose knowledge of engineering, and especially acoustics, had earned him wide respect among Chicagoans. Two years later marked the beginning of the famous partnership of Adler and Sullivan that finally allowed Sullivan's genius to flower.

The early work of the firm was typified by such picturesque and derivative residential designs as the row of houses Adler built for himself, his mother-in-law, and Eli B. Felsenthal, which featured fantastic skylines and facades broken by irregular rhythms and accents in oriels, bays, and gables. It was not until 1886 that Adler and Sullivan tackled problems of a monumental urban scale and realized their first major achievement in their design for the Chicago Auditorium. While Adler solved the engineering and acoustical problems of the auditorium with his usual facility, Sullivan was responsible for the building's final appearance — a sheer, clifflike mass of solid masonry, rising from a base of rusticated granite, and rhythmically grouped under a high arcade. A series of magnificent golden arches spanned the sumptuous interior, giving the auditorium a superb sense of space, and at the same time functioning as acoustic deflectors and ventilation ducts. On the evening of the auditorium's grand opening on December 9, 1889, the capacity crowd was honored by the attendance of President Benjamin Harrison, who during the performance succinctly summed up the city's most brilliant advertisement by whispering to Vice President Morton, "New York surrenders, eh?"

Assisted by Adler, and stimulated by Frank Lloyd Wright, who had joined the firm in 1887 and had become his chief apprentice, Sullivan entered the great period of his career in the early 1890s. Focusing his attention on the skyscraper, he pondered the problem of "How shall we impart to this sterile pile, this crude, harsh brutal agglomeration, this stark, staring exclamation of eternal strife, the graciousness of those higher forms of sensibility and culture that rest on the lower and fiercer passions?" Sullivan's solution was to combine the traditional elements of classic composition—proportion, scale, rhythm, and ornament, to name a few—with the new skeletal structure of the tall commercial building. In his robust Wainwright Building, erected in St. Louis in 1891, "the steel frame was first given authentic recognition and expression." Designed to provide stores on its ground floor and offices above, the structure's elevations consisted of a two-foot base of Missouri red granite, two stories of finely jointed brown sandstone, and red brick piers rising uninterrupted from the third to the tenth floor, where all was terminated by a delightful frieze of red terra cotta ornament. Sullivan's subsequent skyscrapers became more attenuated and lighter, with an increasing emphasis on verticality. The handsome Guaranty Building, erected in Buffalo in 1895, proved to be the architect's most successful composition with its uppermost story dramatically climaxed by round windows sunk in the lush, flowerlike patterns which were so personal and so poetic an expression of Sullivan's genius. Concurrent with his tall office buildings, Sullivan executed such sepulchral masterpieces as the tombs for Carrie Eliza Getty in Chicago and the Wainwright family in St. Louis, and built a residence for his brother, Albert, all of which displayed the same tendency toward classic organization as did his skyscrapers.

When the World's Columbian Exposition opened its gates in 1893, Sullivan was shocked into the awareness that neither his skyscrapers, nor his tombs, nor his houses entitled him to any preferential treatment in his adopted town. Although the organizer of the fair, Daniel Burnham, had invited the eastern architectural establishment to plan the fair buildings in the eclectic manner, Sullivan did manage to provide an effective

Gage Building, Chicago, Ill., built 1899

Teller's wicket, National Farmers' Bank

counterpoint to the prevailing white, classic scheme with his Transportation Building, decorated in richly colored plaster, and containing an entrance of recessed half-circles covered in gold leaf. In his *Autobiography,* Sullivan bitterly referred to the White City as a "lewd exhibit of drooling imbecility and political debauchery." He concluded despairingly that as a result of the fair "came a violent outbreak of the Classic and the Renaissance . . . contaminating all that it touched. . . . The selling campaign of the bogus antique was remarkably well managed through skillful publicity and propaganda. . . . By the time the market had been saturated, all sense of reality was gone. . . . Thus Architecture died in the land of the free. . . . The damage wrought by the World's Fair will last for half a century from its date, if not longer. It has penetrated deep into the constitution of the American mind, effecting there lesions significant of dementia."

Other events also conspired to affect Sullivan's fortunes adversely. The Panic of 1893 had caused Frank Lloyd Wright to leave the firm and establish his own practice. And, when the economic depression finally forced Adler and Sullivan to dissolve in 1895, the sensitive architect no longer had Adler to shield him from the harsh world of business outside the drafting room. His practice soon dwindled—in the last twenty-nine years of his career Sullivan's commissions amounted to about twenty, as contrasted to more than one hundred in the period before 1895. Sullivan was also beset by a series of humiliating personal tragedies that included the failure of two marriages, the loss of his country retreat at Ocean Springs, Mississippi, the auctioning of his art and furniture, and the removal of his offices from the Auditorium Tower in 1918, and he took to drinking heavily. Despite his misfortunes, this architectural Job still occasionally produced a masterpiece. His twelve-story Bayard Building, erected on Bleecker Street in 1898, was one of New York's loveliest skyscrapers, and the city's lone example of Sullivan's work.

At a time when Louis Sullivan felt defeated by cities, he created an exceptional series of banks for small towns in the Midwest. His finest, The National Farmers' Bank built in 1908 at Owatonna, Minnesota, consisted of a nearly cubic block, ornamented with bands of leaves and acorns, and brilliant glass mosaic. Here, at last, Sullivan found compassionate, appreciative clients. The bank's president wrote that its officers "believed that an adequate expression of the character of their business in the form of a simple,

dignified, and beautiful building was due to themselves . . . and their patrons. Further than this, they believed that a beautiful business house would be its own reward."

In the several years before his death in 1924, Sullivan passed the time reading—Walt Whitman's *Leaves of Grass* was a particular favorite—and wrote his *Autobiography*. Toward the end, from his dingy hotel room on Chicago's South Side, the despondent architect cynically confessed, "American architecture is composed, in the hundred, of 90 parts aberration, eight parts indifference, one part poverty, and one part Little Lord Fauntleroy. You can have the prescription filled at any architectural department store, or select architectural millinery establishment," with little thought that he would be remembered.

"Golden Door" of Sullivan's Transportation Building, built for the Exposition of 1893

A Campaign for Improvement

Better Homes for All

In 1897 the well-known novelist (and lady of good family) Edith Wharton and the fashionable architect-decorator Ogden Codman, Jr., collaborated in the writing of *The Decoration of Houses*, a book specifically aimed at improving the lamentable taste all too often evident among the well-to-do. (Mrs. Wharton later referred to the book, with neither reticence nor modesty, as fashion's "touchstone of taste.") The American homemaker, the authors counseled, could achieve satisfactory results "only by a close study of the best models," which were to be found in Paris. Those with limited incomes were not altogether neglected for, as the book pronounced, "When the rich man demands good architecture, his neighbors will get it too." If correct standards were firmly established at society's topmost levels, their beneficent influence would sift down through the lower strata and good taste would prevail at last in America.

There were others who also deplored conspicuous vulgarity among the wealthy, but who chose to start reforms closer to the common level, where more people would benefit more quickly from good advice. Of such reformers, none was more energetic, persistent, and enlightened than the Dutch-born Edward William Bok who, beginning as a young man in 1889, edited *The Ladies' Home Journal* for thirty years. Bok was dismayed by the "wretched" architecture of small houses wherever he traveled in America. Traditionally, houses had been built to serve successive generations, but technological advances—and the rising value of real estate—

Detail of a Bradley design

accelerated a tendency to replace the old with the new at an unprecedented rate. More rapid production and quicker turnovers had reached a point where one planner early in the present century directed that a building to be constructed must be "the cheapest thing that will hold together for fifteen years." Bok determined to improve matters on all counts and in 1895 began the publication of plans for dwellings costing from one to five thousand dollars, providing complete specifications for sound and well-designed structures in a variety of styles, all prepared and certified by reputable architects. He also ran contests for the best homes as part of his campaign. With such features he reached a widening audience over almost a quarter of a century as the circulation of the *Journal* mounted.

Bok continued his program by illustrating furniture designs in "Good Taste and Bad Taste" and offering plans for the landscaping of the small gardens of his small houses. He also offered reproductions of paintings approved by the *Journal*'s editors and available at a low price, suitable for framing and hanging on the walls. (The *Journal* was among the first magazines to publish four-color illustrations.) An indefatigable reformer, Bok attempted to wean American women from Paris fashions, unsuccessfully, and to advise them in matters of sex education, which outraged the delicacy of his female audience. Beyond the home, he fought to banish disfiguring signboards, to save the beauties of Niagara from the power companies, and to improve the furnishings of Pullman cars.

LEFT AND BELOW: THE LADIES' HOME JOURNAL, JULY, 1901. RIGHT: PRINT DEPARTMENT, METROPOLITAN MUSEUM OF ART

"A Small House with 'Lots of Room in It,'" designed in 1901 by Frank Lloyd Wright and published in The Ladies' Home Journal
The main floor plan of Wright's model prairie house (above) showing the free-flowing space of dining and living-room areas

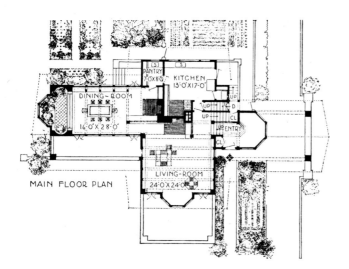

MAIN FLOOR PLAN

BOK, EDWARD, THE AMERICANIZATION OF EDWARD BOK, 1920

"'*Ladies' Home Journal* houses' were now going up in communities all over the country, and Bok determined to prove that they could be erected for the prices given," he recalled in his Pulitzer Prize-winning autobiography. ". . . prospective house-builders pointed their builders to the proof given. . . . The little houses became better and better in architecture as the series went on, and occasionally a plan for a house costing as high as ten thousand dollars was given. . . . It was one of the most constructive . . . pieces of work that Bok did during his editorial career—a fact now recognized by all architects." Over the years designs were presented in a wide variety of styles, enough to fit all manner of preference. The early decades of the present century saw an enormous increase in the use of concrete in construction of all sorts, including houses of every description. One of Bok's concrete dwellings (pictured at left) was built—he estimated—more than 250 times. In July, 1901, Frank Lloyd Wright presented a design for "A Small House with 'Lots of Room in It,'" which was an early model for one of his prairie houses and was to cost just fifty-eight hundred dollars. "The plan disregards somewhat the economical limit in compact planning," Wright explained, "to take advantage of light and air and prospect. . . . The dining-room is so coupled with the living-room that one leads naturally into the other without destroying the privacy of either." At the time it was an original and revolutionary proposal that received the widest possible publicity—and apparently had no immediate effect on the nation at large. That same year Bok commissioned the internationally known commercial designer Will H. Bradley to prepare colored renderings of interiors and furnishings for a complete model home in a strictly contemporary style—designs which were, unfortunately, reproduced in black and white in *The Ladies' Home Journal.*

Ladies' Home Journal *house built of concrete with tile roof*

Design for a living room by Will H. Bradley; part of Bok's campaign to "make the world a better or more beautiful place to live in"

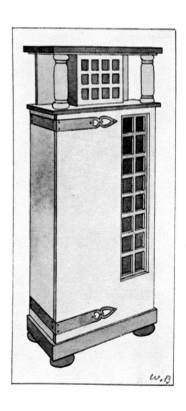

Above: a dining room; an interior designed by Will Bradley for The Ladies' Home Journal
Right: cupboard design by Bradley; like his others, probably not put into production

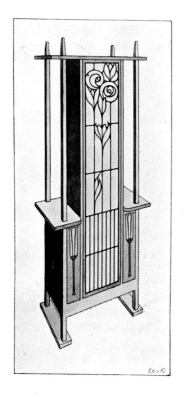

*Above: the furnished and decorated nursery of Bradley's proposed model and modern home
Left: a stylized whatnot, its panels embellished with motifs in the art nouveau manner*

Above: the open hall and staircase of Bradley's house with built-in furniture
Right: a chest; Bok actually printed Bradley's renderings in black and white

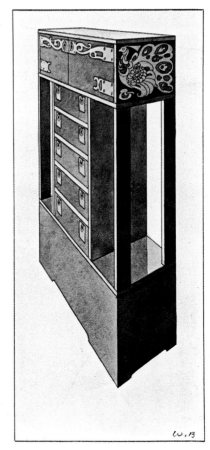

Around the turn of the century the Boston-born Will H. Bradley was creating posters, patterns for wallpapers, and other designs that won him international recognition. Most of his graphic work was in the flowing, organic style known as art nouveau, a style that for several decades enjoyed favor throughout the Western world. In 1896 one critic was moved to declare that although Bradley was classed in the "Aubrey Beardsley" school, he far outdid "his English brother artist" with richer ideas and execution. The original drawings of model interiors and furnishings that Bradley prepared for *The Ladies' Home Journal* show a striking resemblance to the work produced at about the same time by the celebrated Scottish designer Charles Rennie Mackintosh. Mackintosh's skillful combination of geometric forms, restrained curvilinear ornament, and color used with refined intensity strongly appealed to insurgent designers of the time, who were searching for a distinctively modern idiom in design and decoration, especially in Germany and Austria. Because of the influence of his work he is considered a "forerunner, if not an originator," of what we now call modern design. That Bok chose men like Wright and Bradley to address his large, popular audience indicates his own advanced ideas and his progressive editorial policy. Although that audience was predominantly female, "Bok's instinctive attitude toward women," he himself wrote, "was that of avoidance." At another point he declared of intellectual women that "perambulating encyclopedias in the guise of women are very uncomfortable things."

Among the variety of dwelling types suggested by *The Ladies' Home Journal* was the bungalow, an informal design that won great favor during the final years of the last century and the opening decades of the next. Typically, the bungalow was a small one-story house with overhanging eaves that extended over an ample porch and with an almost completely open interior plan. In effect, it was the prototype of the popular ranch house of later years. (The term "bungalow," one magazine explained in 1894, was derived from a Bengalese word referring to certain low, thatch-roofed huts in India that served as hostelries.) *The Ladies' Home Journal, The House Beautiful, The Decorator and Furnisher,* and other magazines of the day extolled the merits of the bungalow as a simple, inexpensive solution to the housing problem, a matter of constantly increasing concern. This type of dwelling, reported *The Decorator and Furnisher,* was "a homely, cosy little country house with piazzas and balconies, and the plan so arranged as to ensure complete comfort with a feeling of rusticity and ease." A few years later one wag described the bungalow as "a house that looks as if it had been built for less money than it actually cost." In 1906 the *Architectural Record* reported the extreme popularity of the bungalow in California, where more and better houses of the type were being built than anywhere else in the country. Just how popular the bungalow was may be judged from a rhyme by Burges Johnson, published in *Good Housekeeping* magazine:

> Oh, a man that's bungalonging
>   For the dingle and the loam
> Is a very bungalobster
>   If he dangles on at home.
> Catch the bungalocomotive;
>   If you cannot face the fee,
> Why, a bungaloan'll do it—
>   You can borrow it of me!

Design for a bungalow, reproduced from an engraving in Radford's Artistic Bungalows

An Era of Period Houses

Eclectic Revivals

The years from just before the outbreak of World War I to the first dark days of the Great Depression have been referred to as the "era of the period house" in America. For those two decades the progressive modernism earlier initiated by Frank Lloyd Wright and a number of his advanced contemporaries was eclipsed by more conservative trends in domestic architecture — trends that looked to "period" styles of proven worth and attraction for solutions to the problems of house design. Wright's work was not altogether forgotten or ignored, but it was often acknowledged as a somewhat nagging presence. Describing Wright's own house at Spring Green (page 321) one highly respectable critic of the twenties concluded: "Force there certainly is in this design, grace not at all. Whether it be beautiful or ugly, we leave to the individual observer and to posterity." The style represented by such a construction, he added almost fearfully, "is spreading rapidly. Its home is in Illinois and Wisconsin, where so many progressive ideas arise to plague us."

However, the day had not yet come when Wright's positive influence was felt to any great extent in America. Meanwhile, most architects of standing looked to safer formulas for their designs, and found them in the older traditions of English, French, Italian, and Spanish architecture — and, indeed, in early American traditions, as already discussed. Writing in 1928, the same critic quoted above exulted in "the vast improvement which has occurred in the last twenty-five to thirty-five years. "In no work," he

Detail, Tudor Revival style

RICHARD WATHERWAX

continued, "is this fact more conspicuous than in domestic architecture, and it is the more gratifying in this field since domestic architecture leans toward the conservative."

In more recent years it has become fashionable to decry any reliance on period styles as a feeble substitute for studied originality, for the demonstration of technological triumphs, or, indeed, for novel effects for novelty's sake. However, the architects of the period house era saw no reason why their structures should not be considered modern work at its best, any more than Alexander Jackson Davis had with his period revivals a century before. To take sound traditions wherever they might be found and adapt them freely to American conditions was truly modern in that it was clearly in the spirit of the times. Rather unexpectedly, H. L. Mencken spoke for most of the leading architects of that day when, in 1931, he scoffed at what European proponents were advancing as their concept of modern building. "If I were building a house tomorrow," he wrote, "it would certainly not follow the lines of a dynamo or a steam shovel. . . . When men . . . begin to live in houses as coldly structural as step-ladders they will cease to be men, and become mere rats in cages. . . . To say that the florid chicken-coops of Le Corbusier and company are closer to nature than the houses of the eighteenth century is as absurd as to say that tar-paper shacks behind the railroad tracks are closer to nature." However, the trying experiences of the depression would bring about fundamental changes in such American attitudes.

In 1918 one distinguished critic felt obliged to point out that "good architecture came to a sudden end in America about the year 1850. . . . It was the machine which crushed out handiwork, it was the machine which killed beauty." There were others, including prominent and fashionable conservative architects, who were not willing to accept that lugubrious judgment, who resisted the "threat" of mechanical science with all the grace they could command. One of these was John Russell Pope whose work epitomized the eclectic revivalism of the period house era. Pope's mansion at Newport, Rhode Island, designed for Stuart Duncan about 1912, freely but scrupulously borrowed from the great Tudor houses in England, although it repeated no one of them. "The worst that can be said of such archaeological treatment," wrote a contemporary authority, "is that it is unprogressive and does not lead to . . . something new. On the other hand, the price is not too great to pay occasionally for a monument of great beauty, especially in a country where historic examples are not available." Pope's last two commissions, the Jefferson Memorial and the National Gallery of Art at Washington, D.C., paid final homage to the eclectic revival.

Right: Tudor-style house built for Stuart Duncan, 1912–18
Below: detail of the Duncan House, designed by J. R. Pope

The interiors of the Duncan House were frankly inspired by 16th-century English models.

Above: driveway entrance of the Peter Cooper Bryce House, Hope Ranch, Calif., by George Washington Smith, 1925–26

Left: the Heberton House, at Montecito, Calif., 1916, the first realized building by Smith in the Spanish colonial revival style

The Greene brothers of Pasadena finished the last of their sensitively designed, advanced houses in 1915. That same year the California-Pacific Exposition opened in San Diego, California, to celebrate the opening of the Panama Canal, and encouraged a trend in building that led in quite a different direction from the Greenes' kind of modernism. A prominent feature of the fair was the California building, an elaborate structure in the Spanish colonial style as conceived by the architect Bertram Goodhue. This was by no means the earliest example of contemporary architecture that revived the old, provincial Spanish tradition on the West Coast, but the exposition served to spur that revival much as the World's Columbian Exposition had stimulated the revival of the classical styles twenty-two years earlier. Like the Anglo-American colonial revival that mushroomed and endured, the Spanish colonial revival quickly became a prevailing theme that, also like the earlier, easternborn revival, set about to recapture the spirit of an all but legendary past—in free variations on the traditional theme. At its best, the Spanish colonial revival style, featured by flat, red-tiled roofs, relatively plain plastered walls, grilled windows, occasional patios, and other reminiscences of the indigenous provincial houses, was well adapted to the nature of the land and the climate—though it was hostile to the independent adventures of the Greene brothers. And at its best, it found expression in the creations of the architect George Washington Smith, who worked in the style from 1916 until his death in 1930, and three of whose best efforts are illustrated herewith. Such houses reflected the tranquil life that visitors and immigrants chose to associate with California.

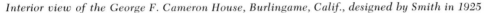

Interior view of the George F. Cameron House, Burlingame, Calif., designed by Smith in 1925

343

One of the houses in the Norman style at the French Village, Chestnut Hill, Pa., characteristic of the "era of the period house"

"There is . . . no type of European architecture so adaptable to our uses in America," wrote one architect in 1928, "as the English or Norman Country House. . . . The style is informal, and hence appropriate to our modern way of living. The interiors of the buildings must necessarily be modified to conform to our American ideas of comfort and practicality, but American architects are masters of the art of planning convenient and liveable quarters. Because of its plastic, informal qualities the English and French architecture can be made to conform to any conceivable interior arrangement." It was much in the spirit of those observations that Robert R. McGoodwin designed the so-called French Village in Chestnut Hill, Pennsylvania, a cluster of dwellings in the "Norman style" that won high praise from contemporary critics. One of the latter observed that such structures were making Chestnut Hill one of the most distinguished architectural districts in the nation.

Above: detail of another of the French Village houses, with typical sharp-pitched roof, circular turret, and lofty chimneys

Left: view of a third example. McGoodwin made fine use of the abundant, easily worked, and attractive local ledge rock.

345

Top: a fieldstone house in the Tudor style, Washington, D.C., designed in 1925 by Russell O. Kluge
Above: half-timbered home, Oak Park, Ill., designed in 1922 by Frank Lloyd Wright for Nathan Moore

The four houses illustrated on these pages, all built between 1922 and 1931, provide a sort of summary statement of the period house era. In 1894 Frank Lloyd Wright, surprisingly, accepted a commission to design a half-timbered "period" house for Nathan Moore of Oak Park, Illinois. The result was unlike anything usually associated with Wright's name. However, after that house burned in 1922 he replaced it with another still bearing some resemblance to Tudor designs, but also revealing clear indications of the architect's own preferred notions. The fieldstone house originally built for Mrs. Arthur O'Brien in Washington, D.C., is a totally different and more pretentious adaptation of Tudor styles. In 1931 the architect Robert O. Derrick designed a house in the manner of the renowned eighteenth-century architect Robert Adam for F. Caldwell Walker of Grosse Pointe, Michigan. Two years earlier Dwight James Baum designed an Italian villa in New York for Anthony Campagna. Variations on period themes were infinite. The eclecticism of the late 1920s, wrote one reporter of the time, "seems at first glance to produce merely a chaos." But, he pointed out, two things gave unity to that chaos: skillful house planning and the endlessly increasing development in the mechanical equipment behind the "borrowed" facades.

Brick house at Grosse Pointe, Mich., designed in the Adam style, 1931
An Italian villa, the Bronx, New York, designed by Dwight James Baum

It was a matter of historic chance that the Spanish settled in portions of the country with a climate not unlike their own. In Florida as in California the environment and old tradition encouraged eclectic architects to look to Spanish origins for the inspiration of their designs. Actually, in both cases the quest led beyond the evidence of colonial tradition in North America. The whole Mediterranean scene—the buildings of Islamic Africa and Italy, as well as of Spain— were tapped as historic sources suitable for adaptation in parts of the New World where the climate was sympathetic to the purpose. However, Spanish tradition was the predominant influence. Writing of current domestic architecture in Florida of the 1920s, one critic observed: "Here, for obvious reasons, the Spanish style has had a tremendous vogue. The modern buildings run through all phases of Spanish, from baroque to comparative academic correctness, from elaboration and great scale to the simplest and most picturesque informal tiny dwellings." One of the most eminent practitioners of the style in Florida was Addison Mizner, an adventurous and much-traveled architect whose designs became established as a guarantee of good taste for clients who could afford his services. There were enough of them in the state during the booming twenties to provide Mizner with plentiful commissions. As the same reporter quoted above said of one of his typical luxurious residences, "The essentials of good Spanish architecture of the most refined type are here combined with the comfort and logic of plan which the modern client demands." With the Depression such displays of luxury dwindled—and the eclectic spirit waned.

Patio of the Munn residence, Lake Worth, Fla., designed in the 1920s by Addison Mizner

A World of Possibilities

Today and Tomorrow

It has been truly said that in America during the last two centuries the single-family house has remained our primary cultural symbol, the one most personal and representative outward indication of our aspirations and accomplishments. Unfortunately, not everyone manages to find or build his own dream house, but almost everyone has plans for one in his mind's eye. Each generation has

Hancock Building, Chicago, Ill.

had its own ideas of what constitutes a livable and attractive house. Fashion, experience, historical circumstance, and technological developments have all played a part in dictating the changing standards by which those matters have been judged. Looking back, our own judgment of what appear to be the best and the most typical examples of any given period is tempered by what we know (or do not know) of the past and by the inevitable bias of the present. The better we understand the relationship of a house to the life of the time in which it was built, the more interesting and meaningful it becomes for us. As time passes, our perspective tends to improve. It is not always easy to appreciate the values of our fathers and grandfathers; in the case of our earlier forefathers our views become clearer. For the better part of a generation, for example, the early pioneering work of Frank Lloyd Wright and the Greene brothers was all but ignored in America. Then, as the isolationism of this country was shattered by the approach and outbreak of World War II, a flow of advanced European architectural ideas and practices—and of some notable European architects themselves—reached these shores. It was then apparent that

the seed Wright had so much earlier sown had found fertile ground abroad. The feedback of the so-called international style from Europe, and the continuing active presence of Wright himself, who was never more inventive or creative than he was in the last decade of his life, brought about a radical transformation of the American architectural scene in the decades that followed. That infusion of new spirit has resulted in such a multiplicity of fresh designs as can barely be suggested in the few pages remaining in this book. The word *style* hardly seems to apply to such varied and novel forms. In eschewing all reference to past periods in their creations progressive architects hoped to express the true spirit of the modern age. An important factor in the growth of strictly contemporary architecture has been the availability of materials that builders of past generations had never heard of—plastics, all manner of glass, laminates, and the rest—as well as revolutionary structural techniques that opened up unprecedented possibilities. One learned and intrepid critic has claimed that "for good or ill, modern architecture has come to seem almost synonymous with American architecture." Actually, it is hard to judge what is specifically "American" about modern American architecture, since similar principles are being applied throughout the civilized world to meet what are the basic human needs of people everywhere. To determine how eloquently this architecture may express the culture of our day will be decided by historians of the future who can view our times in clearer perspective.

Detail of an interior by the Hungarian-born architect Marcel Breuer
Fallingwater, at Bear Run, Pa., was designed by Wright in 1938.

Detail of a house in Alabama designed by Paul Rudolph, a onetime student of the German-born architect Walter Gropius at Harvard
The facade of a New York City town house, built on the existing frame of a hundred-year-old coach house, designed by Paul Rudolph

During the years of the Depression, building activity in America was sharply diminished. Even so, there were both native and immigrant architects, along with the enduring and persistent Wright, who were building houses of advanced design and were gradually eroding the genteel tradition that had dominated domestic architecture throughout the preceeding generation. With the war and its aftermath, that process was enormously accelerated by the arrival of a fresh wave of prominent architects from virtually every country in Europe, men who taught as well as built and whose vital influence, commingling with progressive American forces, continues to be felt throughout the country. During the war years heavy restrictions were put upon construction for civilian needs. But with the war's end those long-dammed-up requirements were released in a flood of new building. The complex crosscurrents of fresh and different ideas, the astonishing developments in technology, and the freedom from traditional restraints have combined to produce a greater diversity in house design than at any time in our past history.

OVERLEAF: *west facade of La Luz, an adobe town house cluster in Albuquerque, New Mexico; designed by the architect and urban planner Antoine Predock. In this highly original concept the windows open on the east side, protected from prevailing winds and strong sunlight.*

Above: house at Darien, Conn., designed by Richard Meier, the architect for Fred I. Smith

Left: "Glass House," designed by and for the architect Philip Johnson at New Canaan, Conn.

In 1938 near Phoenix, Arizona, Frank Lloyd Wright built the desert home and studio which he called Taliesin West and where he "gathered his family and apprentices about him like some Apache chief." Constructed of poured concrete and desert stones, with diagonal redwood rafters and tentlike canvas ceilings, it was his ideal—and last—abode. He died there in 1959. Standing in utter contrast to the massive ramparts of that construction are the glass walls that practically envelop the house Philip Johnson designed and built for himself at New Canaan, Connecticut; the one designed by Richard Meier for Fred I. Smith at Darien, in the same state; and the summer home of Mr. and Mrs. Alan Schwartz at Northville, Michigan, designed by Gunnar Birkets and Frank Straub. The use of glass in architecture has a long and fascinating history, dramatically punctuated by such examples as the great colored windows of medieval cathedrals and the soaring glazed construction of the Crystal Palace at London in 1851. Le Corbusier once referred to the history of architecture as an "unremitting battle" for the window. With modern architectural theory and new types of glass that battle has been won. The most monumental examples of that fact are the great glassed-in office buildings, now everywhere to be seen.

Right: interior detail of a house by Birkets and Straub
Below: a detail of Wright's self-designed Taliesin West

LEFT: BALTHAZAR KORAB, TROY, MICHIGAN. BELOW: PEDRO GUERRERO, NEW CANAAN

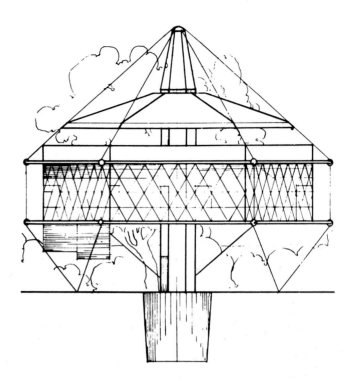

Above: interior view of the Bevinger House, by Goff
Below: exterior of the house showing suspended roof
Right: a design for the Dymaxion House by Fuller

In late years houses have been designed and built that are totally unlike any house known in the past. As early as 1927 Buckminster Fuller conceived his Dymaxion ("dynamic" plus "maximum" efficiency) House, in effect a complex of mechanical services in conjunction with living areas all hung from a central mastlike core. In a quite literal sense he designed a machine for living. Bruce Goff, a western architect, designs every house as if it were the first one in the world. Such is the spiral structure he created at Norman, Oklahoma; a house which coils around a central steel pole from which the roof is suspended. Goff's clients were interested in raising plants indoors among other things, and the architect provided a continuous flow of space without partitions or rooms in the conventional sense. A saucer (gold-carpeted) above the table in the illustration at the left, top, is the children's play area. Other similar saucers, stepped up at intervals of three feet and reached by winding stairs, are used as living and sleeping areas. What the house lacks in privacy it makes up for in untrammeled space. In 1968 another architect, Richard Foster, designed and had built for his own use a glassed-in, circular nine-room house set on a pedestal at a site in Wilton, Connecticut, that commanded breathtaking views in all directions—pine forests, a distant lake, a nearby pond and meadow, and farmland hills. To take full advantage of those various and rewarding outlooks he had his house engineered to rotate in either direction at various controllable speeds about its central axis. The speeds range from five to forty revolutions in twenty-four hours. Seen from the middle distance the structure resembles a moored spacecraft; from within one can dictate the view of sunrise, sunset, moonlit landscape, or whatever from a chosen room with the push of a button.

Opposite: nighttime view of Richard Foster's circular revolving house

Above: a view from the John Hancock Building
Left: Lake Point Tower apartments, Chicago, Ill.
Opposite: looking up at the Marina apartments

In more ways than one, apartment house living is on the rise in America. Around half the housing units constructed in late years have been apartments, some of which have risen high indeed. The three Chicago buildings shown here seem audaciously tall, although there is virtually no limit nowadays to how tall a structure could actually be built. The John Hancock Building, designed by Skidmore, Owings, and Merrill, soars through one hundred stories to a height of more than one thousand feet, combining offices, garages and, above them, forty-nine stories of apartments, a sky-high swimming pool, and miscellaneous other accommodations. One can commute to one's office "downstairs" by elevators that travel eighteen hundred feet a minute. Marina City, built in 1964 with Bertrand Goldberg Associates as architects, consists of two sixty-story towers with parking space on the first eighteen helically designed stories, and with dwelling units, offices, and, again, other facilities above. The curvaceous seventy-story Lake Point Tower, completed in 1969 from the design of George Schipporeit and John Heinrich, is in effect a self-contained vertical inner-city "suburb" with country club built in. In addition to its stores, restaurants, and other convenient features, it has an indoor park with waterfall and lagoon, and a dog-walk area equipped with plastic hydrants. Keeping up with the Joneses requires an ascending way of life.

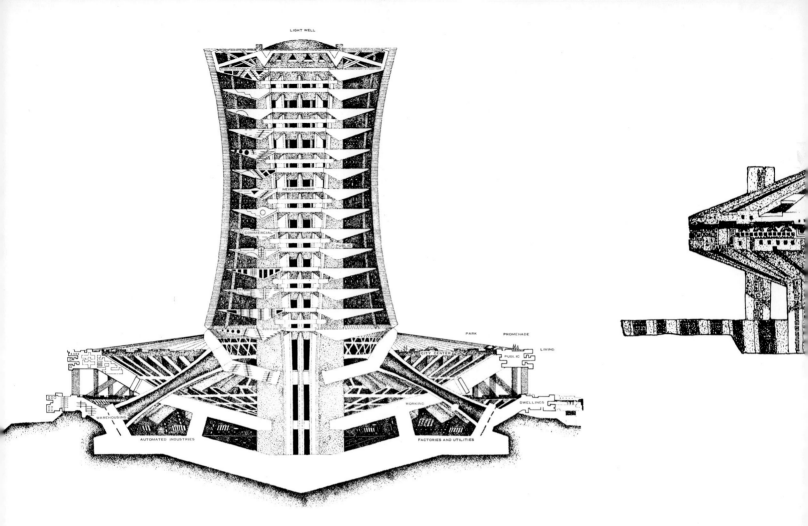

"We cannot all live in cities," remarked Horace Greeley more than a century ago as he watched the mounting tide of humanity that was inundating New York, "yet nearly all seem determined to do so." Today there are more than five times as many Americans as there were in Greeley's time, and a much larger proportion of them are living in cities about the land. In some sizable areas the open countryside has practically disappeared as urban complexes have swollen and coalesced with neighboring swollen urban complexes to form great, unrelieved megalopolitan regions where distinctions between city life and country life tend to dissolve in widespread blight. For some years one visionary planner, the gifted Italian-born architect Paolo Soleri, has drafted schemes which he refers to as "guidelines toward a new option" for modern city dwellers; schemes by which he proposes to restore the traditional balance between city and country by reversing urban sprawl, by compressing all urban activity and services into elaborately multileveled structures—metropolises in the form of buildings, actually—that reach far into the earth and, perhaps, thousands of feet into the sky. "Babel II," as he labels one such design, consists of a mile-high tower with circular platforms supporting whole neighborhoods with streets and residences. Another design, "Babeldiga," would measure over a mile from its underground base to its cliff-level top and house more than a million people. Residents would live primarily near the outer surface of the structure, facing outward toward an unsullied, surrounding environment and inward toward an environment as artificial as that of a city on the moon.

DRAWINGS REPRINTED FROM *ARCOLOGY: THE CITY IN THE IMAGE OF MAN* BY PAOLO SOLERI, BY PERMISSION OF THE M.I.T PRESS, CAMBRIDGE, MASS. COPYRIGHT © 1969 BY THE MASSACHUSETTS INSTITUTE OF TECHNOLOGY

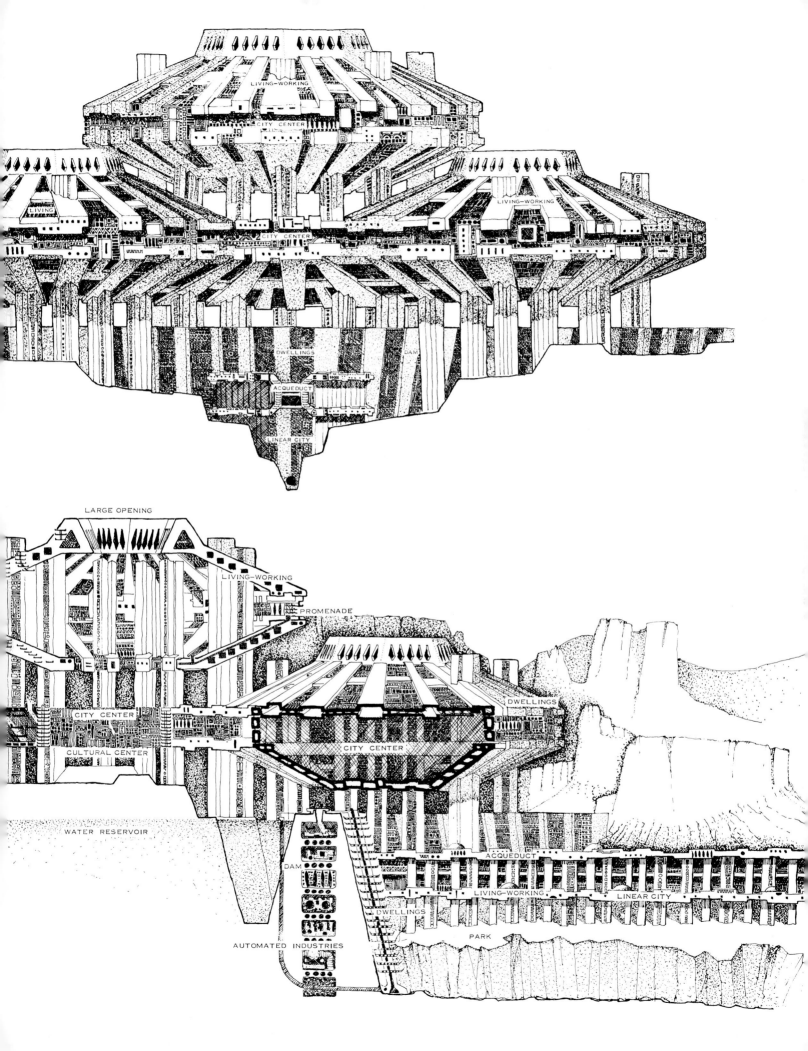

From the 1920s, through the present era, the rectangular form has been the international ideal of modern architecture, despite a few vocal critics who despairingly foresee a time when the American landscape will be reduced to a vast repetition of boxlike structures, stretching from coast to coast. Although it is unlikely that the right angle and the traditional post and lintel system will be outmoded in the near future, architects in recent years have begun experimenting with a richer vocabulary of forms, made possible through engineering innovations and the use of such newly developed materials as plastics and sprayed concrete. Homes, churches, airports, and sports arenas now arise in a variety of shapes, organic and otherwise, that include curved and folded shells, hyperbolic paraboloids, membranes suspended from portal frames, and arches. Among the new modes of expression is the futuristic concept of architectural space evolved by the late Frederick Kiesler. A theoretical designer, concerned more with providing the inhabitants of his houses with rewarding aesthetic experiences than with perfecting techniques of construction, Kiesler devoted much of his career to composing an Endless House, a forty-by-sixty-foot model of which was erected at the Museum of Modern Art in New York during the 1950s. Built of plastic applied to a molded mesh, the dwelling, with its one-piece exterior shell of irregular egg shapes, bore a closer resemblance to sculpture than to architecture. Inside, the Endless House contained no right angles, but walls, floor, and ceiling merged into one continuous plane, and produced the illusion of infinite space. As Kiesler so aptly summed up the new direction, taken by himself and others, "Art can no longer live in mid-air, nor architecture on the ground of business. That's over . . . . to live with and within, that is, directly with art and architecture, is the new concept of art."

Frederick Kiesler's Endless House, displayed at the Museum of Modern Art in 1959–60

Ghosts of the Past

An Epilogue

Although the United States, since the time of the Civil War, has lost none of its distinguished buildings as a result of military action, the nation's historic structures are currently imperiled by a form of destruction more devastating than bombs or artillery fire. In the guise of progress, houses and monuments of irreplaceable architectural value are falling victim, at an ever-increasing rate, to the bulldozer and the demolition expert. As the Englishman Sir Shane Leslie remarked some thirty-five years ago, "The American sign of civic progress is to tear down the familiar and erect the monstrous." Even in the early decades of the nineteenth century, edifices built to serve several generations were leveled, not because of their obsolescence or unfitness for use, but because of the irrepressible American urge to turn a quick dollar by real estate speculation or new construction. In such rapidly growing and changing towns as Boston, for instance, many of Charles Bulfinch's masterful buildings were razed during the architect's lifetime, and the majority of his remaining creations were dismantled in the course of another fifty years. The trend to replace the old with the new was also accelerated by technological advances. In order to keep the machinery of mass production running at capacity, houses and other commodities required built-in obsolescence and the need for replacement. By the beginning of the twentieth century, a writer for *The American Architect* accurately observed that "the best we can do with all the data and facilities at our command is out of date almost before it shows

Abandoned farmhouse in Ohio

DAVID PLOWDEN

signs of appreciable wear. So a building erected today is outclassed tomorrow." And, a contractor candidly noted that a building then being erected had to be "the cheapest thing that will hold together for fifteen years."

The roster of the architectural dead continues to grow. In downtown urban areas, entire neighborhoods are swallowed up in new developments, or are being torn down to provide space for parking lots. All too frequently, isolated and abandoned structures give up the ghost in a blaze of glory, whether in fires strategically kindled to spare demolition expenses, or in accidental holocausts. Some buildings have been so remodeled that nothing is left of their original appearance, while still others have simply worn out from overuse and misuse. In recording the demise of Penn Station, *The New York Times* lamented, "we will probably be judged not by the mouments we build, but by those we have destroyed."

Our architectural past can, in no sense, be recaptured. However, concern has recently been expressed at every level of our society to save what remains of our cultural heritage. Mrs. Lyndon B. Johnson summed up the gravity of the situation in a speech of a few years back. "I was dismayed to learn . . . that almost half of the twelve thousand structures listed in the Historic American Buildings Survey [compiled in the 1930s] . . . have already been destroyed. This is a serious loss and it underlines the necessity for prompt action if we are not to shirk our duty to the future. We must preserve and we must preserve wisely."

Above: an interior view of the abandoned remains of Belle Grove Plantation, La., built in 1856 or 1857 designed by Henry Howard
Opposite: weathered, vine-covered Corinthian columns; all that remains of Windsor Plantation, built in 1861 north of Natchez, Miss.

LEFT: LAMBERT FLORIN, PORTLAND, OREGON. RIGHT: RANDOLPH LANGENBACH, CAMBRIDGE, MASS.

The remnants of what was Main Street, Rawhide, Nev., a once-booming gold-mining center

Discarded fragments of architectural sculpture from Pennsylvania Station, New York City

THE NEW YORK TIMES

The Willows, Manchester, N. H., for exactly 100 years a proud hilltop mansion; recently leveled in favor of still another parking lot

Above: a familiar urban pattern of ruination; the last moments of an apartment house in the course of demolition, New York City

Opposite: recent destruction of the National Presbyterian Church, Washington, D. C.; the violent end of a once-notable monument

LEFT: PHILIP LIEF. RIGHT: NATIONAL TRUST FOR HISTORIC PRESERVATION

Acknowledgments

The Editors appreciate the generous assistance provided by many individuals and institutions during the preparation of this book. They especially wish to thank the following:

American Association for State and Local History, Nashville, Tenn.
    William T. Alderson, Jr.

American Institute of Architects, Wash., D.C.

American Institute of Architects, New York Chapter, New York City

Bohemia, Earleville, Md.
    Mr. and Mrs. W. Harrison Mechling

Boston Athenaeum
    Walter Muir Whitehill

Boston Museum of Fine Arts

Boston Public Library
    Sinclair Hitchings

Colonial Williamsburg
    Jane A. Tyler

Columbia University, New York City
    School of Architecture
        Prof. James Marsden Fitch
        Ronald A. Ramsey
    Avery Library
        Adolf K. Placzek
        May N. Stone

Cooper Union Museum, New York City
    Katharine Frangiamore

George Eastman House, Rochester, N.Y.
    Beaumont Newhall

Essex Institute, Salem, Mass.
    Mrs. Hugh Nelson

Edgar Kaufmann, Jr., New York City

Library of Congress, Wash., D.C.
    Virginia Daiker

Metropolitan Museum of Art, New York City
    Janet Byrne
    Margaret Nolan

Mount Vernon Ladies' Association of the Union, Mount Vernon, Va.
    Charles C. Wall

Museum of the City of New York
    Charlotte LaRue

Museum of Modern Art, New York City
    Richard Tooke

National Trust for Historic Preservation, Wash., D.C.
    Helen Duprey Bullock
    Terry B. Morton

New York City Landmarks Preservation Commission
    Dr. Alan Burnham

New-York Historical Society
    Wilson G. Duprey

New York Public Library
    Donald Anderle
    Elizabeth Roth

New York State Historical Association, Cooperstown
    Dr. Louis C. Jones

Office of State History of New York, Albany
    Lili Reinech

Olana, Hudson, N.Y.
    Albert Fromberger
    Richard Slavin

Clarkson N. Potter, New York City

Preservation Society of Newport County, R.I.
    Mr. and Mrs. Leonard Panaggio

Shaker Village, Hancock, Mass.
    John Ott

Sleepy Hollow Restorations, Inc., Tarrytown, N.Y.
    Joseph Butler

Society for the Preservation of New England Antiquities, Boston, Mass.
    Abbott Lowell Cummings

Staten Island Historical Society
    Dr. Loring McMillen

The New York Times
    Ada Louise Huxtable
    Garth Huxtable

Thomas Jefferson Memorial Foundation, Inc., Monticello, Va.
    James A. Bear, Jr.

U. S. Department of the Interior, National Park Service: Historic American Buildings Survey, Wash., D.C.
    Nancy Beinke

University of California at Santa Barbara
    School of Architecture and Fine Arts
        Randell L. Makinson
    The Art Gallery
        David Gebhardt

Marian Vanderbilt, New York City

Vernon House, Newport, R.I.
    Mr. and Mrs. Quinto Maganini

White House Historical Association
    Hilary Tolson

Henry Francis du Pont Winterthur Museum, Del.
    Karol Grubbs

The Editors also make grateful acknowledgment for permission to use material from the following works:

"An Account of the Town of Boston Written in 1817," by Shubael Bell, from *Bostonian Society Publications*, Vol. III. Copyright 1919 by The Bostonian Society. Published by The Bostonian Society, Boston, 1919.

The American Woman's Home, by Catharine E. Beecher and Harriet Beecher Stowe. Copyright 1869 by J. B. Ford and Co. Published by J. B. Ford and Co., New York City, 1869.

"The Bungal-Ode," by Burges Johnson, from *Good Housekeeping Magazine*, Vol. 48. Copyright 1909 by The Phelps Publishing Co. Published by The Phelps Publishing Co., New York City, 1909.

The Carolina Backcountry on the Eve of the Revolution, the Journal and Other Writings of Charles Woodmason, edited by Richard J. Hooker. Copyright 1953, by University of North Carolina Press. Published by University of North Carolina Press, Chapel Hill, 1953.

Moral Essays, in Four Epistles to Several Persons, by Alexander Pope, Esq., printed in Edinburgh for James Reid, Bookseller in Leith, 1751.

Commissioned photography by Charles Baptie, Annandale, Va.; Jay Cantor, New York City; William Current, Pasadena, Calif.; Richard Glassman, Bethlehem, Conn.; Jerry Goffe, Albuquerque, N. M.; Courtlandt V. D. Hubbard, Philadelphia, Pa.; Paulus Leeser, New York City; Frank Lerner, New York City; Nathaniel Lieberman, New York City; Edwin S. Roseberry, Monticello, Va.; Jay Sacks, Philadelphia, Pa.; Louis Schwartz, Charleston, S. C.; Richard Watherwax, New York City. Commissioned drawings by Cal Sacks, Westport, Conn.; Kenneth Sheller, New York City.

Original drawing on page 1 by Cal Sacks. Photograph on page 2 by Paulus Leeser. Photograph on page 4 by Leo Goldstein. Painting on page 122 from a private collection. Endsheets water color from the Prints Division of the New York Public Library.

Index

Page numbers in boldface type refer to illustrations.

W

WADDELL HOUSE, New York, N.Y., 201

WAINWRIGHT BUILDING, St. Louis, Mo., 331

WAINWRIGHT TOMB, St. Louis, Mo., 331

WAITE, EZRA, 83, 84

WALKER HOUSE, Grosse Point, Mich., 347, **347**

WALTER, THOMAS U., 179, 180, 280

WARE HOUSE, Augusta, Ga., 149, **149**

WARNER, CHARLES DUDLEY, 234

WARNER HOUSE, St. Louis, Mo., 261; interior, **260–61**

WASHINGTON, GEORGE, 60, 73, 74, 79, 109, 125, 126, 130, 132, 153, 171, 294, 316; inauguration, 118, **118**. *See also* Mount Vernon

WASHINGTON, LAWRENCE, 130

WASHINGTON, MARTHA, 130, 132

WASHINGTON, D.C., 139

WATTS SHERMAN HOUSE, Newport, R.I., 266, **266**

WEBB HOUSE, Wethersfield, Conn., 109

WEBSTER, NOAH, 16, 117–18

WEDGWOOD, JOSIAH, 59–60

WELLS, H. G., 117

WENTWORTH HOUSE, Portsmouth, N.H., 112; interior, **112**

WEST ST. MARY'S MANOR, Md., 57, **57**

WESTERN ARCHITECT, THE, 319

WESTMINSTER ABBEY, London, 175

WESTOVER, Charles City County, Va., 64, 67, **67,** 69, **70–71,** 87, 92; detail, **93**

WETMORE, WILLIAM. *See* Château-sur-Mer

WHARTON, EDITH, 283
The Decoration of Houses, 333

WHIPPLE HOUSE, Ipswich, Mass.: detail, **28–29;** garden, **32,** 33

WHISTLER, JAMES McNEIL, 306

WHITE, STANFORD, 239, 265, 270, 284, 296, 304, 308

WHITE HALL, La., **156–57,** 157

WHITE HOUSE, THE, Washington, D.C., 122–25, **126–27,** 128, 134; interiors, **127–29;** portico, **126**

WHITFIELD HOUSE, Guilford, Conn., 40, **40**

WHITMAN, WALT, 179, 319, 332

WHITMAN HOUSE, Farmington, Conn., 22, **23**

WILCOX-CUTTS HOUSE, Orwell, Vt., 188, **189**

WILLIAMSBURG, Va., 62–63, 64, 311, 316; governor's palace, 62–63, **63;** lamp, **311**

WILLIS, NATHANIEL P. *See* Idlewild

WILMINGTON, MASS., Cape Cod house, **167**

WINDSOR PLANTATION, Natchez, Miss., ruins of, **365**

WINTHROP, JOHN, 9, 15, 36, 40, 107

WINTHROP, JOHN, JR., 22, 33, **33,** 38

WOOD, WILLIAM, 34

WOODMASON, CHARLES, 73

WOOLLETT, WILLIAM M.: *Old Homes Made New,* 252

WOOLWORTH BUILDING, New York, N.Y., 305, 310

WORKS IN ARCHITECTURE OF ROBERT AND JAMES ADAM, ESQUIRES, THE (Robert and James Adam), 119

WORLD'S COLUMBIAN EXPOSITION, Chicago, Ill., 239–40, **240,** 282, 303–4, **304,** 307, 331, **332,** 343

WREN, SIR CHRISTOPHER, 62, 63, 86, 105

WRIGHT, FRANK LLOYD, 239, 272, 306–10, **308,** 313, 319–24, 326, 330–31, 334, 339, 346–47, 349, 350–51, 355; designs by, **307, 323, 334**

WYTHE, GEORGE, 134

Y

YOUNG BUILDER'S GENERAL INSTRUCTOR, THE (Lafever), 186; plan from, **186**